Dear Roberto —

I hope this adds
a little to your
intellectual capital!

Best wish

Frances Horibe

Aug. 2003

MANAGING KNOWLEDGE WORKERS

MANAGING KNOWLEDGE WORKERS

New Skills and Attitudes to Unlock the
Intellectual Capital in Your Organization

Frances Horibe

JOHN WILEY & SONS
Toronto • New York • Chichester • Weinheim • Brisbane • Singapore

John Wiley & Sons Canada Limited
22 Worcester Road
Etobicoke, Ontario
M9W 1L1

Canadian Cataloguing in Publication Data

Horibe, Frances Dale Emy
  Managing knowledge workers: new skills and attitudes to unlock the intellectual capital in your organization

Includes index.
ISBN 0-471-64318-1

1. Knowledge workers. 2. Knowledge management. 3. Intellectual capital.
I. Title.

HD8039.K59H67 1999   658.3'044   C99-930033-4

Production Credits

Cover design: Interrobang Graphic Design Inc.
Printer: Tri-Graphic Printing

Printed in Canada

10 9 8 7 6 5 4 3 2 1

DEDICATION

To my family but especially to my father who was
my first model for a worker who put his head,
hands and heart into what he did.

TABLE OF CONTENTS

୫ଔ

ᘒ

The Hot Job Market

For those of us who have survived the downsizing, rightsizing, and outsizing of recent years, it's hard to get our heads around the idea that things have changed. Instead of showing you to the door, they're chasing after you. For example, if you have SAP experience (a finance system which is becoming the corporate standard), your signing bonus can be $100,000. Microsoft has a signing bonus too but not just for its employees. If an employee stays more than two and a half *months*, the recruiting firm gets performance pay. One of Northern Telecom's subsidiaries, FastLane Technologies, recently made front-page headlines when it offered $1000 to anyone, anyone off the street, who referred a high-tech worker who stayed for more than a month. High-tech companies' turnover is running at about 30 per cent[1] annually.

So what does this tell us? With some 478,000 high-tech jobs in the US unfilled[2] and a further 20,000 in Canada,[3] it's pretty clear high-tech workers can pretty much call their own tune. But high-tech is simply leading the way. In many other areas, the demand for workers is great and growing. The standard signing bonus for a graduating MBA is now $20,000 to $30,000. Class of '98 liberal arts grads can expect to make 6.5 per cent more than their peers did just the year earlier. In a survey done by the National Association of Colleges and Employers, nearly 70 per cent of companies plan to increase the number of college graduates they hire.

And the need is not just young people with the new skills. In 1997, the demand for executive talent rose 45 per cent over the previous year and indications are the demand will stay strong for a

---

[1] Anne Fisher, "The 100 Best Companies to Work for in America," *Fortune,* (January 12, 1998): 70.

[2] Leslie Kaufman and John McCormick, "The Year of the Employee," *Newsweek,* (July 20, 1998): 39.

[3] *The Globe and Mail,* (March 12, 1998).

ile.[4] Even the lowly middle manager whose very existence was being called into question just a few short years ago is in demand to run the cross-functional teams which are becoming standard operating practice. The consensus seems to be that, "We are sitting at the beginning of an employment boom and the specific shortages that we are witnessing today are likely to spread widely...to other fields."[5] TD Bank chief economist, Ruth Getter feels that this is the best job market in 10 years. The talent shortage seems likely to continue for at least the next couple of years.

So, if you're looking for a change, the time has never been better to sharpen up the old résumé. But if you're a manager trying to attract or retain good people, you're in trouble.

Actually, it gets worse. For one thing, not as many workers are being forced back onto the job market; layoffs are the lowest since the 1991 recession. In addition, there is a growing phenomenon, particularly among baby boomers but not restricted to them. As baby boomers can see the end of their work lives, even if it's some distance off, they're beginning to wonder if they're running out of time to accomplish their life goals. With those thoughts, some are opting out of the traditional corporate world and this is reflected in *Fortune* magazine articles like "Is it Time to Bail from Big Company Life?" Other major business journals reflect the same trend when they feature alternate careers like blacksmithing in articles like, "Forget the Suit, Get me an Anvil".[6]

All of this has created a situation where more than half of US companies say they have recently lost so many talented people that their ability to compete has been severely compromised.[7]

What's happening? After all, a huge chunk of the population hasn't suddenly withdraw from the workforce. There aren't an inordinate number of people retiring. Even the oldest baby boomer is just in her early fifties and even if some are dropping out, most seem to be planning to work until 55, 60, 65 or beyond. So why the demand?

If you look carefully, you'll see that demand is not uniform across all occupations. There were still about half a million lay offs in the US in 1997[8] and still a substantial number of people unemployed. The demand is almost exclusively for *knowledge* workers.

---

[4] "The Executive Demand Index: Sizzling," *Fortune*, (March 2, 1998): 221.

[5] David Berman, "Who's Hot? You Are" *Canadian Business*, (November 14, 1997): 52.

[6] Harvey Schachter, "Forget the Suit, Get me an Anvil," *Canadian Business*, (April 1997).

[7] Anne Fisher, "The 100 Best Companies to Work for in America," *Fortune*, (January 12, 1998): 69.

[8] "Why Layoffs are Getting Lighter," *Fortune*, (March 2, 1998).

What Is a Knowledge Worker?

I'm sure there is a whole crew of people somewhere arguing about this definition, but at its simplest, knowledge workers are people who use their heads more than their hands to produce value. They add value through their ideas, their analyses, their judgment, their syntheses, and their designs. They still use their hands, of course, but it's more likely to be inputting into a computer than lifting a 50-pound sack.

The knowledge component of jobs like accounting and research is obvious and is also evident in occupations like management and sales when you think about it. For example, Xerox salespeople don't sell copiers, they sell document solutions. They have to know their customers' businesses and the Xerox product line well enough to be able to propose a suite of products and services which meets individual and specialized needs.

But even jobs which have traditionally been more hands than head, like manufacturing, have changed radically. Hourly workers making Dove soap don't spend most of their time stirring vats and adding perfume. Instead, they sit at a space-age console which runs the process. They use Histograms, Pareto charts, and Ishikawa diagrams to improve product and process quality.

Knowledge workers already form a large part of any organization and their percentage is growing. It is estimated that by the year 2000, knowledge workers (e.g., sales, managerial and administrative, professional and technical) will be 59 per cent of the workforce.[9]

The bottom line is that knowledge workers make up the bulk of most organizations and there aren't enough of them to go around. Let's look at why knowledge workers are suddenly so important.

The New Economy

I don't think there's a management book today which doesn't have a section called "The New Economy." That's because the new economy—this flood of information coming at lightning speed—really is changing almost everything. How we buy, how we sell, what we make, when we make it, what we value, and where we live. Information

---

[9] Stephen R. Barley, "The Turn to a Horizontal Division of Labor: On the Occupationalization of Firms and the Technization of Work," paper prepared for the Office of Educational Research and Improvement, US Department of Education, January 1994.

is now the driver of wealth creation and those who have it (knowledge workers) are the keys to this new way. To understand why they're so critical, let's talk about "book value."

"Book value" is the term used by economists and stock market types to identify the hard assets of a company such as the buildings, inventory, machines, etc.—all the things which, in an industrial society, were needed to turn out products. This has traditionally been considered a rough measure of a company's worth. Of course, it has always been recognized that there is some measure of human contribution to this equation and this was usually lumped under the heading of "goodwill." That might include the value of your brand name, the experience of your people, the value of your customer base. Goodwill was the "fudge factor" to account for all the mushy bits which played a part in worth but couldn't be counted easily and were not so important that imprecision was a problem.

The equation ***Company Worth = Book Value + Goodwill*** worked pretty well when most of what needed to be counted, could be. That is, when there was a more or less straight line relationship between the assets you invested (machines, raw materials) and what you got as a result (fridges, stoves).

However, over the course of the last 10 or 20 years, the fudge factor has gotten bigger and bigger. A study done by the Open Business School, the business school arm of the Open University in England, showed that in 1992, only 60 per cent of a firm's worth could be accounted for by its book value.[10] Margaret Blair, a Brookings Institution economist, looked at the same issue for manufacturers. In 1982, book value accounted for 62 per cent of a company's worth; in 1992, it was just 38 per cent.[11] Whatever this goodwill was, it was getting more and more important.

Similarly, a study of large companies showed that their market value (what they were sold for) was 4.4 times their book value (what their assets were worth). Microsoft stock trades at 10 times book value. That is, only 10 per cent of Microsoft's worth is in hard assets. The fudge factor is now the most important part of a company's valuation.

---

[10] Leif Edvinsson and Michael S. Malone, *Intellectual Capital: Realizing Your Company's True Value by Finding Its Hidden Brainpower*, (New York: HarperBusiness, 1997), 4. As measured by its selling price.

[11] Thomas A. Stewart. "Trying to Grasp the Intangible," *Fortune*, (October 2, 1995): 157. The difference in the two numbers may be due to using only manufacturers in the Brookings study and a more broadly based set of companies in the Open Business School study.

With goodwill now constituting up to 90 per cent of a company's worth, and traditional accounting methods capturing only the other 10 per cent, this changeover to the New Economy has understandably caused a lot of angst among accountants. But beyond that, it brings home the fact that wealth is being created in an entirely new way. Wealth, jobs, and competitive advantage are no longer primarily a matter of machines and tools but of brains and harnessing those brains. The old economy was about "'congealed *resources'*— a lot of material held together by a bit of knowledge"[12] such as a dishwasher or table. The new economy is about "'congealed *knowledge'*— a lot of intellectual content in a physical slipcase,"[13] such as software; the value is not the diskette itself but the brainpower you access when you buy it.

Thus value and competitive edge are created by the knowledge your people have and how they apply it to their work. In fact, there seems to be a growing consensus that developed nations can continue to enjoy their high standard of living only by concentrating on knowledge-dense products and services. [14] The knowledge, or intellectual capital, of your company, has become the most important aspect of your business.

This realization has sparked much attention in the business world. In a recent survey, four out of five managers believed managing knowledge is essential or important.[15] Big organizations like Dow Chemical, Hughes Aircraft, and the Canadian Imperial Bank of Commerce[16] are starting to act. About one in five Fortune 500 companies employ a chief knowledge officer.[17] And not just big business needs to take notice: many small businesses depend entirely on the talents of their employees. They often have few tangible assets and shallow pockets. Almost their only competitive advantage is their people.

Understanding, growing, and managing intellectual capital are the most important jobs you have no matter the size of your business.

[12] Thomas A. Stewart, *Intellectual Capital: The New Wealth of Organizations*, (New York: Doubleday, 1997): 16. Stewart is quoting an interview he did with Brian Arthur, an economist at Stanford and the Santa Fe Institute. By the by, the Stewart book has an excellent explanation of how the new economy creates wealth.
[13] Ibid.
[14] Philip Siekman, "Brains are Powering US Exports," *Fortune*, (February 3, 1998): 70[B]
[15] Thomas A. Stewart, "Brain Power. Who Owns It ...How They Profit From It," *Fortune*, (March 17, 1997): 105.
[16] Leif Edvinsson and Michael S. Malone, *Intellectual Capital: Realizing Your Company's True Value by Finding Its Hidden Brainpower*, (New York: HarperBusiness, 1997), 18.
[17] Thomas A. Stewart, "Is This Job Really Necessary?," *Fortune*, (January 12, 1998): 154. Titles may vary but the function is similar.

What This Book is About

The field of intellectual capital is large and expanding. We're beginning to explore its relationship to strategic plans, how to measure it, and the computer systems and databases required to support it. All these are important but Leif Edvinsson—one of intellectual capital's gurus and early proponents—believes that "...only the human factor interpenetrates the others, serving as the active agent operating upon all the others. Without *a successful human dimension*[18] to a company, none of the rest of the value creation activities will work, no matter how sophisticated the technology. An unhappy company is a worthless company; an enterprise without values has no value." [19]

Without that successful human dimension, building intellectual capital won't work and you won't create wealth. So that's what this book is about: the human aspects of intellectual capital; creating and sustaining a company where employees want to contribute their ideas, innovations, and analysis and which receives them willingly. It is about building an organization which truly values its people and demonstrates this belief in both its management style and systems. It is about all the mushy things, like trust, involvement, communication, and personal change that are difficult to quantify, impossible to define but clearly indispensable in this new age. And while managers can turn a little faint when conversation shifts to these areas, Jack Welch, famed CEO of General Electric summed it up best: "Without very high trust you will never get maximization of brain potential."[20] Without all of these "soft" skills, you won't be able to manage the new challenges you face. Because wealth creation is now in people's heads rather than in their hands, your success will depend not only on your ability in managing the workflow but on your talent in enticing from each person his best ideas, judgments, and effort.

You Can't Just Throw Money at the Problem

Big signing bonuses, an increase whenever a knowledge worker looks cross-eyed at a competitor, stock options, profit sharing—that's how many companies are trying to retain their intellectual capital. And at

---

[18] my emphasis.
[19] Leif Edvinsson and Michael S. Malone, *Intellectual Capital: Realizing Your Company's True Value by Finding Its Hidden Brainpower* (New York: HarperBusiness, 1997), 123.
[20] Geoffrey Colvin, "The Changing Art of Becoming Unbeatable," *Fortune,* (November 24, 1997): 299.

some level it makes sense. After all, you usually pay more for a scarce resource. The chapter on rewards (Chapter 12) will discuss the role of money in tapping the intellectual capital of your organization, but here are a couple of things to consider right now.

Paying more and more for the same resource is a zero-sum game. It's like the inflated salaries for hockey and basketball players. You're paying more for the players but you're not necessarily getting better players nor improving the game.

In addition, money might be the solution if knowledge workers composed a relatively small proportion of your workforce. However, when they're the majority, as they are now in most companies, continuing this strategy is a fast road to insolvency. What's worse, paying more doesn't work over the long term, even if it seems to in the short term. Even with all the salary one-upmanship going on in some quarters, *Fortune* magazine found that "One of the most vexing problems facing entrepreneurs in all fields of business—from biotechnology to manufacturing to research consulting—is dealing with employee defections."[21] So even with these inflated salaries, turnover in high-tech firms is running at an unacceptable rate. Huge salaries and bonuses don't retain your intellectual capital. In fact, they may not even be necessary, if you look at examples of companies which can do amazing things without amazing salaries.

Careerware, a business unit of ISM, one of Canada's largest high-tech services companies, produces career guidance software for the educational market. Their software is updated yearly and includes many leading-edge improvements. Given that, their programmers are constantly being beckoned into dark alleys and shown how much better they could do elsewhere. But most programmers have stayed with Careerware for five and six years even though the salaries are not above market average. The employee satisfaction rates *and* the customer satisfaction rates are out of this world (97 per cent and 95 per cent respectively). Happy employees, happy customers and all with just average salaries. Barb MacCallum, the director of Careerware, attributes their success to an organization which truly feels committed to creating an environment where people feel excited about what they do and feel their ideas are welcomed.

BrockTel, part of the Nortel telecommunications family, recently won a Canada Award for Excellence. They have exceptional customer

---

[21] Lori Ioannou, "Putting Them on Ice," *Fortune,* (March 16, 1998): 156[C].

and employee satisfaction rates but pay under industry norms as a deliberate part of its strategy. BrockTel has brought their plant back from the edge of shutdown by producing components for older Nortel lines at substantially cheaper prices. They do it by streamlining the original production process and by paying their employees less than what their education might command elsewhere. They realize that this is a fine line to tread. However, they attribute their continuing success to their staff's willingness to trade off some wages for a competitive position in the market place and a job where their ideas are encouraged and valued.

Hewlett Packard considers itself among the leaders in pay but not *the* leader, with a fairly traditional compensation package. Yet its attrition rate is usually half the average in the labor market where it operates; in the 1990s attrition has actually fallen by a third. They believe that the secret of their ability to retain high demand workers is building good relationships.[22]

So it isn't all about money. In fact, in a recent study of high tech-workers, money was the *sixth* most important factor in their work, with the challenge of the job, exposure to new technology, career opportunities, work environment, and on-the-job training coming before it.[23] This was confirmed by a survey of people in *Fortune's Best 100 Companies* who turned down job offers from competing firms. Their reasons for staying? The chance to work on cutting edge technology, to change careers within the same company, to have a shot at a challenging overseas assignment, for promotion, flexible or reduced work hours or truly terrific benefits. Nobody mentioned money. [24]

Summary

There are companies which pay either average or even below market value for their knowledge workers and are able to retain them. I'm not trying to suggest that paying below market is an objective. If there is a huge and continuing gap between what you pay and what others will pay, you will get more drain on your intellectual capital than you want. But thinking you can solve the problem of attracting,

---

[22] Thomas A. Stewart, "Moi? Gray Flannel Suit?," *Fortune,* (March 16, 1998): 76.
[23] *The Globe and Mail,* (June 5, 1998).
[24] Anne Fisher, "The 100 Best Companies to Work for in America," *Fortune,* (January 12, 1998): 70. Okay, there might be one which is money-related-that of benefits.

retaining and tapping into your intellectual capital using only money is kind of like trying to play a symphony with just a violin. You may play long, loud, and even exceptionally well but it still doesn't work. You need all the instruments of the orchestra playing together to produce a complete, full sound which delights the ear and the heart. And this book will discuss the other instruments you can use to make your company sing.

To start off, the next chapter will be a Cook's tour of intellectual capital, just hitting the highlights but using them to point out the kinds of human management challenges it generates. After that, we'll examine the techniques you'll need to adjust to this new kind of worker.

Main Points

- The driver of success in the New Economy is knowledge.
- Demand for knowledge workers is great and growing.
- A knowledge worker is one who uses her head more than her hands to produce value.
- About 60 per cent of all jobs are knowledge-based.
- Managing the human dimension of knowledge work is the most important job a manager has.

ACKNOWLEDGEMENTS

৩০

As is usual with any book, there are many people beyond the author who make its publication possible. There are those whose early encouragement and comments made the book better than what it would have been otherwise and also urged me to continue the long route to publication. Among those I wish to thank for that early belief in me and the book are: Claude Bernier, John Butcher, David Carlson, Chanlun Chan, Margaret Coshan, Barry Davy, Michel Desjardins, Mont Doyle, Helen Durand-Charron, Doug Gahm, Ken Henry, Brett Holt, Martha Hynna, Tony Johnston, Carolyn Levy, Michael McFaul, Diane McGarry, Mike Norman, Maureen Scott, and Katita Stark.

In addition, there are those who helped to create the book by slogging through many chapters and their revisions, investing their time and wisdom in a way which I can never thank adequately but for which I will always be grateful. My very special thanks to Cliff Cullen, Stephanie Howard, Barb MacCallum, and Janet Mairs for their insights and willingness to contribute their intellectual capital.

Finally, my thanks to my agent, Daphne Hart, whose belief in the worth of my book sustained me when nothing else did and to my editor, Karen Milner, and all those at John Wiley and Sons Canada, Ltd. who have consistently been both pleasant and professional as they applied their special knowledge to mine.

Intellectual Capital: What Is It And Why Do You Care?

We have been discussing how the new economy is driving a demand for knowledge workers—people who produce value with their brainpower rather than their hands. Organizations that can harness the intellectual capital of these knowledge workers will be successful in the information age. To illustrate, let's use an example of knowledge at work.

Gordon Feeney, vice chairman of the Royal Bank Financial Group, is very aware that knowledge and knowledge workers have permeated the way we do business. The Royal Bank Financial Group has over 200 different product and services, ranging from telephone banking, to deposit instruments, automobile loans, mortgages, and mutual funds. To handle much of this business, they employ more than 2000 people at call centers. Although these call center operators don't command the heady salaries of computer programmers, they are nevertheless knowledge workers since the Royal's objective is to handle 80 per cent of all calls without referring them to anyone else. Thus, they must be able to understand, synthesize, and integrate an enormous amount of knowledge to serve customers well. In addition, they need to be alert to opportunities to interest the client in other Royal services that both meet the customer's need and are profitable for the bank. Call center operators must be willing to use their abilities of analysis, synthesis, integration, and innovation to make each call as profitable as possible.

An example of this happened one Saturday afternoon at a Royal call center. An operator received a request for the exchange rate on the peso. She provided it and then asked, did the caller need a calculation? Yes, the caller agreed, that would be helpful. The conversion from pesos yielded several million dollars. The operator offered help again—did the caller want to deposit or transfer the money? "Actually," said the caller, "I want to invest it." Using the bank's listing of investment counselors, the operator connected the client with the appropriate people and by Monday morning, two or three people were working on making profit both for the client and the bank.

When knowledge workers invest their intellectual capital in an organization, the results can be both satisfying for them and profitable for the company. And if they don't, withholding their intellectual capital can create serious problems. As Gordon Feeney points out, "It would have been easy for that call operator to stop after giving the exchange rate. After all, that was all the client was asking for. If she hadn't been willing to go further, we would have missed that opportunity and would never even have known."

That is the key difference between knowledge workers and other workers. Because so much of what is valuable occurs in knowledge workers' heads, *whether* they are using their intellectual capital to best serve the organization can usually only be assessed at a time well past the point that a company can do anything about it. For example, with so much information and the pressure of calls—the Royal's call centers handle between 50 and 60 million calls a year—it is easy to see how call center operators could be tempted simply to process whatever the customer asks for and no more. However, if they do that, the sales will be unsatisfactory and managers will likely spend many months trying to figure out why. It could be that the operators aren't using their intellectual capital, but it could also be that the services aren't ones that the customers want, or that other banks have equally attractive offerings at a lower cost or more conveniently available.

Some organizations have tried to compel employees to use their intellectual capital by imposing sales quotas and monitoring calls with customers. And while they have some success, both suffer serious flaws. Quotas or targets allow the company to meet revenue targets but don't encourage or perhaps even allow for the possibility that customers don't want a product or might want another which either isn't targeted or doesn't yet exist. It assumes that some senior person who is not talking directly with the customer knows what the customer needs and will buy better than the customer herself or the person dealing with her. If the targets are not met, it's not clear whether the fault is the operators' or an unrealistic target.

Monitoring the operators' calls to ensure they are spending the time needed to assess the customers' needs is also a possibility but unless a call center is willing to effectively double its staff, it's not possible to monitor every one. Only a small percentage can be, which still leaves operators with many opportunities to choose whether to invest their intellectual capital in their calls.

So while quotas and monitoring might have some success, the most effective way to ensure that knowledge workers use their intellectual capital in service of the organization is to convince them that they want to. That isn't to imply that sales quotas and monitoring will be unnecessary but it will mean that they will not be the drivers of profitability but simply ways to measure how well the company is doing. True success will come when your knowledge workers *want* to make an investment of their intellectual capital in the organization.

Thus, we all need to pay attention to how to leverage the intellectual capital of our organizations. To do this, let's first discuss the types of intellectual capital in your organization and then the management challenges that each type generates.

Broadly, intellectual capital is divided up into three large areas. The first is *human capital* or the knowledge and experience people bring to the workplace. It is another way to say "people" but thinking about them as human capital points out how brainpower has effectively replaced asset capital as the driver of wealth. Human capital is the wellspring of the new economy. In the example above, the call operators' use of their abilities to analyze, synthesize, integrate, and innovate is the organization's human capital.

Of course, these characteristics have always been important to an organization, but the difference is that they were usually only truly necessary for the top echelon of the company—those who were seen and saw themselves as being responsible for doing the thinking for everyone. In traditional manufacturing operations, the division between thinking and doing was very sharp. Managers analyzed the market, synthesized the data, and decided what new products were required. The workers manufactured the result of that thinking. Even in service outfits, the tradition has been that managers decide what needs to be done and workers do it.

It was possible and probably even most effective to use only managerial intellectual capital when there were few products or their variations minor. Then, managers had knowledge to make those decisions. But when the products and services an organization offers grow and the knowledge needed to produce them is also growing, the idea that a relatively small number of people in the organization can or should be the only ones to use their intellectual capital is no longer viable. Everyone's intellectual capital must be used.

The second type of intellectual capital is *structural capital*. To tap human capital, organizations have to use more of what their people know. One part of structural capital is building systems like databases that allow people to be connected to and learn from each other. It avoids reinventing the wheel and, in addition, promotes the synergy that comes when two or more like-minded people work together. In our example, the call operators have access to information on-line (e.g., a list of investment counselors), that they might otherwise have to research themselves. They are able to make use of other people's knowledge because it has been housed in some structural capital—in this case, a database—which allows easy access.

However, beyond connecting people, there is another equally important function of structural capital. As more and more of what is valuable resides in the heads of people, organizations are becoming aware that if the people leave, the value leaves also. They are trying to find ways to capture this knowledge so others can use it and the organization can retain it. Some ways are standards and procedures as well as hardware and software. In summary, structural capital is the infrastructure that helps to convert human capital into wealth for the organization.

Organizations know that customers are the pivot of their livelihood. Customers create wealth. If they don't buy, you don't prosper. So the third pillar of intellectual capital is *customer capital*. Customers have always been important to any company but like voters, they are becoming both more demanding and crankier. To capitalize on your customer base and continue to generate revenue, you need a new relationship with them. This relationship increasingly needs to be long term, stretching over many years and many repeat sales rather than a one-time, one-off contact, and how your knowledge workers deal with customers will drive whether customers are willing to enter into this continuing connection. If the call center operator is rude or appears to be selling product rather than meeting the customer's needs, that customer will not be willing to enter into a long-term relationship with the bank. However, if the customer believes that he was treated well by the call operator, he is more likely to buy the next time, creating customer capital for the company.

Managing different types of intellectual capital well is the key to your company's competitiveness. However, it also prompts new management challenges,[1] and we'll discuss them in this chapter. The three types of capital are:

- Human Capital
- Structural Capital
- Customer Capital

Human Capital

The more computers dominate our landscape, the more those exclusively human characteristics of judgment, analysis, synthesis, and innovation are important. This change requires nothing less than a rethink of the relationship of knowledge and position power. In most organizations, the higher your position, the more power you have. Simple, obvious, almost pre-ordained. However, focusing on the creation of wealth through knowledge can change that. Suddenly, *who* is important in an organization shifts. It's the working level knowledge workers whose moods, needs, and interests become most important. They are the ones who both have the most up-to-date knowledge and are closest to the customer. Thus they have a substantial influence on a company's success through their ability to transform knowledge into wealth and to build customer capital. It is the job of every manager to pay attention to these knowledge workers because they control the levers of wealth creation.

The usual response to the previous sentence is something like: "Of course, people have always been our most important resource." We've heard it from every corporate executive who's swept in to lay a blessing on the troops on his way to more important matters. But in fact, in most organizations, it has never been true. It is our bosses' moods, needs, and interests which rivet our attention, not our employees'.

---

[1] Or ability to fulfill your mandate. I realize that in non-profit and public sector environments, competitiveness will not be as relevant. However, the principles to be discussed have as much relevance in terms of delivering on your mission.

We might have an interest in our employees' moods and needs, but let's face it, it's usually optional. If you don't deliver results, caring about your employees doesn't cut the mustard. But the information economy has moved this focus on employees from optional to mandatory because caring about your employees is becoming *the* way to deliver results.

New Management Challenges with Human Capital

So, dealing with knowledge workers has major implications for who you're going to worry about keeping happy. But there are other challenges in managing the human side of human capital. Its effective use requires:

- Encouraging new knowledge to come forward.
- Tapping everyone's knowledge.
- Managing knowledge you don't understand.
- Encouraging people to learn.

Encouraging New Knowledge to Come Forward

In the olden days (i.e., when we first started working), there was usually a set body of knowledge we all worked from. There were designated new knowledge gurus like researchers and engineers and by and large, knowledge spread through the organization in a steady and organized fashion.

Today, knowledge comes at the organization from all sides—the Internet, greater media coverage, plus all the old ways, like conferences and business articles. What's more, the competitive advantage today is not the slow, sure building of knowledge, but the breakthrough innovation which might come out of left field.

Given this, one of the most important jobs managers have is to encourage new knowledge to come forward. And while we all think that we do that, in practice, many of our systems and mind-sets prevent it. For example, I was brought into a consulting firm that had an excellent track record for attracting new customers but needed a line of services to keep them buying. I had a body of new knowledge that could provide that next wave.

However, there were hiccups. Consultants "owned" certain customers with whom they had a relationship and from whom they derived their revenue. The new knowledge I had was the logical next step for most customers, but if the consultant recommended me to a client, who got credit for the resulting revenue? The original consultant who recommended me or me, since I had the knowledge the client needed? If I got it, why would any consultant want to use the new knowledge, since he lost both the revenue and the client? If he got it, what was in it for me? Since we were both judged on how much revenue we brought in, it caused some heartache and more importantly, jeopardized the ability of the organization to introduce the new knowledge.

"Business as usual" is the way an organization usually deals with this problem. It's also the death knell for new knowledge. New knowledge demands changes, not just in what knowledge is used, but in the systems and structures which have grown up around the use of the old knowledge. It can be, and often is, very disruptive but unless you learn how to manage these changes, new knowledge will be prevented from infusing your organization even if it is critical to your competitive advantage.

Chapter 2 will show managers ways to encourage employees to bring forward their new knowledge.

Tapping Everyone's Knowledge

In recent years, with the advent of better educated workers, it is recognized that the philosophy that managers think and workers do no longer fits organizational needs. There has been some push to share responsibility for thinking in all its elements—analysis, synthesis, innovation, and strategy—with more people in the organization.

The information age will push this requirement even further. In a world of increasing knowledge, it's no longer possible for one person (like the CEO) or one set of people (like managers) to take in enough of the relevant knowledge to make the decisions in the same kind of isolation as was possible in the past. Thus, employees need to be consulted and involved in decisions beyond the scope of their immediate jobs. It is in the best interest of the organization not simply to access its employees' know-how, but also to increase their willingness to commit to the strategic direction. Knowledge workers who don't want to invest their intellectual capital in an organization, don't have to, and that unwillingness can be hard to detect as in our example at the Royal Bank. So while consulting with and involving employees can provide insights into the running of the business, they can also be a compelling invitation to employees to donate their intellectual capital to the organization.

Chapter 3 will outline how managers can help employees understand the company's strategic direction and its implications well enough to make informed decisions and recommendations. Chapter 4 will cover how to consult employees on company-wide issues and Chapter 5 will discuss how to involve them in corporate decision making.

Managing Knowledge You Don't Understand

As knowledge proliferates, it also specializes. In most academic fields, the knowledge is so great that you can only become truly proficient if you go down deep. One of my colleagues in graduate school did his thesis on color preference in chicks (baby chickens). Honest.[2]

The requirement for a narrow but deep focus has been less extreme in business environments but most of us still had to decide at some point in our careers whether to be generalists or specialize in one function like finance, marketing, sales, or operations. But today, even within a specialty like finance or operations, there are levels of expertise that cannot be conquered by everyone. For example, in a manufacturing operation, you could have experts in process improvement whose depth of knowledge about *how* you re-engineer may be unparalleled. Exceptional proficiency in one area is often at the expense of breadth of understanding, but it still means that, in that niche, you have no equal.

An unsettling corollary for managers is that, more and more frequently, employees are doing things you don't really understand. That is, you may understand the broad outlines, but you don't have enough knowledge to know whether it really is wisest to zig when your inclination might be to zag at a particular point.

This in turn leads to uncomfortable questions like: "If I don't know what they're doing, can I direct them?" And even worse, "If they know more than I do, do I have a real job?" The answer, you'll be glad to know, is "yes" to both questions. How you get there is covered in Chapter 6.

---

[2] They prefer red.

Encouraging People to Learn

In a static world, the need to learn isn't very great. You generally do a lot when you're young and stop after a certain point. But in an uncertain world, learning never ends. As we all come to terms with what that means to us and the work world, companies need to make a concerted effort to help knowledge workers to continue to add to their store of knowledge. Those at the leading edge of the knowledge are the ones who create competitive advantage. A haphazard, well-meaning approach to this learning is not enough. Chapter 7 will cover how to establish a learning program in your organization.

As you can see, the rise of knowledge workers in the workplace will make profound changes in the way you manage. When position isn't important anymore, how do you direct? When you supervise people whose job you don't fully understand, how do you lead? If new knowledge is easy to stifle but critical to long-term success, how do you encourage it? When knowledge wants to be free, how do you keep a competitive edge? And these are just the management challenges for human capital. There are more in the next section on structural capital.

Structural Capital

Structural capital—the infrastructure side of intellectual capital—often gets the most management attention, probably because it's the most concrete. Building computer systems or databases fit the way we're used to working—put it on a time line and get it built. Human and customer capital enter that much mushier realm of innovation, trust, and interpersonal issues. You can't put them on a time line ("you will have a breakthrough idea by 0800 hours tomorrow").

Most organizations have more structural capital capacity than they need.[3] The role of structural capital is to *support* the real knowledge network: that of people talking to other people. All of your structural capital needs to be assessed in this light. In fact, leaders in the field of intellectual capital are unanimous that "without strong underlying human capital, any amount of structural capital is all but worthless."[4]

There is no point in an elaborate infrastructure unless you address the following management issues which structural capital generates.

---

[3] Leif Edvinsson and Michael S. Malone, *Intellectual Capital: Realizing Your Company's True Value by Finding Its Hidden Brainpower* (New York: HarperBusiness 1997), 57.
[4] Ibid, 46.

New Management Challenges with Structural Capital

While building and maintaining the structural capital infrastructure is an important contribution, it is not sufficient if you want to leverage your organization's intellectual capital to maximum advantage. Effective management of the human side of structural capital requires:

- A free flow of information.
- A freer flow of knowledge and people.
- A willingness to share and learn.
- Rewarding knowledge.
- A willingness to change.

A Free Flow of Information

If I'm a stock clerk and you want me to use my knowledge for the good of the company, you need to help me understand exactly what that means. For example, unless I know we're having trouble financially, I may not bother redesigning the inventory controls so that they're cheaper and simpler. Of course, I know, based on the exhortations of all the higher ups, that I'm always *supposed* to improve my job, but let's face it, I've got a life outside stock clerking. I'm only going to do it if there is a compelling reason to pay attention. Knowledge and innovation cannot be ordered, but only invited. The challenge for all managers is to make the invitation so irresistible that all will respond. Some part of that compelling invitation is ensuring that knowledge workers know what is happening in the company. This often entails releasing information that has hitherto been largely management's province (e.g., financial and other confidential information) and helping people to understand how it relates to their jobs. Chapter 8 will cover what information you need to release and how to do it.

A Freer Flow of Knowledge and People

If your structural capital is working for you, you can envision a system where you type in "statistics—graduate level" and get the names of several knowledge workers who have those qualifications. You call one, explain the help you need and work together. You get the project done faster and learn something. It sounds great but this idyll is predicated on a system or mind-set that doesn't exist in most organizations. Let me sketch what usually happens. Ken, our statistician, does statistical analysis full-time. As with any other job, he's got a full plate of activities. The first time someone from outside the section asks for Ken's time, it may not be a problem. However, as the number of requests or the amount of time needed rises, Ken's boss starts asking, "So just when are you going to do the stuff I need?" Unless this can be resolved, Ken will be told to quit responding to these requests unless they come through official channels (i.e., his boss). And the network is prevented from working as intended. Unless managers can resolve the problem of sharing resources, you may run into an untenable situation: you know where the experts are; you just can't talk to them. Chapter 9 will address this issue.

A Willingness to Share and Learn

You can build a beautiful database, but if no one inputs any data, what good is it? Say I'm a whiz at writing bids for contracts. I know the requirements cold, and even the quirks and preferences of all the major customers. If I think that my job or my feelings of worth depend on having a unique competency, why would I want to load this knowledge onto a database for all to use? By making it widely available, I cheapened the value of my knowledge (and maybe of me).

For databases or any other type of structural capital to be effective, employees must believe it is in their best interests as well as the company's to share what they know. This belief cannot be compelled or mandated. Oh, you can order me to share, but since by definition, I know more about the contracting process than you do, just how do you know whether I've shared all I need to? Probably only after it's too late—when a bid has been unsuccessful after someone else besides me tried to use the data in the database. It's like a chef who gives you the recipe for his to-die-for chocolate cake, minus one ingredient.

Because sharing is always voluntary, the challenge is to create an environment in which people both want to share what they know and make use of what others know. Otherwise, databases and other structural capital are just expensive ways to keep the IT department busy.

In addition to getting people to learn, there is another, equally important challenge. The example used above assumes that everyone is dying to get this new knowledge and it's our old processes and attitudes that are getting in the way. But in fact, that's not always the case. Sometimes, people need to be encouraged to learn.

Let's return to the example of the consulting firm. One stumbling block was the compensation system but another was just plain human dynamics. Consultants are the purest form of knowledge worker since knowledge is the only thing they have to peddle. Like most knowledge workers, they're proud of their expertise and rightly so. However, this pride can make it more difficult to accept new knowledge. It can be a direct attack on the body of knowledge I've already mastered. Admitting I need to know something new may prompt me to wonder whether I really was doing the excellent job I always thought I did. And, to learn this new knowledge, I have to choose to be incompetent for a period while I struggle to understand, integrate, and use it. For those who have drawn self-worth and recognition from their expertise, it's a distasteful situation.

Most of us take pride in what we know and learning new knowledge can be both threatening and unsettling. Unless we're in an environment and with a boss where being temporarily incompetent is okay and where the new expert doesn't suddenly displace everyone else as the favorite son, it's less likely the new knowledge will proliferate quickly. Chapter 10 will tackle this topic on an individual basis and Chapter 11 will deal with it in a team setting.

Rewarding Knowledge

We've already discussed the problem some organizations are getting themselves into by assuming that the only lever they have to attract and retain knowledge workers is money. Money is of course an important element in maintaining your human capital but it is only one of several types of rewards which you can and should use. Chapter 12 will deal with money's role and other incentives to acquiring and using knowledge.

A Willingness to Change

As you can see, tapping intellectual capital requires substantial personal change of both managers and staff. Whether it's giving away decision-making power or overcoming resistance to new knowledge, these are challenges in and of themselves and we'll deal with personal change in Chapter 13.

Ensuring that structural capital really contributes to your store of intellectual capital requires people who are willing to share their knowledge, a free flow of information among all levels of the organization, a freer flow of people than traditional, and a willingness to learn from others. A network of structural capital is a necessary but not sufficient condition. Managing what goes into and comes out of your infrastructure is the source of true leverage.

Customer Capital

I bought my first PC when the term "PC" was a brand name. It didn't even have a hard drive and almost anyone else with a home computer was a geek-in-training. They were interested in how it operated and why. I just wanted it to work. I could care less about what was on the inside and the less I had to know, the better. I was a modern consumer, ahead of my time. Like me, today's customer has come to expect that products and services will be easy to use, practically indestructible and instantly repaired. Oh yes, and cheaper the next time he buys. And over the course of the last decade, companies have delivered on these expectations. However, given the demands for low price and high quality, it's not surprising profit margins are squeezed. With each individual sale producing less profit than previously, a company can stay in business only if customers will buy and rebuy. Customer loyalty is an important component of your success.

But customers are a fickle lot. Xerox conducted a study reported in *Harvard Business Review*. On a five-point scale, going from one (completely dissatisfied) to five (completely satisfied), customers who were fours (thoroughly satisfied) were six times more likely to defect than fives.[5] Imagine, even customers who call themselves thoroughly satisfied will drop you like a hot potato! They have to be at the I-love-you-and-nothing-will-ever-break-us-up stage or they're not loyal. Yet their loyalty is critical to your viability.

---

[5] Thomas A. Stewart, "A Satisfied Customer Isn't Enough," *Fortune* (July 21, 1997): 112.

New Management Challenges

The kind of fanatical loyalty you need to succeed in this volatile marketplace is not solely a function of price or quality. They're important of course, but all your competitors will eventually match them and, as we know, competing on price is a no-win game. As *Fortune* columnist, Geoffrey Colvin points out, you need to compete on service and innovation, "both of them nearly magical results of human interactions that will never be easy to engineer or even understand."[6] So, what human management challenge does this new relationship with customers generate? Customer capital requires:

Employees Who Build Loyalty

So how do you get these magical interactions that produce customer loyalty? Sears has done an interesting analysis that indicates employee attitudes about the job and company are two factors that predict their behavior in front of the customer, which in turn predicts the likelihood of customer retention and customers' recommending the company to others, the two factors that, in turn, predict financial performance. So loyal customers are a result of loyal and satisfied employees. Thus, you need both to build loyalty in employees (Chapter 14) and know how you're doing on building it (Chapter 15).

Will all this focus on the human dimension of intellectual capital really make a difference to the bottom line?

A good question and an important one. Asking managers to focus on amorphous issues like sharing and learning is difficult enough as it is—it needs to have a payoff. And the research shows there is one.

- Using the 61 publicly traded companies of the 100 named "Most Admired" in *Fortune's* 1997 poll, 45 yielded higher returns to shareholders than the Russell 3000 (an index of large and small companies that mirror the 100 Best). The 61 companies averaged annual returns of 27.5% vs. 17.3% for the Russell 3000. Ten-year patterns were the same. Russell 3000 annual returns of 14.8%; publicly traded Best companies, 23.4%.[7]

---

[6] Geoffrey Colvin, "Art of Becoming Unbeatable," *Fortune* (November 24, 1997): 299.
[7] Linda Grant, "Happy Workers, Happy Returns," *Fortune* (January 12, 1998): 81.

- Gallup matched employee attitudes with company results. Four attitudes, taken together, correlate strongly with profits: workers feel they are given the opportunity to do what they do best every day, they believe their opinions count (and simply you saying they do, is not enough), they sense their fellow workers are committed to quality, they've made a direct connection between their work and the company's mission.[8]

- Sears found that if a store increases its employee-satisfaction score by five measuring units in a quarter, the following quarter its customer-satisfaction score would go up by two units. This in turn leads to a revenue growth of .05% above the national average.[9]

So yes, this concern about the human side of intellectual capital does make a difference to the bottom line. It makes a difference now and it's going to be even more important as the information age picks up speed.

From Common Sense to Common Practice

We've done a quick tour of intellectual capital and the new people management challenges it generates. For your intellectual capital to be a competitive advantage, you must have employees who are willing to offer new ideas, share their own knowledge, learn from others, and create customer loyalty. The way to invite people to donate their intellectual capital to the company will involve revisiting and reworking many of the concepts such as shared decision making, creating a team, and employee loyalty that have been floating around organizations for years.

At this point, some of you may be thinking: "Been there. Done that. Got the T-shirt." However, when managers say they've *done* trust, involvement and communication, it reminds me of when Total Quality Management (TQM) was being launched. I knew how gut-wrenching and revolutionary TQM was if an organization was serious about improving its quality. It was a long and never-ending journey with a 70 to 80 per cent failure rate. So when I heard executives say, "Quality? Oh ya, we did that last year," I knew not only had they not, but whatever they had done, it wasn't going to improve quality.

---

[8] Ibid.
[9] Sherman Stratford, "Bringing Sears into the New World" *Fortune* (October 13, 1997): 183

But when I heard, "Quality? We're trying but it's hard! We're not making as much progress as I'd like but there is some movement," I knew there was something there.

It's very similar with intellectual capital. It is difficult, not conceptually but in practice, to put a system into place which actually delivers the results you want. Moreover, it's easy to be fooled into thinking that the level of sharing and learning going on in your organization is what is actually needed to have a competitive edge. Allowing people to go on courses doesn't making an organization a learning one, anymore than people occasionally pinch-hitting for each other makes it a sharing one. The level of sharing and learning we're talking about is much more profound than most organizations have experienced.

So if you're tempted at points in the book to say, "Yes, but that's just common sense," you're right. It is often common sense but it is rarely common practice. The focus of the book is on what you need to *do* in order to turn common sense into common practice. And that is more of a challenge than I think anyone can imagine.

Summary

Just as information technology is causing a revolution in almost everything we do and think, so it is prompting an upheaval within organizations. New management challenges arise from the demands of working with knowledge, including the need to decrease issues of turf and increase employee loyalty.

This chapter has given you an overview of the human management challenges which intellectual capital brings to an organization. The next chapter will start to delve into each of these in more detail, starting with encouraging new knowledge to come forward.

Main Points

- Intellectual capital consists of human, structural, and customer capital.
- The human capital management challenges are encouraging new knowledge to come forward, tapping everyone's knowledge, managing knowledge you don't understand, and encouraging people to learn.

- Managing structural capital well requires a free flow of information, a freer flow of knowledge and people, a willingness to share and learn, and a willingness to change.
- The management challenge related to customer capital is creating and maintaining loyalty among employees who in turn determine whether customers are loyal.

S e c t i o n   O n e

The Human Side of Human Capital

While building intellectual capital has many components—technology, systems, and measurement—the most important is the human dimension. Managing human capital to leverage its worth for the company requires:

Encouraging New Knowledge. Even if your people know a lot, if they can't or won't apply this knowledge to their jobs, it can't create wealth. Chapter 2 deals with how managers can encourage new knowledge to come forward from individuals.

Pushing Down Complexity. The days when managers made all the decisions and workers did all the work is long since past. In order to leverage the human capital in the organization, managers must help employees understand the company's strategic direction and how it applies to their work. They can do this by pushing down complexity (Chapter 3).

Tapping Knowledge Throughout the Corporation: Consultation. Once employees understand the business environment, their input into corporate decisions can be invaluable both for the specialized knowledge they can bring to bear and to increase their commitment to the organization's goals. However, while valuable, the process of consultation needs to be managed carefully. How to do this is covered in Chapter 4.

Tapping Knowledge Throughout the Corporation: Involvement. Similarly, asking employees to decide or recommend on the big business challenges of the day can have important pay-offs for the company, but ensuring that the involvement process builds rather than destroys commitment and trust lies in careful implementation. This process is discussed in Chapter 5.

Managing Knowledge You Don't Understand. As the amount of knowledge available grows by leaps and bounds, workers must increasingly specialize in order to master a particular niche. Managers are faced with more and more employees whom they must direct without an in-depth understanding of what the employees do. Chapter 6 will consider how to deal with this conundrum.

Encouraging People to Learn. Intellectual capital is only a sustained competitive advantage if it continues to grow. Thus, the people in the organization must be able to enhance their store of knowledge and skills through on-the-job learning. However, a learning program is more than a few courses and Chapter 7 will cover how to set one up which will encourage the kind of continuous learning an organization needs.

CHAPTER 2

ᏮᏇ

Encouraging
New Knowledge

There are plenty of epochal stories of missing the boat on great new knowledge. The Swiss invented a mechanism that counted time in digits but couldn't see how it applied to watches. The Japanese saw it in an exhibit of interesting curiosities and the rest, as they say, is history. Talk to Xerox people and they'll freely admit—in fact it's part of their folklore—that their research facility at Palo Alto came up with truly breakthrough technology (e.g., the mouse, icon technology, laptops). None of it was exploited because Xerox management couldn't see its market value. Apple did.

But there are some success stories too. 3M Post-it notes were the result of a scientist creating a glue that didn't stick well. The genius was not just that scientist, but in the company's ability to recognize usefulness. In hindsight, it's easy to shake our heads and say, "How stupid, how short sighted," and to believe we're more like the 3M manager who gave the go-ahead for the Post-it notes or Steven Jobs who saw the potential of the Palo Alto research.

But encouraging new knowledge can be a tricky thing. The glue used on Post-it notes failed 3M's standards. In some companies, that kind of "failure" would have prompted the response, "Throw the stuff out and start again." Great ideas are great *because* they don't fit into our current way of thinking. Truly creative people often link items that *we know* don't make any sense to join. So, encouraging new knowledge or ideas[1] to come forward can be a difficult thing and all great missed opportunities probably started with one manager shaking his head and saying, "I don't think it'll work."

This chapter will discuss three major things a manager can do to address this issue. The first actively solicits employee's ideas. The second and third activities are more about the culture that you need to create so that the ideas will continue to come forward. They are taking a new view of failure and admitting mistakes.

Encouraging Employees to Generate New Ideas

A friend told me about a meeting where the people were asked to offer ideas to solve a particularly thorny problem. They were tossing around various options when one participant, Kirk, came up with a real blooper. Kirk's boss came back with, "Well, that's not a good idea," and Kirk, to save face, said, "Oh, you wanted *good* ideas...I hadn't realized that." It's an amusing story but on second thought, it's a cautionary tale because it captures exactly the problem managers have in encouraging new ideas.

If we all had worlds enough and time (and money), the best way to encourage new knowledge would be lots of leeway for experimentation and dumb ideas. You'd always be able to say, "Hey, I don't think it'll fly, but what the heck, give it a try!" But we can't. We have a business to run. You can drive an organization into the ground if there's too much going on that isn't valued by your customer however interesting it might be or however much it might ease your life. A judgment call is necessary about what's worth pursuing and what isn't.

In the past, that call has usually been yours. And realistically, that's probably going to continue. However, there are a couple of problems. For one thing, your call is based on your assumptions of what works in your business. As illustrated above, even whole crews of smart, committed executives can be left standing at the station when the train pulls out. Relying exclusively on your own ability to think outside the box doesn't tap all knowledge and innovative capacity in your work unit. In addition, your ability to know what will fly may be compromised because the knowledge needed is deeper and more specialized. You may not know whether an idea really is dumb or whether it just looks that way.

---

[1] I'll use the terms "new knowledge" and "new ideas" interchangeably in this chapter.

It's sort of daunting. You want to encourage new knowledge, but you don't have unlimited resources, and you can't necessarily tell what's going to be useful. There are some ways you can still do it:

- Help employees understand how the strategic direction applies to them.
- Let employees work on things you don't agree with.
- Listen vigilantly.
- Kill an idea when it isn't going to work.
- Help employees understand your role.

Help Employees Understand how the Strategic Direction Applies to Them

If people really understand the strategic direction of the company— not just words on the page, but how it intimately connects with what they do, they're more likely to generate ideas consistent with it. In the next chapter, we'll discuss how to do that.

Let Employees Work on Things You Don't Agree With

I know this sounds wrong and inefficient. Shouldn't everyone be aligned to the same target? Yes, but 3M has been very successful in part because they give researchers permission to spend up to 15 per cent of their time and company equipment and supplies to pursue lines of interest to them but with no obvious relationship to the company's goals. It's not experimentation gone wild but it does recognize that you don't have a corner on all the good ideas and that your judgment might even be wrong.

This suggestion creates immediate and understandable objections. 3M is a big company, they can afford this kind of thing. I have deadlines and production to meet. And any number of other good reasons. But what about this idea: we've all dealt with an employee who proposes an idea we had to put the kibosh on. However, a week or a month later, he comes back with, "Boss, you know that idea I had? I did a little more work on it and..." Or it might come up casually that he's been spending time on it. Your first reaction might be "What part of 'no' didn't you understand?" You might be tempted to shut him down to show him the issue has been settled.

But instead, what about:

You:	*I didn't think you were working on that.*
Employee:	*Ya...well...I know I wasn't supposed to, but...*
You:	*OK, well enough said. What did you find?*
Employee:	*Really? Well, actually, it's pretty neat...*

This exchange signals your willingness to allow latitude in what people work on. Of course, not every employee idea will turn into gold. But allowing a greater degree of freedom will allow for the possibility that that breakthrough idea will come forward.

Some managers may be concerned that they'll lose control of their operations if everyone is running off, ignoring direction. But it's not all that likely to happen. If employees really understand how they can contribute to the strategic direction, their ideas, while perhaps not strictly in line with yours, will probably be going in the same general direction.

Naturally, we're not talking about problem employees who consistently do what they want rather than what's assigned but about the normal worker who delivers what's expected. Even if you can't officially give these people a set amount of time to pursue their own interests, you can signal that you're willing to support some of that work.

And—don't treat this "unapproved" idea like a pariah. Once you know about it, inquire occasionally on progress. This signals you don't punish people for showing some independence.

Listen Vigilantly

New knowledge is rarely an eureka! type discovery. It's more likely a wallflower than the life of the party. What gives new knowledge the confidence and room to grow into that huge idea is someone responding, "That's interesting..." or "Why don't you give it a try?" The best ideas often come in tenuous packages. So you need to get into the habit of listening vigilantly to what people say and trying to stifle automatic responses like, "You're right...that'll never fly" or "Well, it's a good idea but it'll cost too much" or even "I'd like to do it but the powers that be will never go for it."

All these statements may be true and you may have to say them eventually. But it's a question of timing. If you say them while the idea is being born, you'll probably kill it. The employee will shrug and turn to other things. However, if you say something like, "Well, that's interesting. Tell me a little more" or "I think that would be great. How do you think we can solve the cost problem?," you encourage the employee not just to come forward with the idea but to think about how to expand it into a great one.

You may do some of this already but consider whether you do it as much as you need to or if you do it with everyone. When you've worked with a group of people long enough, you start to form opinions of whose ideas are worth listening to and whose aren't. Of course, you shouldn't spend inordinate amounts of time listening to Charlie who has never really understood the difference between what he likes and what your customers like. But try to listen a little more vigilantly, even to those whose good-idea-to-dumb-idea ratio is quite low. After all, you only need one great idea.

Kill an Idea When it Isn't Going to Work

A corollary of letting people develop new ideas is knowing when you need to kill the project. If you don't, you get into exactly what you feared—people working on things that don't create wealth. Before the employee starts, agree how long the development phase will last. After you discuss the great new idea Angela has, you might ask, "So, do you think a couple of weeks will be enough time to get a fix on whether this will fly?" When the time's up, the two of you can make a judgment call.

Conversations about killing a project can be difficult, especially when the employee's put a lot into it. If the idea hasn't worked out in the time period you agreed to, she'll probably push for more time or resources. If you agree with the potential, no problem. However, if you don't, the conversation needs careful handling. Let's think about how that might roll out.

Angela:	*I just know I could get this to work if I had another month or so.*
You:	*Angela, I can't see how it's going to make a difference. It just doesn't look like the idea will fly.*
Angela:	*I think you're wrong.*

You:	*That's always a possibility, but right now, I need you to concentrate on the other things you've got on your plate.*
Angela:	*Barbara, I'm sure this is a great idea. I don't want to let it die.*
You:	*Well, Angela, help me with my problem. I need you urgently on the Myers and O'Keefe projects. In addition, I honestly don't think the idea's feasible. From my point of view, it just doesn't make any sense to continue.*
Angela:	*What if I cleaned off Myers and O'Keefe and then went back?*
You:	*That would help in the short-term but it wouldn't make any difference to feasibility. Can you think of a way we can get around that?*
Angela:	*But if I had even two more weeks, I could prove it was feasible.*
You:	*So, if you had the two weeks, you'd spend the time working on proving feasibility and not just on developing the idea itself?*
Angela:	*Sure, if that's what it takes.*
You:	*Well, if you do the other projects first, maybe we can live with that. But if it's not feasible, then we'll drop it, right?*
Angela:	*Oh, absolutely.*

You may think this is a cop out. After all, if you really don't think an idea will fly, why give Angela more time to prove it? There may be other reasons which make it impossible to give her more time. But remember, new ideas don't necessarily look like good ones right off the top, and you don't have a corner on the knowledge and vision to always assess their true potential. This may mean allowing experiments on things which, deep in your heart, you don't believe will work.

In the above scenario, it's quite possible that even after the two weeks, the idea still isn't working. You may feel Angela's wasted the time. However, that's not necessarily so. For one thing, her "failure" may help her think how she can make the idea work at some later date.

In addition, and perhaps even more importantly, you've signaled to her in a very tangible and important way that you're willing to support her innovation, that you don't believe you have the corner on all the new ideas. You're showing her you value her intellectual capital and you want her to use it.

So the question really is: "Is it worth the two extra weeks to keep Angela trying to come up with new ideas?" Sometimes the answer has to be no, but if the answer can be yes at strategic moments, you'll demonstrate your willingness to encourage new knowledge to come forward.

Help Employees Understand Your Role

Sometimes, you just have to say no. However much you'd like to give Angela more time, you can't. Saying no may also occur when employees ask to move their idea up the food chain or for more resources to fully develop the idea. If the employee takes the no well, you're in business and no more said. But sometimes, a no can take on a meaning for the employee that you don't want.

Employee:	*Matt, what about that suggestion I made last week for shorter production runs? What's happening with that?*
You:	*Oh, ya, Art. I've been meaning to get back to you about that. I looked over your figures and I don't think it's a go.*
Employee:	*Why not? It'll save us a lot of work.*
You:	*But it'll cause problems in shipping. We're just shifting the workload.*
Employee:	*I thought you wanted ideas on efficiency. Here I come up with one and you won't buy it. Brother, talk about mixed messages!*
You:	*Well, what did you expect? Just because you had an idea, I'm supposed to OK it, no matter what? Come off it!*
Employee:	*Well, fine. Forget it then. I knew this "we want your ideas stuff" was a crock anyhow.*
You:	*It wouldn't be if you'd come up with good ideas ....*

You can see that this conversation doesn't augur well for future donations of intellectual capital. It's also easy to see how you might walk away thinking, "He just doesn't get it."

Naturally, you aren't going to implement a poor suggestion just to encourage innovation. However, there were two separate issues in this conversation. One was the suggestion itself; the other was the perception that your support of new knowledge is merely lip service. The first was addressed in some fashion. The second wasn't, and if you ignore it, the employee will believe you really don't want new ideas. Your real intent is almost irrelevant. If the employee believes it's just window dressing, he'll keep his great ideas to himself, no matter what you say.

There's a temptation to say, "That's their problem. My heart and conscience are clear." However, if it matters whether or not they believe you, you need to take some action. Let's go back to the situation outlined above and have another run at it.

Employee:	*I thought you wanted ideas on efficiency. Here I come up with one and you won't buy it. Brother, talk about mixed messages!*
You:	*Wait a minute, Art. I do want your ideas and I thought there were some real possibilities when you suggested it. But not every idea is going to fly.*
Employee:	*But this would have improved our efficiency by 15 per cent. It was all in my analysis.*
You:	*You're right and that's pretty impressive. But if we create downstream problems, the company as a whole doesn't win.*
Employee:	*Well …I guess.*
You:	*So, I appreciate your work and I wish it were feasible. I'd love to see that kind of improvement. But this one just doesn't look like a go.*
Employee:	*OK, OK. Too bad.*
You:	*Absolutely. If it had worked, we would have been heroes. But, before you go, can I talk a bit about the mixed messages thing?*

Employee:	*Oh that. Forget it. Just blowing off steam.*
You:	*Sure, I understand, but I think it's important. I need to know if you think I'm not giving you the straight goods.*
Employee:	*No. No problem.*
You:	*OK, so it makes sense I need to check out new ideas? Some will be a go right off the bat, some might need work, and some may not fly. But that I'm not talking out of two sides of my mouth if I do?*
Employee:	*Well, really, that's your job, isn't it?*

You may need to push a bit to make sure the implicit message is addressed. If you deal with the overt issue, it's typical for people to think you're done. And since Art jumped to a conclusion about your motives, he's not all that keen to keep talking about it. But don't lose this opportunity to clarify what to expect of each other.

When you say no, people need to understand you're saying no for this project only and not to all new ideas. As demonstrated in the example, you can help by explicitly addressing your role with respect to new knowledge.

It Is Important Not to Punish Failure

So there are several ways to actively encourage new knowledge to come forward. But even more importantly, there are things you need to do to keep the ideas flowing. One is not punishing failure.

There's an interesting phenomenon in the high-tech sector. Developing the information age on the ground has meant a series of experiments and failures, with companies starting up and failing with great consistency over and over until the industry gets it right. Christopher Meyer at Stanford University believes that the high-tech sector succeeds partially *because* "failure here is understood to be an integral aspect of the growth process."[2] In fact, venture capitalists effectively reward failure by preferring to invest in companies whose executives are "seasoned"— i.e., have been involved in one or more start-ups that didn't fly.[3]

---

[2] Robert J. Samuelson, "Secrets of Success," *Newsweek Special Issue* (Winter 1997/98): 79.
[3] Leif Edvinsson and Michael S. Malone, *Intellectual Capital: Realizing Your Company's True Value by Finding Its Hidden Brainpower,* (New York: HarperBusiness, 1997), 28.

It's quite a different spin on failure—not punishment but reward. How can you apply that logic to your setting? First, think about the reasons for failure or mistakes (I'll use the terms interchangeably). Here are some:

- Because you're incompetent.
- Because you don't care.
- Because it seemed to make sense at the time.
- Because you were learning.
- Because you were trying something new.
- Because you didn't know.

There are many different reasons for failing, but the consequences always seem to be the same. If it's a really big boo-boo, the axe comes out swinging and heads roll. If it's big but not lethal, there is some anger and then the issue is buried, with embarrassed silences whenever it's inadvertently raised later. If you've failed, you get the clear, although often unspoken message that you shouldn't be looking for any plum assignments in the near future. The punishment is usually related to the gravity of the error not the reason for it. In no case is there anything like rewarding failure.

But some reasons for failing may stem from exactly the characteristics you want to encourage in knowledge workers. You want people learning and trying out new things. If they don't, their knowledge can't grow and neither can the company. So to try to keep innovation alive, you need to focus on the reasons for the failure rather than its gravity. Did they fail because they were experimenting or because they didn't care? Did they make a mistake because they didn't know the consequences or didn't think about them?

Getting at the real reasons can be difficult. After an error, big or small, people are more likely to tell you what will get them off the hook or save face rather than what really happened. This is particularly true if they believe they'll be penalized. You can up the chances at understanding what really happened if you lower the threat by always assuming a failure is due to positive intentions—that is, it happened because someone didn't know or was experimenting.

"Whoa!" I can hear you saying, "I should assume that every time someone messes up, it wasn't his fault?" No, but when someone makes a mistake, neither she nor the organization can learn unless you can talk about it. However, if she is mired in self-justification or defensiveness, it'll be hard to explore the issue. Your assumption of positive intentions makes it easier to open the discussion.

Here's how a conversation could go. The company is bidding on a substantial government contract which you have a good chance of winning. The proposal deadline was 2 p.m. Friday. Bill, a fairly new employee, submitted the proposal at 2:05 p.m. and the government official refused to accept it. The revenue you were counting on for the next two years has just gone up in smoke.

If you assume negative intentions, the conversation is likely to go something like:

You:	*You idiot! Do you know how much you've cost the company? And if you think I'm taking the rap for this, you've got another think coming!*
Bill:	*But I didn't know...*
You:	*Don't give me that. It was your job to know...*
Bill:	*Anyhow, it wasn't my fault. Marie didn't get her part finished in time...*
You:	*What? How come?*
Bill:	*I dunno. But it was her fault.*

And then you go off to jump all over Marie. But what if you assumed positive intentions? First, you need to go into an enclosed space and rant and rave. Say all the things like, "That incompetent! How am I going to tell Ralph? How dare he put me in that situation!" And so on. Once you've gotten your blood pressure down, talk to Bill by saying:

You:	*Bill, how could this happen? Do you realize how much you've cost the company?*
Bill:	*I know. I'm sorry... but I didn't know...*
You:	*You didn't know what?*
Bill:	*I didn't know they were so strict about deadlines. I mean, I was only five minutes late.*

You:	*Then you should have left more time.*
Bill:	*Yes, I should have. I'm really sorry. But I didn't know that it was so important.*
You:	*You didn't know? How come?*
Bill:	*In my last job, we didn't bid on government contracts. I just didn't know it was that important.*

There is a difference, as you can see, but it is almost entirely in your willingness to assume that there is a reasonable explanation. In the first instance, Bill tried to shift the blame to Marie. In the second, he told you the real problem. It's a horrible mistake but it's not actually his fault. The problem was the training/briefing or supervision he got. Punishing him for the mistake doesn't solve the problem and assuming he was incompetent wouldn't have identified the source of the true problem.

But what about the people who make mistakes because they really don't care or are incompetent? These types constitute a very small percentage of the working population, but they do exist. The difference between them and your average employee is the frequency and nature of the mistakes. Someone who consistently makes the same kind of error is either incapable or unwilling to learn and these people need to move out of the organization. But for the majority who can learn from their mistakes and want to, using the assumption of positive intentions can go a long way to helping both them and the organization.

Not Using Gravity of Error as the Criteria for Failure

Gravity of the error does of course make a difference. If a doctor causes a death or a chemical company is criminally negligent, there are sanctions even if they had the best of intentions. If your business has life and death consequences, you may not be able to apply all these ideas. However, even in these settings, there are probably plenty of instances where the gravity of the error can be balanced with the need for people to be free to learn and to try out new behaviors. This isn't easy, but organizations need to consider how to do it if they're truly trying to encourage new learning.

Rewarding Failure or Admitting Mistakes

Many people may agree about not punishing failure but what about actually rewarding mistakes? In most corporate settings, it's probably not rewarding the mistake but rewarding *admitting* the mistake. Sometimes you're fairly sure a mistake has been made, but you don't have all the facts and the employee can't or won't supply them. If people admit a mistake, you can work on ways to avoid it in the future. If they deny it, you can't get any farther in the learning and knowledge building process. To encourage these admissions, you can do several things, not all of which are appropriate in all circumstances.

Praise Him at the Time of the Admission

When someone admits a goof, you can say: "Well, Andy, I admire your honesty. It must have been tough to do, but it means we can get it cleaned up that much faster. Thanks."

Prevent Others From Throwing It in His Face

If the error has been big, substantial or particularly embarrassing, the colleagues of the person may make jokes or otherwise use it in embarrassing or even threatening ways. (Should he be given this new responsibility, given the recent screw-up?) You can discourage this with: "It was an honest mistake and Andy stepped up to it. Cut the ribbing; it might as easily have been you."

Refer to the Positive Effects Admitting the Mistake Has Had on the Business

At some point it may be appropriate to say something like: "You know, if Andy hadn't pointed out that capacity miscalculation, we'd really be in the soup now. I'd hate to think where we'd be if he hadn't."

Give the Admitter a Plum Project

By doing this, you signal that openly admitting mistakes doesn't damage a career and may even enhance your confidence in the trustworthiness of the person. Of course, don't do this if it was really a stupid mistake. I'm not asking you to reward stupidity but honesty.

But even if it was a stupid mistake, you can still use all of the other techniques to encourage people to be open about the problems they're having.

In short, you can, and should, use your position power to support the change in the way people view mistakes.

Thou Shalt Not Disagree with the Boss

It's critical to avoid rules which stifle new knowledge, but when's the last time you saw "Thou shalt not innovate" hanging on a corporate wall? No one actually ever makes up rules with the intent of stifling new knowledge, but there are plenty of unwritten rules that do exactly that. One that is anathema to tapping intellectual capital is a pretty common: "Thou shalt not disagree with the boss," or variants such as "Thou can disagree in private but never in public." These unspoken rules are just as, if not more powerful, than the overt ones.

Of course, life is easier in the short-term if there is no dissent. It's very tiresome having people always objecting to what you do. And a continued high level of dissent in an organization means it can't carry out a shared purpose or vision. However, the paradox of dissent is that having too much or too little has the same effect. In both cases, the organization becomes stalled, unable to move forward. When there is too much dissent, the paralysis is obvious. But when none is allowed, it simply goes underground and shows up in more insidious forms such as malevolent obedience or withholding one's intellectual capital.

Dissent is an important part of encouraging new knowledge to come forward. People have to be able to feel free to say to their boss, "I think you're wrong." The crux is not whether *you* believe people can tell you you're wrong, but whether your subordinates believe it.

An obvious way to signal that you're open to criticism is to acknowledge the possibility that you could be wrong when someone challenges you. However, someone actually has to say, "I think you're wrong," before you can demonstrate how open you are. It's possible you aren't getting a lot of expressed dissent because you already have a very efficient unwritten rule that the king is always right.

To get around both problems, you need to model your willingness to integrate new knowledge. That usually means demonstrating that you can be wrong and, more importantly, that you know it. You admit your mistakes.

Admitting a Mistake

Some managers would rather sell their first born than openly admit an error. It seems better to hide it, deny it, or step around the problem rather than say, "I made a mistake," but saying it demonstrates your willingness to change your ways when new knowledge or understanding becomes available. In addition, as a leader in the new world without readily apparent solutions, the ability to admit you were wrong allows your group to abandon a path which isn't leading anywhere and frees everyone to search for a way that does. Still, managers have a terrible time doing this. Why?

Your Credibility Will be Damaged

This is a common fear, but when you think about it, the only way admitting a mistake affects your credibility is if you always have to be right and always perfect. It's a way of thinking you shouldn't encourage in yourself or in your subordinates. It's an intolerable and ultimately undeliverable expectation. You were never perfect or always right (I hope this doesn't come as a shock to you). The only difference is that now you're admitting it.

Someone Will Use It Against You

Without a doubt, there are people in an organization who will try to use a mistake against you. Your boss might deny you an interesting assignment because he assumes you must have *really* messed up if you're admitting it. These people are probably relatively few in number but they may be influential.

You Usually Have to Rectify It

If you deny the mistake, you don't have to do anything to fix it but if you admit it, you usually do. That rectification may not be of your choosing either in solution or timing. At the very least you have to justify why you aren't acting the way others think you should.

These appear to be pretty compelling reasons for not admitting a mistake. But if you don't, you lower the likelihood your employees will admit theirs. You can admit a mistake in a way that is honest but won't stumble too far into the deterrents noted above. Let's talk about each one.

The Credibility Issue

You need only say: "Okay, I goofed up. Just goes to show I'm human. So, what can we/I do to fix this?" If this seems too facile, you may still believe you always have to be right. Think about how important the whole issue of admitting mistakes is to you. If it's important, you may need to start taking the first small steps to encourage that belief.

Using It Against You

This is the tricky one. How do you admit an error without jeopardizing your reputation? One possibility is to say something like: "I always thought people admitted mistakes only because they'd be found out anyway. Now I've realized it's just part of being a team." Might work, might not. If you're in a really entrenched culture or work for a very conservative boss, you'll have to tread carefully. You might try admitting your mistakes to your staff but not to peers or bosses. Educating your bosses about a change in their attitudes will help, but may not be feasible. If it's not, take it slowly, keep it small and the circle circumscribed.

Rectifying the Mistake

If you admit a mistake, you usually have to fix it. But the solution doesn't have to be what others propose. If the solution urged on you doesn't fit, it's perfectly okay to say: "Thanks, that's a good suggestion. But I want to think about it some more. I'll keep your comments in mind." Just stick to that, no matter how much people persist.

How to Start Making the Change

Sometimes you'll realize on your own that you've made a mistake. These are the easiest to correct. You just do it and move on. The most difficult times to admit a mistake are when someone else points it out—when you're criticized. Here's how that might start out:

Employee:	*Andrea, how come you didn't let me know about the meeting on the new product launch?*
You:	*The one yesterday?*

Employee:	*I needed to be there and I had to find out from Mike. Talk about open communication!*
You:	*But Bob, why did you need to be there?*
Employee:	*Well, this is always the attitude. You never include me in important meetings.*

From this point, one of three possibilities kicks in. The criticism is ill-founded, it's correct but you didn't realize you were creating a problem, or deep down you know it's true. Let's examine each one.

It's Not True

COMMENT	CONVERSATION	
Bob is upset. Address that first, then ask for more information.	You:	*I'm sorry you feel that way. Why do you say that?*
	Employee:	*Well, it's pretty obvious isn't it? You have ops meetings I'm not invited to.*
If you're really calm, you could also ask:	You:	*So you think you should attend the Tuesday meetings. Anything else?*
	Employee:	*And what about the last executive retreat? I should have been there too.*
Before you jump in with the answer, keep asking.	You:	*Tell me why you think you should be there.*
	Employee:	*Well, Ron is and I'm the same grade. If he can, why can't I?*
So now you understand the problem.	You:	*But if you remember, Ron's part time on re-engineering the marketing function. He's there in that capacity, not because of his regular job.*

	Employee:	*Oh... I guess I did see that memo.*
Bob is admitting he's wrong. Let him off lightly.	**You:**	*Well, there's a lot of stuff flying around these days. It's hard to keep track.*

If the employee's wrong, it's tempting just to jump in and correct him. And when it doesn't matter, it's probably the most efficient too. However, if the employee doesn't think it's minor (even if you do), spend time making sure you understand the problem. It will assure the employee that you are listening.

This type of problem is easy to solve but for one big pitfall. Sometimes, people will use spurious logic to avoid criticism. This happens in personal as well as work life. An example: a guest complained about the difficulty in finding the hotel. The hotel manager pointed out the map on the back of the confirmation sheet. The guest looked at it and harrumped: "Yes, but it's not to scale." He's saying, "It's not true," to avoid admitting he was wrong. There will certainly be times when the criticizer is mistaken, but you need to be careful you aren't searching for ways to ignore that kernel of truth.

You Didn't Realize It

This may also be relatively easy. An employee points out an unexpected consequence of something you did. Let's pick up the conversation from the point you've gathered the information you need.

COMMENT		CONVERSATION
	You:	*And tell me why you think you should be there.*
	Employee:	*Well, once you guys make the big decisions, who makes all the physical arrangements—the meeting space, materials, booth setups? My guys. How can I plan if I don't know what's coming up? Just like we always do things around here.*

Maybe you think Bob has a point. If you do, you just say:	**You:**	*Sorry Bob, I guess I wasn't thinking. You're right of course.*

On the other hand, you may feel you can't keep adding people to the table who aren't the decision makers. Even if the employee has identified a real problem, you don't have to use his solution. You might try:

Acknowledge the need and then talk solution:	**You:**	*I can see you need to know. And so does HR. Frankly, I'm a little reluctant to add more people. We're already at 10 and it's getting pretty unwieldy. But we could commit to having the minutes out that afternoon so you can get the info ASAP.*
	Employee:	*Well, I suppose. But it would be better if I attended.*
You can't expect he'll love the solution, but you can stick to your guns:	**You:**	*Yes, I realize that. But I still have the size problem. Let's try this for a while. We can revisit if it's not working.*
	Employee:	*Well, okay. Let's try it for a while.*

See, it's not that hard. You need to distinguish between justified criticism and implementing the solution proposed. They don't have to go together. You can admit a mistake has been made but solve it in a way that works for you.

The next one is more difficult. You know you've left someone out who should be included. It may be this person is ineffective, hogs the floor, or just plain gets on your nerves. Meetings run more smoothly without him. However, he is right. He should be there. Let's look at a conversation that goes wrong and then a more constructive one. Let's take it from when the employee first approaches you.

You Knew It Deep Down

CONVERSATION		COMMENT
You:	*But Bob, why do you need to be there?*	(These comments will be mostly on the effect of your words.)
Employee:	*Well, this is always the attitude. You never include me in important meetings.*	
You:	*Oh come on, Bob. Aren't you being just a little sensitive?*	• personal attack—it must be your fault you're feeling this way.
Employee:	*What do you mean, a little sensitive? I think I should be included.*	
You:	*Well, everyone does, don't they? But I can't be including everyone just because they have an urge to know. I mean, we'd have to have the whole company at retreats.*	• ridicule as a method of silence
Employee:	*I'm not talking about the whole company. Everything you're talking about has huge admin implications but I'm not there to advise you.*	
You:	*Well, we have a pretty good grip on the logistics stuff. I mean, we're all experienced managers, you know.*	• devalue Bob's work • imply Bob is attacking others' competence
Employee:	*Yes, but.....*	

Yes, the manager has successfully eluded the issue. He can't use facts and logic (since they reside on the employee's side this time), so he has stooped to spurious reasoning (Bob wants the whole company at the meetings), turning the tables (Bob is criticizing his colleagues), personal attack, ridicule, and devaluing.

If the intent were to create winners and losers, I'd say congratulations! and move on. But such defensive maneuvers, however useful they might be in the short term to avoid embarrassment and discomfort, are immensely destructive in the longer term. They keep you in the status quo and in the tension inherent in any situation where true motives are underground, masked by silly excuses which no one dares challenge. It signals to this employee (and to others who hear the story) that you're exempting yourself from learning, and moreover, that pointing this out is a sin. In fact, it's business as usual, no matter the rhetoric.

If you want to create an environment which is supportive and encourages new knowledge, you must engage in a process in which you, as well as the employee, are changed. Let's hit the conversation again.

You Knew It Deep Down (Reprise)

COMMENT		CONVERSATION
	You:	*But Bob, why did you need to be there?*
	Employee:	*Well, this is always the attitude. You never include me in important meetings.*
It's easy to get your hackles up. Try to suppress it and say:	**You:**	*What makes you say that?*
	Employee:	*Well isn't it obvious? The ops meetings, the last retreat, and now there's another off-site and I'm not on the list.*
You're getting a queasy feeling that he's right. If this is sticky, don't feel compelled to settle it right away. Instead, say:		
Set a particular time and place.	**You:**	*I can see this is an important issue to you. I need to think about it. Why don't we talk again tomorrow? How about 1:30 in my office?*

It's certainly best to deal with the situation immediately but not if you need to think through your options.

OK, you're back in your office. You don't like Bob and you don't want him at the meetings. He is disruptive or ineffective. But his criticism is justified and it prompts two unpalatable trains of thought: you might have to admit you were wrong and this may be a comment on how you deal with conflict.

You Might Have to Admit You're Wrong

All kinds of corollaries come up. There is the embarrassment of course, but in addition, you might have to admit you don't want Bob at the meetings because he'll push for things he's been hinting around about. Well, he might, but you can keep saying no as appropriate. Yes, it would be easier if he knew not to ask, but he doesn't. He can only learn what you'll support by seeing how you react to his suggestions. If he lacks judgment, and doesn't have other compelling positive qualities, he may need to be replaced. On the other hand, if this is a minor (but annoying) flaw, he needs your coaching to become the employee you need in that position.

So admitting the mistake may mean you have to invite him to the meetings. If that's true, then your role is to coach him on being more effective.

This May Be a Comment on How You Deal With Conflict or People You Don't Like

The criticism may force you to confront more fundamental issues. Is this the way you deal with people you don't like? Is this fair? Is it effective? Does it reflect the kind of manager you want to be? Is this true personally as well as in your work life?

These are not questions anyone wants to look at. Most people would rather dismiss the criticism rather than embark on questioning fundamentals about themselves. It is understandable that you'd want to avoid them but these moments sitting quietly at your desk with the door closed or at home raking leaves, have more power than any others. They are when you choose to learn and embrace the future or when you choose the immediate relief of denial.

Even if you choose the thornier path, you don't have to trumpet your conversion. You may have concluded you don't deal well with conflict and may even be planning how to tackle it. But you don't have to admit that. In the follow-up conversation with Bob, stick to only one unpalatable part: acknowledging the mistake and rectifying it.

You:	*Bob, we were talking about the ops meetings and the retreats.*
Employee:	*Yes, Andrea. I need to be there. How can I support the company if I don't know what's going on?*
You:	*Well, Bob, you may have a point ...*
Employee:	*Great! You don't know how long ...*
You:	*However, I want to talk about some things you do in meetings that I'd like you to work on.*
Employee:	*Like what?*
You:	*Well, for example, I don't feel you consistently make suggestions which are workable or feasible.*

I could go into more detail but the point is made—you can respond to the criticism by making a change, but you don't have to go into the soul searching which accompanied it. As long as you rectify the error, you can keep to yourself how you got to that conclusion or what it means about you.

Finally, don't make Bob's personal change a condition of attendance. He should be there, period. In addition, he needs to work on his effectiveness. You need to distinguish between rectifying your mistake and helping the employee be more effective. One shouldn't be a condition for the other.

Summary

Encouraging new knowledge to come forward can call for some uncomfortable changes. You may have to tolerate more divergence of opinion and even encourage it. You need to rethink your automatic reactions to failure and start to move toward a different way of doing things. None of this is easy, but if you truly want to encourage new learning to come forward, you need to make sure the door is open and the way in is inviting. How you act will make a difference. Another way to encourage people to contribute their intellectual capital is to help them understand the challenges the company faces. We will deal with this in the next chapter.

Main Points

- It's easy to discourage new knowledge coming forward without meaning to.
- You can encourage it if you:
  - Help employees understand how the strategic direction applies to them.
  - Let employees work on things you don't agree with.
  - Listen vigilantly.
  - Kill an idea when it isn't going to work.
  - Help employees understand your role.
- Other ways to encourage new knowledge include:
  - Not punishing failure.
  - Rewarding admission of mistakes.
  - Admitting mistakes yourself.

CHAPTER 3

❦

Pushing Down Complexity

In the last chapter, we discussed how important it was for new knowledge to come forward. But sometimes when a new idea is offered, managers feel that employees just don't "get it." Yes, it is an exciting and fun thought—it's just not profitable. Yes, it will improve the quality but it will get us into the market too late. And then, occasionally, there is some egregious error. The admin person sends out the figures on what the job actually cost rather than what you were billing. Now you have to tell the customer the bill is 15 per cent more than invoiced. Or, you know that the most influential VP can only stay half an hour at your big presentation. Ted was supposed to handle the logistics but you spend the first fifteen minutes trying to get the computer to display your overheads.

Incidents like these often leave managers feeling, "Am I the only one with a brain around here?" You know how important everyone's job is but sometimes people don't act as if they knew or cared. Some of the errors and unrealistic demands may not be due to lack of caring or willingness to think but to a lack of understanding. If the admin person doesn't know how the company operates and just pushes paper and numbers, it's not surprising she wouldn't realize that the figures she was sending out didn't look right. Similarly, if Ted hasn't linked setting up computer presentations with the success of the business, it's also not all that astonishing he didn't put his heart and soul into another meeting setup.

Yes, they should be doing these things because it's their job, but knowledge workers—even ones with less complex knowledge as in these examples—don't work that way. Knowledge workers need knowledge to do their best—in this case, the knowledge of what's going on in the company, how it affects them, and how they can contribute. Managers are pivotal in making the links for them or pushing down complexity.

What is Pushing Down Complexity?

Knowledge workers' intellectual capital is valuable *only* if it operates within the reality of your environment. Pushing down complexity is helping employees integrate the company's strategic direction and competitive environment pressures into what they do and how they do it. For example, they must be convinced that today's world demands speed *and* innovation not speed *or* innovation. If they aren't, their sense of urgency in the work will be less than you need it to be and, moreover, they will believe you want shoddy work when you ask for a quick response. Pushing down complexity is a way to help employees understand the intricacies and ambiguities of today's business world.

But why is it so important for employees to understand today's business world? Why can't we operate as we always have, with the managers taking care of strategy and the workers doing the rollout? There are four reasons I can think of. First, as we've already discussed, encouraging new knowledge is predicated on people experimenting and innovating. Since most of this innovation occurs in their heads, managers can only be sure that it is in the service of the company if employees understand the business environment in which they are operating. Otherwise, their ideas will be unusable. Secondly, as we will see in a later chapter, an important way to deal with the explosion of knowledge and the need for rapid market response, is to share decision making with employees. Again, they can only make sound decisions if they are conscious of the political and other realities in which the decision must live.

Thirdly, if employees truly understand how complex and volatile the business environment is, they will develop a greater tolerance for decisions you make which may need to be altered to meet changing market conditions. With this tolerance, they will understand why today you want the new product launched through regular channels and tomorrow you change your mind when you see a competitive product being offered through the Internet. In the past, such shifting of decisions would have been seen as a sign of a weak or indecisive manager. Today, it is the sign of one who understands the need for flexibility and nimbleness. But unless your knowledge workers believe that, they will be reluctant, in fact will resist, frequent changes in direction and moreover, will hesitate to invest their intellectual capital in what looks like a doubtful enterprise. They will understand the true situation only if you have pushed down complexity so that they accept—in their hearts and not just in their heads—that success today means moving forward even in an ambiguous and complex situation.

Finally, and perhaps most importantly, you need to push down complexity in order to increase your employees' commitment to the organization. As we will see in the next chapter, because the donation of intellectual capital is always voluntary, the donors (i.e., your employees) must have a compelling reason to do so. A way to provide that reason is to consult and involve them in the important business decisions of the day. However, they can only provide intelligent and useful input if they understand the context. Without it, their advice will not be useful, executives will stop asking for it, the opportunity to increase employees' commitment will be lost, and their willingness to invest their intellectual capital with it.

For all those reasons, it is critical that managers are actively engaged in pushing down complexity so that everyone can integrate the good of the entire corporation in their actions. If you can engender this corporate thinking mind-set, employees will be more willing to innovate, will make better decisions themselves, will be more willing to make quick changes in direction, and be more committed to the strategic direction. Without it, you'll run a constant rearguard action, trying to force people along a strategic path that they don't believe in, aren't committed to, and moreover, don't have to do. You'll spend your time policing rather than moving forward which is neither fun nor ultimately useful.

The Stages of Pushing Down Complexity

Generating corporate thinking in everyone is a difficult task, made all the more so because it doesn't happen overnight. While we would all prefer it if we could just explain the situation once, have everyone salute and move forward from there, it won't happen. People need to pass through four stages before they can begin to integrate corporate thinking in their way of operating:

- Stage 1: I understand the challenges facing the company.
- Stage 2: I realize the challenges are difficult.
- Stage 3: The solutions may not be 100 per cent in my interest.
- Stage 4: I'm OK with that.

Let me demonstrate the steps with an example. In a human resources function I was working with, a group of employees was asked to recommend a new model of doing business, given that their resources were being drastically reduced but the clientele drastically increased. Obviously, the task could not be completed usefully unless the recommendations took into account the strategic direction and challenges the company faced and to do this, each member of the team had to pass through the stages outlined.

Stage 1: I understand the challenges facing the company.

To assist the group, the VP of HR spent several hours outlining her perspective on the company. She explained that the executive committee had decided to shift many more resources into directly serving clients. This being the case, all corporate functions like HR, finance, technology, and legal were being reduced. At the same time, the company was also merging with another. The responsibility for the second company's corporate functions would be assumed by this company but without an adequate increase in staff to handle the increased workload.

Stage 2: I realize the challenges are difficult.

To help people understand how the company's problems might affect HR, the VP shared her concern that the executive committee might consider outsourcing the HR function completely if it was perceived as too much overhead. This would jeopardize all HR jobs and in addition, the VP didn't believe it was the right move for the organization. However, she also noted that the competitive pressures on the company were enormous and if things didn't turn around in the near future, the whole company would be in trouble.

At this stage, people need to be allowed to ask questions, put forward proposals, and offer solutions no matter how inappropriate. Some group members were angry that the executives had gotten the company into this state. They said things like, "We wouldn't have this problem if we had leaders who could lead. We need a new CEO." After allowing the venting, the VP addressed each comment. For example, she reminded the group that their whole industry was experiencing similar problems which had more to do with shifts in the marketplace than executive mistakes. This stage doesn't have to last long but people have to have the opportunity to be assured that everything that might have reasonably been done to avert the problem was done. They also need to understand that the solutions will be complex. To start people thinking about that, the VP asked the group to consider some of the trade-offs ("How can we ensure a minimum standard of quality in HR practices while allowing managers maximum flexibility?").

Stage 3: The solutions may not be 100 per cent in my interest.

In addition to understanding that the solution will be complex, employees also need to accept that it will be a "best fit." That is to say, it may solve the problem but will probably not satisfy everyone nor be without some undesirable consequences. For example, in the original company, the regional operations were quite small and all HR functions were performed at head office to take advantages of economies of scale. However, the reason for the merger was to acquire a more extensive regional operation that in turn would allow the company to be closer to its customers. After the merger, it could now make sense to assign HR people to each of the regional offices.

Employees in the task force must struggle with the knowledge that this recommendation will have major impacts on themselves, on their colleagues, and on the way they do business. It will mean relocation for many and a long-distance relationship with their HR colleagues, very different from the present ability to drop in on someone to talk through a problem in person.

Unless employees can reach the stage of understanding that a solution may be a good one even if it has undesirable consequences for them personally, they are likely to avoid considering certain options. And if they do, they may well reject the best solution for the company in favor of the best solution for themselves and their colleagues.

Stage 4: I'm OK with that.

Employees must accept—not just with their heads but in their hearts—that the right solution is not always the best one for them. If they don't, they will continue to resist the idea and might even try to sabotage the implementation. It takes time, and in the example we're discussing, other options which would not involve such dislocations were extensively explored. Employees understood the challenges facing the company, so they eventually rejected options like continuing business as usual or demanding more resources, because they saw that it would not help the company and, in the longer term, might even contribute to its demise. These were not easy discussions but they took place and helped people to truly come to the point of accepting decisions that were both personally and organizationally challenging.

As you can see, simply announcing *why* a new direction needs to be adopted will not be sufficient if you need people to not only accept it but also to commit to it. It is critical that employees move through all four stages if they are to think corporately. If a significant proportion of employees or managers stall at a particular stage, everyone will suffer. For example, at Stage 1, unusable solutions are generated. "What this company needs to do is fire all the bean counters and auditors." If at Stage 2, the solutions will protect those making the decision even if it doesn't actually solve the problem.[1] "Yes, I realize that customers won't like it, but any other way will force layoffs." Stalled at Stage 3 creates continued or prolonged anger, bitterness, or cynicism with feelings of betrayal and an urge to blame someone— anyone— for the problem. It is only at the final stage that people and organizations can integrate the strategic direction into ongoing activities.

Is Getting to the Final Stage Possible or Even Desirable?

Can people actually get to the final stage? Is it possible? And even if it's possible, is it a good idea? Good questions and let's deal with both.

Let's talk about whether people can actually reach Stage 4. To do so, employees have to struggle with difficult issues that touch them

---

[1] Although this step looks like it would apply only to managers, front-line employees show their "stuckness" by generating all kinds of reasons [some of which may be valid] why a particular solution cannot be implemented.

where they live. It is natural to assume that they won't be capable of making decisions which materially affect their own well being, that they won't be able to see the larger good if their own circumstances will be adversely affected. If I hadn't seen it myself, I'd be skeptical too. It is possible. If given the time and support, employees can do it.

In fact, it shouldn't be all that surprising that people can make difficult decisions that affect them personally. People at all levels of the organization deal with significantly more complex issues in their daily lives. How to deal with a daughter's drinking, come to terms with a dying parent, or accept the signs of their own aging. These are weighty problems, but they cope. It's only at work they don't get a chance to exercise these skills. Because they've been shut out from dealing with similar levels of work complexity, they will need your help to apply their skills to the change, but they can do it.

But let's talk about the second objection: even if it is possible for people to reach Stage 4, is it necessary or desirable? It is important to remember *why* you are pushing down complexity. Knowledge workers have to understand and accept the strategic direction, not as some plaque on the wall, but as a way to guide their individual actions and thoughts to make better decisions and be willing to be as flexible and nimble as the market demands. Because what knowledge workers produce is from their heads, you cannot compel better decisions or more flexibility but only invite them. Pushing down complexity is a way to invite knowledge workers to do just that.

How to Push Down Complexity

So, pushing down complexity is an important way to help employees make decisions that are good for the corporation and also be willing to change directions as quickly as the market demands. To do this, they need to both understand and accept the challenges and solutions the organization is faced with. You can help employees do this by providing three things: information, implications, and involvement.

Information

You definitely need to provide information on what's happening to the company, the industry, sector, and even country. It needs to be stated in a way that helps employees understand how complex the problem is. So, it's not just "We're getting a lot of pressure from foreign markets," but "Our major competition is coming from the third world, where they can produce our products at half the price. Of course, wages are extremely low and even production costs can be significantly lower. So, we're faced with a product that can be made, shipped, and sold in our markets at 20 per cent less than we can do it. We're trying to figure out what to do in these new circumstances. Got any suggestions?"

If the company has been communicating well, it has done much of this work for you. If it has not, you need to do it for your people.

Implications

Once employees have information, they need to understand the implications for their work and their lives. I'll use a relatively contained issue to illustrate.

The situation: The company goes to teams and cuts out a level of management. Twelve people now report to the manager. An employee complains that the manager isn't providing enough personal recognition.

Employee:	*I don't get much appreciation for what I do around here.*
Manager:	*How so?*
Employee:	*Well, my old manager used to drop by to tell me when I'd done well. No big deal. But it felt good.*
Manager:	*I'm sure it did. But didn't Van have six people reporting to him?*
Employee:	*About that. Five after Shelley left.*
Manager:	*With this new structure, I have 12. It's harder to know what everybody's doing. And given they're self-directed, I'm really not supposed to get involved.*
Employee:	*But Van used to come by every once in a while and just shoot the breeze. That's how he kept up.*

Manager:	*I'd like to do that, too. But with 12 people who need my attention, I don't seem to have the time I'd like to. In fact, I'm beginning to wonder if we aren't running into something new. If I'm not supposed to be involved in the day-to-day, I can't know what's going on, and if I don't, I can't give you the recognition you need and deserve. I don't know the answer. Do you have any thoughts?*

This is a relatively small problem and the conversation will go on. They may try to increase recognition from the manager or look to meet the need in other ways. Whatever the outcome, the conversation helps employees understand how a strategic decision can have complex implications and consequences which are difficult to resolve.

To engage in the process, remember to:

- pose the trade-offs
- ask employees what they would do, given the same parameters and constraints
- don't accept: "I don't know, but there must be a way."
- keep your temper and keep explaining the problem
- don't expect this to be accomplished in one or even several sessions.

Involvement

Once people have the information they need and understand its implications, they may overreact. The outside threats may become so important and real that they feel either hopeless ("We'll never close the gap between Wedgies and us") or overwhelmed ("This is too big to tackle"). You can use your greater experience in dealing with ambiguity to help identify what parts of the situation employees can control. In fact, the more control you allow them, the more likely it is they'll both commit to the mission and want to contribute to it. *How* to do this is covered in the next two chapters.

Pushing Down Complexity is a Thankless Job

Pushing down complexity is important organizational learning and will make your job easier in the long run. However, don't expect any thanks while you're doing it. Strong reactions are usual when people begin to understand they may not get everything they want. Let me sketch a typical scenario. You've already explained the realities under which the company is operating. An employee approaches you.

Employee:	*I don't get this. The VP told you to cut SURGE?*
You:	*The whole executive group decided, yes, that given our present difficulties, SURGE was a lower priority.*
Employee:	*A lower priority? Are you telling me my work for the last two years doesn't matter?*
You:	*No, certainly not. But we've had to make hard decisions. The choice isn't between things that don't matter and those that do. We're prioritizing among the essentials.*
Employee:	*Then why pick on SURGE?*
You:	*Well, like I was saying—when we look at the market, we think new products like INNOVATION will position us better.*
Employee:	*But didn't you point out how much customers like SURGE? Didn't you fight to keep it? I mean, this is a time for leadership.*
You:	*Of course we discussed it. But we agreed SURGE's demand has plateaued. We can't assume it'll continue to grow.*
Employee:	*So, you let the marketing and sales guys walk all over you.*
You:	*No, I agree with the executive team. Nobody walked over anybody.*
Employee:	*How do you know this INNOVATION thing will work?*
You:	*Well, of course, there are no guarantees—the market's pretty volatile right now.*
Employee:	*So, you axe a product you know sells for one you're not sure will? Does that make sense?*

You:	*We've got to respond to where we think the market's going. Do you think we've read it wrong?*
Employee:	*Don't you know? I mean if you don't, how are we supposed to? If you don't, we must really be in trouble.*
You:	*Well, we think we're right, but I'm open to other solutions.*
Employee:	*If you guys had been on the ball from the beginning, we wouldn't be having this conversation now.*

This rather nasty confrontation is, unfortunately, quite typical when people are faced with unpleasant and unwelcome realities. A natural first reaction is to blame someone, and the natural target is you. And, to be honest, we've contributed to this outcome. Just as managers have traditionally seen their jobs as: here's the problem, here's the solution, this is what you need to do, we've conditioned employees to expect it. They could bitch about the solution and agitate to do it differently, but at least there was one. The more ambiguous and complex the situation, the more likely employees are to crave a way to stabilize a world at tilt. Instead, they get constant changes, with Plan A this week and Plan B the next. Helping employees learn to tolerate the ambiguities of the world better is an important way to help leverage your organization's intellectual capital.

Summary

People's intellectual capital is valuable only to the extent it helps the organization address its challenges. But unless employees understand the complexities of the business environment, they can't invest their intellectual capital wisely no matter how willing they are to contribute it. By pushing down complexity, a manager can help employees understand the ambiguities and implications of environmental pressures and how these apply to everyday work. If employees can think corporately, then their input into company-wide decisions will be invaluable. How to tap that resource is covered in the next two chapters.

Main Points

- Knowledge workers' intellectual capital is valuable only if it operates within the reality of your environment.

- Pushing down complexity helps employees integrate the company's strategic direction and competitive environment pressures into what they do and how they do it.

- People can't instantly think corporately because they must understand and accept that a solution can be right for the company without being totally right for them personally.

- To help push down complexity, managers need to provide information, implications, and involvement.

Tapping Knowledge Thoroughout the Corporation: Consultation

In the first chapters of the book, we explored how pivotal knowledge and knowledge workers are to the success of any organization. Knowledge is the raw material of today's products and services and you need knowledge workers to transform that raw material into wealth. To be competitive in today's knowledge environment, you need people's best synthesis, analysis, integration, and innovation.

But because these wealth creation activities occur in a domain which you can neither control nor see—people's brains—you have to find a way to engage people in such a way that they will freely and enthusiastically donate their intellectual capital to the organization. They won't do it just because you need the donation badly, nor entirely because you pay them to do it. They have to want to.

They will invest their intellectual capital if they feel they can influence what goes on. If you remember, a Gallup study found that employees' belief that their opinions counted was one of four factors which predicted a company's profitability.[1] Gore-Tex, which *Fortune*

---

[1] The others were being given the opportunity to do what they do best, the sense that their fellow workers were committed to quality, and making a direct connection between their work and the company's mission.

magazine ranked as the seventh best company to work for, has consultation as one of its guiding principles. They believe that consultation is an important element in creating an environment of creativity, initiative, and innovation. They understand that employees need to believe that you're listening to them and respect their opinions if they're going to commit their intellectual capital to your collective endeavor.

An employee's conviction that she is being heard will also materially affect how satisfied she is with the company, and as we will see in Chapter 14, this will influence whether you can keep your customers loyal.

Engaging Employees

So what exactly does "being listened to" mean? One important method has already been covered in a previous chapter—the individual manager plays an important role in encouraging individual employees to use their knowledge. However, the employees also need to believe that their opinions are respected at the company level, that they can and are welcome to influence its overall direction. Otherwise, their loyalty will be to a particular boss but not necessarily to the organization. While that's helpful, you don't want a bunch of fiefdoms with excellent access to their own intellectual capital but little urge to share it corporate-wide. Convincing employees that they are heard needs to happen both at the unit and the corporate levels.

Organizations can demonstrate their willingness to listen through various forms of employee engagement. Employee engagement means giving employees an active role in influencing the future of the company. It's not just about letting employees know what's happening. That's a given. It is about encouraging employees to consider and be heard on the issues which affect the profitability and viability of the organization.

Of course, engaging staff has always been part of a manager's kit bag. There have always been managers who listened carefully, but using engagement to tap your intellectual capital is not just about an individual effort; it's about an organization-wide commitment. To transform your organization into one that makes effective use of its intellectual capital, employee engagement has to move out of the realm of a nice-to-do individual good management practice to a need-to-do systemic way of management life.

There are two forms of employee engagement: consultation and involvement. While both are useful, they differ quite sharply. The table below outlines the differences.

CONSULTATION	INVOLVEMENT
• employees have two or more clear options on a substantive decision	• employees make a decision or recommend on a substantive issue
• wide canvas of opinion through some kind of questionnaire	• assigned to a team of employees representing all facets of the organization
• issue-specific and usually one-time	• issue-specific but may be ongoing
• final decision is with the management group	• final decision *may* be with the management group

The pivotal difference between consultation and involvement is that, in consultation, the final decision belongs to the management group. In involvement, it may or may not. I'll discuss consultation in this chapter and involvement in the next.

The Consultation Process

Consultation is a process by which management seeks the opinion of employees on important issues of the day. It is primarily about testing the waters since, with consultation, the right to decide the issue is with management. Consulting allows employees to express an opinion about their future.

Although that seems a fairly straightforward idea, running a successful consultation can be a tricky thing. Let me tell you about one consultation which went wrong to show you some of the issues involved. For simplicity's sake, only one person was consulted in the following story; however, the principles are the same whether you're consulting one person or a thousand.

I was involved in the merger of two large organizations. Each had extensive regional operations that were to be amalgamated. A regional manager—I'll call her Lynn—was asked by her boss, Alex, to work on these plans, including the location of the regional headquarters in the new territory. The only viable options were Lynn's city or the other company's regional quarters. She was worked on her recommendations when Alex called to say that the other regional site had been chosen and she would report to the manager at the other site.

Lynn felt betrayed and unvalued. Why have her work on recommendations when he had no intention of considering them? She even suspected her counterpart in the other company of politicking to have his site chosen. She became cynical about the whole process and told anyone who would listen. Not only that, but she began actively looking to take her experience and expertise elsewhere.

Alex gave Lynn a substantive issue to tackle. However, he overlooked an important requirement of consultation. You've got to use the results produced. You don't have to accept them in their entirety, or at all, but you have to consider them seriously and respect the work invested. By consulting Lynn and then pulling the rug out from under her, Alex negated any good he might have done by assigning the task.

You might be thinking, "Well, I can see how this came up. Probably something happened which forced the decision. Maybe Alex didn't know it at the time. Or maybe he didn't think Lynn could make an objective assessment, since her job was on the line."

All of this may be true. However, if Alex doubted her objectivity, why assign the task in the first place? To give it and then take it away is surely worse than never assigning it at all. Even if Lynn had campaigned for the assignment, Alex would have been better to take the heat up front by refusing than look underhanded later. If some external issue forced the decision, presumably Lynn should have been told since it obviously affected her recommendations. Or, if the situation was that volatile, perhaps Alex shouldn't have assigned the task at all.

The issues on which employees are consulted must be substantive, but must also be ones on which management is willing to listen. If one or the other doesn't apply, it's not an appropriate issue. There are many that might not be. If you conclude a manager is unable to deliver, you wouldn't consult employees on his fate. Similarly, an edict from the corporate level doesn't require employee consultation, although its rollout could.

So if you're asking employees their opinion, the issue needs to be both substantive and one on which you are able to listen to the conclusions.

While consulting employees on company issues certainly has the payoff of increasing their commitment to the organization and through that, their willingness to invest their intellectual capital with you, it is still a process which needs careful handling. The next section will deal with how to run a successful consultation.

Running a Successful Consultation

It is possible not only to avoid the disaster Alex experienced but to run consultations that really do increase people's feeling that they are being listened to. However, running a successful consultation requires the following five steps:

- Deciding Whether to Consult
- Getting Agreement from the Executive Group
- Briefing Employees
- Running the Consultation
- Dealing with the Results

We'll discuss each one of these steps in some detail. Since I used an individual consultation example above, I'll use a corporate-wide consultation example as we work through these steps. Let's pick up the example we have already discussed—a large HR organization facing significant challenges from increased workload and decreased resources.

Deciding Whether to Consult

There is of course the basic decision of whether you want to consult employees on a particular topic. If you remember, a task force within HR was asked to design a new way of operating which would take into account the new realities. As part of that process, the VP of HR was considering consulting employees on how to configure the HR service so that it best served clients. For this consultation to be effective, several conditions have to be met.

First, the issue for consultation must be substantive but not yet decided. Keeping reassignment of employees to yourself and letting them decide who gets what parking spot is all right, but it isn't consultation. Employees can tell the difference between true consultation and fluff. The issue has to make a difference to the future of the organization and to the employees. Also, the decision makers can have opinions, leanings, and thoughts but these cannot yet have solidified into a decision. In our example, the issue for consultation is substantive—the structure of the new organization—and the VP had not made a decision on which model to use.

Second, the issue for consultation must be amenable to being expressed in relatively well defined options. If the options are vague or seem similar (even if they're not), it will be difficult for employees to make informed choices. Issues without clear options may not be good candidates for consultation unless you can do a lot of up front work to explain the subtleties. If the issue is important enough, it may be worth doing.

In our example, three different models of how service might be delivered were designed for use in the consultation. The models ranged from a centralized HR function to a completely decentralized one. Consulting on models of service is preferable to asking a question like, "Do you think centralized or decentralized HR functions are better for the company?" since many people would not understand the implications of the question. With the models, people could see that the highly decentralized HR model meant almost all the staff would report to line managers. This made it clear to employees that some geographic relocations would be necessary since line managers were spread across the country.

Thirdly, to affect employees' belief that their opinions count, the consultation must make a difference. This sounds obvious, but organizations sometimes get carried away when they get the consultation bug. The sidebar on the following page illustrates that.

The executive in our example was clear that the employees' opinions would make a difference. It wouldn't drive the decision (see the point below), but she was open to being influenced by employee reaction. It is important to have that mind-set. The question to ask yourself is: "If 100 per cent of the employees voted one way, would it make a difference to the decision?" If the answer is yes, then great, go ahead and consult. On the other hand, if the answer is no, and you consult anyway, you're setting yourself up for failure if you have to disregard the employees' opinions.

Finally, the issue for consultation is one on which you prefer to retain the final decision. There are lots of these. You might consult employees on what they would like in a benefits package or whether they'd prefer a buffet or standard approach. But the package's exact composition will also depend on what the organization can afford and wants to provide. It's quite in order to tell employees that you will make the decision but seek a broad base of views to help you in your deliberations.

Consulting With No Influence

While many organizations are doing many wonderful things with respect to intellectual capital, there are others that are doing exactly the wrong thing. So occasionally throughout the book, I'll highlight an example, sometimes for comic relief, but just as frequently, to illustrate how an organization can go wrong as we all struggle to leverage our people's intellectual capital. Here's one story.

A self-contained business that wasn't really in the mainstream of the large corporation's mission was trying to decide whether to evolve into a separate entity or remain part of the larger company. In a well-intentioned but misguided moment, the executive asked employees to vote on which of the two options they preferred.

Although it was done with the best of intentions, such an action is fraught with danger. The decision was largely a financial and strategic one and was not going to be based on majority employee vote. By consulting employees, the company gave the impression people would have some influence in the outcome. When they didn't, they were understandably angry and confused. Thus, the credibility and trustworthiness of the company's executive was needlessly damaged when the factors that would be used to make the decision were not announced up front. Had they done that, most reasonable employees would have seen the logic.

Getting Agreement From the Executive

As you can see from the examples, consultations are usually on issues which, in the past, executives decided on their own or with the input of a few trusted colleagues. Opening these issues to public debate can cause some angst and this needs to be dealt with early in the process if a consultation is even going to get off the ground.

Sometimes, executives don't want to consult employees because they have the same misconceptions about consultation as employees (see Briefing Employees, below). Once these are discussed, most resistance should dwindle. However, there may be other objections. Here are some and how you might deal with them.

OBJECTION	POSSIBLE RESPONSE

• *There isn't enough time to consult.*	• Always a problem and sometimes legitimate.
	• Some counters:
	  – It won't take much time to get the results.
	  – Can you afford not to? Will you have to do so much damage control you might as well have consulted to begin with?
	• Lack of time is often a red herring. Lack of priority is usually closer to the truth.

• *I don't want to change my mind about what I want.*	• Nobody ever actually says this, but this is often the root. If you ask someone's opinion, you're likely to get it and if it doesn't fit with yours, you have to respond in some way. However, if the executive group understands the difference between consultation and approval (see "Briefing Employees"), this may not be a problem. • If it still is, point out that knowing how employees feel is valuable *especially* if it is opposite to the executives' preferences. It cues them that they have work to do to convince people that the direction they've chosen is right.
• *It holds up the decision-making process.*	• True, however *making* the decision is only one part of success. If you need willing compliance to roll the implementation out, the delay and inconvenience may be worth it.
• *It'll give ammunition to the opposition.*	• Managers fear consulting employees will provide ammunition to oppose the decision once it's made. • Employees react to a decision even if it's after the fact. Since ramming the decision through is not the point, providing its pros and cons will help the debate.

Trying to retain as much control as possible is an understandable urge as the organization embarks on this new relationship with its knowledge workers, but it is important to remember that none of this will work unless there is a real intent to be inclusive rather than exclusive. It is the job of the CEO and the people who report directly to her to require this behavior both of themselves and of others.

Briefing Employees

Employees must have a clear understanding of the parameters of the consultation *before* the consultation to avoid negative feedback *after* it. It is a critical step which is often omitted and having been omitted, causes no end of trouble and suspicion. That's the bad news. The good news is that this step isn't hard to do and is usually well accepted by employees.

There are two common misconceptions that you need to discuss with employees to help them identify the parameters. They are: 1) consulting is approval, and 2) consensus is necessary.

Consulting Is Approval

Managers are sometimes reluctant to consult because, like employees, they assume consulting means you have to accept the advice. This is not the case, any more than consulting a friend on whether to accept a job offer implies you must do what she advises. Consultation issues are ones on which you wish to retain final say but welcome input. Make this clear up front by saying something like: "I welcome your opinions on this issue. I'll need to take into account other factors (name them if you can) but your input will be considered very seriously in the decision."

Employees will only be annoyed and suspicious of your motives if the rules of engagement aren't clear and their unspoken, implicit expectations are violated.

Consensus Is Necessary

As people began to study the models in our HR organization example, they realized that two of them implied relocations of staff. They were uncomfortable with the idea that their opinions might result in forcing some of their colleagues to relocate. Thus, they urged the executive to get consensus before moving forward. While the senti-ment is understandable, it's not feasible in today's fast-moving envi-ronment.

You're looking for opinion, not consensus. A majority would be nice but it's not a showstopper if it doesn't materialize. That there is a minority of people who disagree with the decision and are affected by it, is unfortunate but doesn't change the decision.

Again, although people will generally see the logic, they need to be reminded. You can say: "This is an exercise in opinion gathering but not necessarily in consensus. Although I'd like everyone to agree, these issues are so complex and there are so many possible paths, I think it's unlikely. What I hope for is a thoughtful consideration of the issues and your considered opinion on them. And even though we don't have a unanimous opinion, we can still move ahead."

Running the Consultation

Our HR organization distributed the three models of service delivery about a month prior to the consultation. They prepared communi-cations materials for managers and ensured that they understood the ramifications of each model. The newsletter and other communica-tion vehicles provided the questions. Employees were encouraged to ask their managers or HQ staff about the models. About a week before the consultation, the VP sent an e-mail to all staff, reminding them that this consultation was not about approval nor was consen-sus necessary.

In general, there are some rules of thumb about running consul-tations. First, make the consultation as wide as is possible and well publicized. Trying to reach every employee is a worthwhile goal, but since the consultation process is both voluntary and anonymous, a 100 per cent response rate is unrealistic. In fact, professional survey-ers are thrilled with a 30 per cent return (if they are using a fairly large target population).

You can influence the return rate by the method used to collect the information. A print-based medium (memo, e-mail) tends to have the lowest return, although 30 per cent is still possible. Being consulted in real time (by telephone, in meetings) has the highest rate but is also usually the most costly. In addition, timing is impor-tant. Summer vacations and peak work periods may make a differ-ence in the response rate but shouldn't be the driver of whether you do the consultation. If the question needs to be decided promptly, it's better to do a consultation with fewer people rather than not to consult at all.

Pose the options in the consultation as simply and concisely as possible. Keep reading levels in the organization in mind. If they can't understand the question, they can't give you an informed response. Finally, tell employees what you will do with the results— who will analyze them, when the results will be ready, who'll get them, and when they'll be folded into the decision.

Setting up a consultation is much like an employee survey although the consultation document can be more informal, since it is a one-time event and you don't need to compare year over year results as you would with an employee survey. However, read the chapter on employee surveys (Chapter 15) for other suggestions.

Dealing With the Results

In one organization I know of (not the HR one cited above), the results from the consultation were disappointing. The executive group had expected rousing support for their new customer focus initiative and suggestions on how to improve it. Instead, they got a barrage of complaints. Employees disliked working the longer hours needed to be more accessible to customers; they objected to the monitoring of customer interactions and they were incensed that no recognition had been given to the greater effort that this new initiative required.

The executive group was shocked and, although they were reluctant to admit it, hurt too. They knew this new initiative was vital to the organization's long-term health and therefore, the existence of everyone's jobs. But instead of being praised for their insight and strategic thinking, they were criticized for the necessary fallout from this new direction. Given the disappointing results and the fact that few good suggestions came out of the consultation, the whole thing was quietly buried.

In consulting employees, you do more harm than good by asking the question and then falling silent if you don't like the answer. Employees understandably feel that they are being manipulated if you ask for their advice and then seem to ignore it. Make a commitment before the results are compiled that you will distribute them and when. If possible, accompany the employee results with the decision that has been taken and how the employee results were used in the decision process.

Even in the case of these disappointed executives, the same process of feedback should be used. Tell employees when they can expect to see the results, and what improvements, if any, will be implemented as a result of the consultation. In addition, however, the executive group also needs to address the message about the customer service process. The response might be information sessions about why this new initiative is necessary or more involvement in how the new initiative is implemented (see the next chapter for discussion on this). Whatever the response, you need to give feedback on the answers both to the questions you asked and to those you didn't.

While you retain the right to decide in consultation, pay special attention if you get a very strong message that employees prefer a choice you don't. For example, to return to our HR example, employees were against decentralizing the function, even though management felt that, on balance, it was the best way to get closer to its customers. Getting employee feedback contrary to your inclinations doesn't mean you should go with a decision that doesn't feel right. But you need to explain to the employees what factors made you decide to go against their expressed views. If you don't, they'll suspect you've ignored the feedback. If you do explain, you'll minimize the disgruntled feelings. In our example, the executive decided to go with decentralization and spent a considerable amount of time explaining why they felt they made the right decision.

Tell Me Again Why All This Is Worth It?

Sometimes it's not a matter of inviting or convincing people of the right path but of simply saying, "We're going in this direction." Period. And there are still times when this is necessary. The difference is frequency. The number of times you can just point in a particular direction and expect the troops to salute and rush off are getting fewer and fewer. In the past, it was much easier to detect whether the troops were following—they were either lined up behind you or they weren't. But the deeper we get into the information age, the less clear it will be. Are they really following or just saying they are? Because what workers produce is no longer so tangible, you often won't be able to tell until it's too late to correct. Unless you truly engage people's minds and hearts, you won't have access to either.

Summary

If employees are to commit their intellectual capital to the organization, they need to believe that their opinions matter. One way to demonstrate this is to consult them on important issues. While this will help employees realize that they are valued, the consultation process must be managed carefully in order to produce the desired results. The same can be said for another employee engagement technique—involvement—which will be discussed in the next chapter.

Main Points

- Employees will only commit their intellectual capital if they believe their opinions count.
- One way to show employees that their opinions matter is to consult them on corporate issues.
- Issues on which employees are consulted must be both substantive and amenable to influence.
- Employees must understand that they are being consulted, not asked to approve a decision, and that consensus is not necessary.

CHAPTER 5

ꙮ

Tapping Knowledge Throughout The Corporation: Involvement

Centralized planning, power concentrated in the hands of the few, dissent denied or suppressed. What does that sound like? Totalitarianism, dictatorship, Communism. But in many organizations, you could also add, "Where I work." It's interesting, isn't it, that features which caused revolutions in the political sphere are still so prevalent within organizations? But the revolution is coming to where you live. The power is shifting from the few to the many who now not only control the levers of wealth but embody them. Without brainpower, the company doesn't have anything to offer the world and no reason for existence. The balance has shifted.

However, many organizations are still running under the old rules that tacitly assume, official pronouncements to the contrary, that power is in the hands of the few and that divergent opinions are not welcome and are moreover punished. Organizations can continue along these lines for some time but not forever. Let me tell a story about an early example of knowledge workers. I was working with the president of an animation company when computers were first introduced to that industry. Before that, each cell of the cartoon had to be colored by hand—a painstaking and laborious task. The company saw the possibility for a huge cost saving with computers but when they were introduced, production costs didn't drop. While eliminating the repetitious aspects of animation, the computers also allowed animators to produce much more complex and realistic cartoons. Creating more visually interesting cartoons absorbed the time saved by computer. In fact, the animators were being *too* creative for the target market (low-cost Saturday morning cartoons). It was a difficult situation and unfortunately, this CEO approached it in the way we've all grown up with. He announced a standard of production to meet his goal of cheaper cartoons and began to track the number of cartoon cells produced per hour by each animator.

Over the course of several months, his best animators left. He shrugged this off with, "Well, some people can't cut it." But over the next several years, things got worse and the company eventually went out of business. The loss of animators was not the only reason but it contributed to the downward spiral. When the market swung to prime-time higher-end animation, the company couldn't take advantage because it no longer had sufficiently skilled staff.

So, you see, the old style didn't work for the animation company and it won't work for anyone else dealing with knowledge workers. When wealth is created in their heads and you can't control their heads, you must find other ways to invite them to join you along the organizational path.

As we have already seen, some part of this invitation is accomplished through consulting and encouraging new knowledge. Another important way is by involving employees in the company's big decisions. By involvement, I mean asking them to decide or recommend on major challenges. Not only will this approach bring to light more of the implicit knowledge people have of what might work, it will also challenge their creativity and reinforce their belief that you value their opinions and knowledge.

It has many positive benefits but poorly implemented, it can also backfire. So, while involving employees is an important way to release intellectual capital, it needs to be done with finesse.

The Types of Decisions Appropriate for Employee Involvement

The types of decisions employees can be involved in run a wide gamut. Harris Farinon, a supplier in the cellular and telephone markets and a recent winner of the Canada Award for Excellence, has developed its capacity to involve employees to a very high degree and with very great success. When they needed to overhaul their manufacturing operation, they gave the project to a team of employees whose task included deciding whether or not the floor needed supervisors. The team revamped the operation and, in addition, concluded that supervisors were still required. Harris Farinon was able to demonstrate the high degree of confidence they had in employees and they repaid them with a serious and thoughtful plan which kept the company's needs uppermost.

Other topics that might benefit from employee consideration are HR policies, strategic business decisions, or revamping outdated processes. The comfort level of the executive group usually drives what is chosen, at least initially. At the beginning, it's usual for them to choose a topic (e.g., what policies need to be put in place to support individual employee learning) which is important but not vital to the immediate success of the business. As they get more comfortable with the process and the process itself starts to produce valuable results, they are usually more willing to allow an involvement team—a group of employees representing all parts of the organization—to tackle more strategically critical issues (e.g., how to increase customer loyalty or, as in our example, a revamp of a major operation).

Whatever topics are chosen, they need to be ones on which employee commitment is sought. If it's not necessary to have employees implement the decision, they probably don't need to be involved in working out *how* to do it. I can't think of many strategic decisions that would fit that bill in today's knowledge economy but there are many nonstrategic ones (e.g., no employee cars in the visitor parking) which simply require adherence to the rule. Also, it's not always necessary, and sometimes not even advisable, to ask employees to consider some questions like the new direction of the company. However, it would be very appropriate to involve employees in *how* the new direction should be rolled out.

In addition, as with consultation, the decision must make a difference to the organization. If the executive group is nervous, it's all right to start out with topics that are perceived to make only a marginal difference to the corporation's success, like decreasing absenteeism or increasing the safety record. However, for knowledge workers to truly believe that their opinions count, the strategic nature of the topics in which they are involved must grow over time. Also, as with consultation, the executive group cannot have already made the decision, however informally. If they have, it is a waste of the employees' time and moreover, will create a great deal of resentment among staff.

A good topic for an involvement group is one where the implications of the decision must be thought through operationally, logistically, systemically, and so on. This is work executives don't usually have time to do well and may be more familiar territory for front-line employees. Process re-engineering is a good example. Employees know the processes they work in at a much finer level of detail than their managers and they are the logical ones to be involved in streamlining the work.

Also, the decision should affect more than one function. There are still lots of decisions that affect only one function in the organization, be it finance, marketing, sales, or operations. These should continue to be made within it. However, today's work is more and more interdependent. HR needs IT to tailor the HR on-line system to its needs; IT needs HR to develop special incentive packages to avoid losing its programmers. For decisions that will affect other functions, either as part of their work specialty or as employees of the corporation, an involvement group is an excellent vehicle.

In the table below, I've listed some decisions appropriate for involvement and some which are probably not.

Table: 5.1

POSSIBILITIES	ISSUES PROBABLY NOT APPROPRIATE
• models for new service • design of delivery function • how to revamp systems to get closer to customer • revamping HR policies to reflect strategic mandate • identify and make business cases for new growth areas/markets • identify process used to lay off staff (how they're identified and/or how they're treated)	• removal of a direct report • mission of organization • financial goals • how to deal with board of directors • union negotiations

You may not agree with the items either because they give away the shop *or* they are too restrictive. If you don't, that's okay. As mentioned earlier, the "right" topic will be determined by the needs of the organization at the moment and how much control executives are willing to let go. If the involvement task groups go well, you'll probably want to expand their scope but it's perfectly appropriate to start small. But start.

Deciding or Recommending?

You can ask an involvement group either to make recommendations to a more senior body or to make the decision themselves. Whatever you decide, don't leave any doubt. If the employee group hares off to implement a decision when the executive group expected them to check first, all will be unpleasantly surprised.

Whether you give the group recommendation or decision power is not necessarily driven by the topic they are working on, but by how confident the executive group is that the task group will take into account all the strategic, political, and other considerations necessary. It can be perfectly appropriate to give the group recommendation power only. In one organization I worked with, the task groups were asked to recommend on very important issues (e.g., the process used to lay off people, the process by which managers would be chosen) but they were never allowed decision-making power. Because the issues were important to both the employees and the organization, the employees had no trouble with the idea that the executive group had the final say.

The rule of thumb on whether to give an involvement group decision or recommendation power is: is the executive willing to implement whatever the employee group decides? There are times when that might be true. For example, you might ask an employee group to identify ways to increase safety that don't adversely impact production and cost no more than a certain amount a year to implement and maintain. If they come up with measures that meet those parameters, you might be willing to go with whatever they decide.

However, there are other times when you won't be willing to implement an outcome without considering it yourself. An example might be ways to increase customer loyalty. It's perfectly all right to keep the final decision as long as the employee group is clear about that before they start. Don't give them the power to decide and then second-guess them. If you think that might happen, give them the power to recommend only.

Getting Executive Agreement

If the issues are both important and strategic, it's a little nerve-racking for the executive to involve employees no matter how much they support the principle. This nervousness can express itself in objections. In addition to all the fears and concerns covered in the previous chapter, executives may also challenge the idea of involvement in the following ways:

Objection: *If they're going to make the decision, what's my job?*

Even if the employee group only has the power of recommendation, this fear may still underlie the executive's resistance. When issues that have traditionally been the bailiwick of executives are assigned to employee groups (such as, how to revamp customer delivery or streamline a major process) executives will have questions such as: "If I don't have a role, do I have a job? Even if I do, do I want to just be the implementer of what somebody else decides? Is this what I struggled up the ladder for all these years?" The fear that they won't have a role in this new way of doing things, that their expertise and experience won't be valued, is compelling and needs to be addressed. If these questions were rolling around in your head, you'd be a little reluctant too.

Possible Response

In fact, executives have a leadership role that is as challenging and satisfying as any in the past. This new role is more coach and teacher than doer, more strategic than operational. They add value to knowledge workers' work by being tapped into the changes in market forces and customer preferences and helping knowledge workers incorporate these understandings into their work. Once they realize that this new role is as satisfying and valuable as the old one, the fear will subside. This realization will take time, however, and until it happens, executives may well be quite resistant.

Unfortunately, as with consensus, you can't always wait until people have reached the point where they should be before you press on. You may need to start these involvement groups before every executive is completely convinced both of their worth and the role he can play. You can encourage the executive team to move into this new area by ensuring that the team is:

- mandated for recommendation only
- given terms of reference approved by the executive group (see below)
- chosen by the executive

Objection: *Employees won't be objective. They're too emotionally involved.*

This is the pot calling the kettle black. Executives are just as emotionally involved; they're just more practiced in packaging it. However, there is some validity to the objection. Employees are usually new to this level of thinking and like all new things, first efforts are likely to be a little rough unless they get help. Unfortunately, the quality (or acceptability) of these first decisions often determines whether the whole process will continue.

Possible Response

One way to address this concern is by explicitly stating the trade-offs and compromises inherent in the topic that the employee group needs to consider. For example, if the employee group has been asked to tackle customer loyalty, some of the trade-offs they might be asked to consider are: How do we maintain or improve the quality of what we offer without increasing the price? Customers demand greater accessibility to services, but how do we address employee morale if we go to longer business hours? Customers need extremely knowledgeable sales people, but how can employees stay current without spending all their time in training and learning? The employee group would be asked to respond to questions like these explicitly and in addition to their recommendations. When they do, the executive group can follow the reasoning and be assured that all aspects of these difficult questions have been adequately considered. Another way to assuage concern is to have the employee group discuss progress with the executive group at regular intervals during the course of the project.

The more employee teams provide helpful and well considered recommendations, the more confidence the executive group will have in the process, and the more they'll be willing to cede actual decision-making power. However, even if the executive committee never gets to this stage, these task groups can still be a powerful force in releasing the intellectual capital of the organization. Knowledge workers need to believe that their opinions count if they are going to donate their intellectual capital, but they are usually both logical and mature enough to understand that the executive group can—and needs to—play a role in guiding the overall direction. Therefore, in important issues, most employees have no problem with the executive making the final decision, as long as they also believe their recommendations are seriously considered in that process.

Terms of Reference

Although this may seem overly formal, I urge you to have terms of reference for each employee team. Because this is new territory, a written document covering what is to be delivered, when, by whom, and with what parameters helps clarify the task. For example, you may want to specify that the recommendations cannot entail spending any more money than a preset amount or that they must be able to be implemented within a certain time period. The format you can use is on page 79, with an example filled out.

Sometimes, the executive group is inclined to direct the employee group to consider only certain options (e.g., whether increasing hours of service would increase customer loyalty) and not others (e.g., building more stores in downtown areas). By and large, try to avoid forbidding the employee group to consider certain avenues. Otherwise, you may leave the impression that their work is just window dressing.

These considerations are quite legitimate but should be addressed in a different way. One is to strike a group to specifically consider the ramifications of increasing store hours instead of a group on all facets of customer loyalty. Another way is to reflect the concern in the scope of the task. For example, you might specify that the recommendations can't cost more than $1 million to implement and maintain.

Terms of reference are invaluable in ensuring that both the employee group and the executive understand what is expected. If the mandate is too loose or unclear, the results may be off track or otherwise unusable. Once all that work has been done (no matter how minimally useful the outcomes), rejecting the recommendations will cause anger, frustration, and cynicism in employees. This can be avoided by spending time at the beginning defining the exact nature of the project.

Table: 5.2

TERMS OF REFERENCE FORMAT

OBJECTIVE:

• *what the team is to accomplish*	• To increase the loyalty of customers as demonstrated by increased repeat sales and increase in customer satisfaction ratings.

SCOPE:

• *what area is to be covered (the whole company, restricted, etc.)*	• All product lines should be considered with particular emphasis on the products on the market for less than three years. • Products with a projected launch date of later than six months from now should not be included.

DEADLINE:

• *when the recommendations have to be ready*	• Final recommendations are six months from now. • Monthly status reports should be tabled at the first executive meeting of each month. • In three months, the project leader will discuss the conclusions the group has reached on the trade-off questions posed (these would be attached to the terms of reference).

TEAM MEMBERS:

• *who's on the team, who's the team leader*	• One representative from marketing, finance, human resources, sales, operations, and strategic planning and two representatives from field offices will constitute the team.

Table 5.2 cont'd

- The team leader will be Susan Markel from marketing.
- The team members will be chosen by the VP of their respective divisions.
- Other members may be added if the team decides this is warranted.

CHALLENGE FUNCTION:
- *someone without a vested interest in the outcome*

- Cliff Elgin will act as the challenge function.

PARAMETERS:
- *any restrictions, constraints which define the boundaries of the project (money, decisions already made)*
- *any subset issues which require a solution*
- *any direction on level of risk/radical thinking expected*

Recommendation must:
- Include input from customers and other stakeholders.
- Be able to be implemented within the next two fiscal years.
- Not involve an increase in head count.
- Cost no more than $1 million, and no more than 50 per cent to be incurred in any one fiscal year.
- Consider the impact of the recommendations on our strategic direction.
- Not be constrained by present organizational structures or processes.

LOGISTICS:
- *if they need support or research help, where do they get it?(from themselves is an acceptable answer)*

- Clerical and other support for the task group will be provided by marketing.
- The budget for this task is $10,000 to be administered by team leader and used to fund pilot studies, short-term research, etc.

Setting Up the Team
How to Pick Team Members

Have the executive group pick the team members using specific criteria, such as one representative from each function (e.g., field operations, marketing) that will be affected by the recommendations. In addition, the choice should consider characteristics such as the ability to work well with others. Managers and supervisors should not be on the team unless their expertise is essential and if they must be, no other team member should be in a direct reporting relationship in their regular jobs.

Who to Pick as Team Leader

The team members can pick their own leader or it can be the representative of the function most affected. In our example, the marketing representative was chosen because her area would be most affected by any changes recommended. The executive committee will probably have an opinion and with the first few involvement teams, will probably want to make the choice. That's all right, although hopefully they will eventually feel comfortable enough to allow the teams to pick their own leader.

Avoid joint leadership if at all possible. This is sometimes proposed because several senior managers want their representative as head. Usually, these groups have a limited time in which to deliver their recommendations and often are doing this work in addition to their regular jobs. If there is joint leadership of a project—especially one which is contentious or on which there are many conflicting views—the group can waste time while the two project leaders fight over who will have the upper hand and an atmosphere is created in which it is difficult to reach workable conclusions. So even if joint leadership works politically because it increases the perception of control for more than one executive, it doesn't work practically and should be avoided.

Be prepared for some real difficulty in choosing the team leader. In the first task group I tried to set up, the VPs were so bound up in turf protection that simply having a representative was not enough. Several believed that unless their candidate was project leader, the recommendations wouldn't be what they wanted. As control wasn't an acceptable overt objective, it was played out by attacking any candidate but theirs. The meeting descended into character assassination and the final compromise resulted in a leader whose main virtue seemed to be that the VPs were fairly certain they could push him around. It was such an inappropriate choice that the CEO later vetoed it.

Although it was appropriate for the executive committee to make the decision, if I were to do this over again, I would have insisted the discussion focus on the qualities people *had* rather than those they didn't. This was a perfect—if unpleasant—example of how groups unused to thinking on behalf of the whole corporation, aren't very good at it.

Some of you might be thinking, "Right. A bunch of control freaks! Just like my guys!" Well, yes, they were. The need to control one's environment is common to everyone, no matter their position; it's just that senior managers define their environment as covering a lot larger territory than front-line people. But while their need to control comes from the same urge as anyone else's, its expression often needs to be tempered for the good of the company. In order to have knowledge workers commit their intellectual capital, they need to feel that their opinions will be listened to. To demonstrate this, executives must cede some of their control so that employees can have more influence. It's an important contribution to encouraging the flowering of intellectual capital, but it's not easy. So while it's required, it should also be acknowledged that it's a risky step for those in power.

Executives Sitting In

If some members of the executive group are very concerned about the outcome of the employee group (or even secretly opposed to the whole idea), they may want to "just sit in" or even appoint themselves as their function's team representative. This is not a good idea, particularly early in the process, when the team isn't at all sure whether they're being involved or manipulated. If a high-ranking person sits in, this heightens the suspicion. Because senior managers are used to taking charge, they are unhappy, uncomfortable, and unable to let a group struggle with a problem if they think they know the answer. Without meaning to do so, they can dominate the meeting and confirm the team's suspicions that they're being manipulated into ensuring the executive committee gets what it wants.

Once this process is well established, it can work to have a member of the executive group participate. However, three conditions need to exist: (1) the organization has had some positive experiences with this process; (2) the executive member can act as a team member; (3) the executive member has an expertise welcomed by the group.

If these apply, the executive's participation can be a very positive sign of interest and involvement. But be careful of doing it too early in the process.

How can involving a small number of employees in a decision make all the organization's knowledge workers more committed to the company?

An excellent question. It makes intuitive sense that the employees who are actually involved in the topic will be quite committed to their recommendations. However, it's harder to see how it would make a difference to anyone not in that group. That would probably be true if only one task group was ever struck. Even if their recommendations were accepted, it's unlikely that that one group will influence whether all the company's knowledge workers feel their opinions count.

The power of involvement comes when employee teams are a regular part of the decision process. For example, with Brocktel, which won the Canada Award of Excellence, striking a task group to solve a problem is how they do business. Employees believe their opinions count because there are countless and continual reminders of it through these involvement groups.

In addition, the influence one employee has on another should not be discounted. If an employee is working on a big issue and his recommendations are seriously considered, he'll be telling his colleagues in the neighboring cubicles. In this way, others start to believe that management is serious even if they themselves haven't been in a group.

So involving a small number of employees can increase the belief that knowledge workers' opinions matter if this involvement is repeated again and again until it is standard operating procedure.

The Challenge Function

In our example, the involvement team was asked to recommend ways to increase customer loyalty. The rep from the strategic planning unit raises the option of increasing the hours of store operation. Although no one says anything, the HR rep is thinking of all the disgruntled employees who will have to work the longer hours and the possible union drive as a result. The field rep is thinking of the flack he'll get from his colleagues if he agrees. The sales rep is wondering how to support a field operation with increased operating hours. The finance guy is shuddering about the overtime costs. For all these reasons, no one responds to the strategic planning rep's suggestion, and the group moves rapidly to a less contentious possibility.

What if longer hours are the key? It may also have all the problems that the group fears, but if the option isn't fully discussed, there is no opportunity to decide whether many or all of these obstacles could be overcome. An idea that might positively affect customer loyalty never sees the light of day.

Burying uncomfortable issues is an understandable and even common activity of groups trying to deal with difficult problems. However, if they do so, they are unlikely to produce anything very different from the status quo. Sometimes they don't even resolve the issue they've been assigned. To address this aspect of working in a group, there is enormous benefit derived from the presence of someone who isn't really part of the team.

The person plays the role of a challenge function. This challenge function is the one on the involvement team who doesn't necessarily know the content and doesn't have a stake in the outcome. His primary function is to keep the group focused on what's good for the company. He is not a management plant since the group's only responsibility is to listen to what the challenger has to say. Even if the group is heading toward an unworkable solution, his only role is to point out that it doesn't fit the objectives in the terms of reference. The group doesn't have to act on his observations.

In order to fulfill his role, he would question the sacred cows and traditional ways of doing business and push the group to consider off-the-wall options. It can be an advantage to know little or nothing about the problem since it frees the challenger to ask those "stupid" questions which sometimes hide hitherto ignored solutions. In the group, the person would do the following types of things:

- Ask group members to take the larger view when they get mired in myopia. "We seemed to be into the details of store layout before we've decided the objective for the layout change. I wonder if it might make more sense to tackle that first."

- Support the project leader in keeping things focused. "This is really interesting but I think it's a little off-topic. Perhaps Jane and Alan could discuss that some other time."

- Point out when proposed solutions are not heard or discussed. "I notice that Brian has raised the idea of longer store hours a couple of times and nobody has addressed it. Why do you think that is?"

- Highlight avoidance behavior. "We've spent almost an hour discussing whether or not to do a videotape about our project, and we haven't spent any time talking about the possibility of layoffs in the eastern regions if we implement this plan. Is there some reluctance to discuss this?"

- Remind the group of its mandate when it is straying. "The solution proposed has a great many merits but won't it cost more than the $1 million outlined in the terms of reference? What do you think needs to be done about that?"

- Point out when the recommendations may be being influenced more by emotion or group think than by logic. "It's really unpalatable to think about closing down the satellite offices. Even if the company offers all those employees other jobs, they'll have to move. It'll be really hard on people who have lived all their lives in those small towns. But is it the right decision for the long-term health of the company?"

It might look like the project leader can, and maybe even ought to, do these tasks, but she is as interested in keeping things free of conflict as is any team member. In fact, her ticket to the next big job may ride on it. The team needs someone whose reputation or credibility is not tied up with the production of the recommendations and can stand outside the debate.

In summary, the team is responsible for content; the challenger is not. It is also accountable for the outcomes; the challenger is not. The challenger's job is to raise uncomfortable issues and the team members' is to hear what the challenger has to say. They can choose not to act on it, but they shouldn't ignore it just because it's not what they want to hear.

If a challenge function is used with involvement groups, it increases the chances that the recommendations will be useful to the executive committee and that the employee group's work can be implemented.

Helping the Process

In addition to providing terms of reference and a challenge function, you can increase the chances that the involvement team will produce a valuable product by making sure it understands the complexities of the context it is working in and by training them to work together.

Make Sure the Team Understands the Complexities

Executives often don't want to use involvement teams because the employees don't have a big enough view of the complexities and small "p" political realities. It is true that a good decision needs to take into account these factors and, moreover, that many employees don't have that perspective. However, this isn't an argument for avoiding involvement teams. Rather, it is another reason why communications and pushing down complexity activities are so critical. If you're already using the techniques discussed earlier, this part of your job has been done.

Train Them to Work Together

There seems to be a myth circulating that teamwork comes naturally. It just isn't so. Professional sports people have always known this. The NHL doesn't just put together a great group of athletes and then say, "Gee, fellows, good luck on the season. I'll really be rooting for you." They practice, build skills, and get coaching. There is an intense attention to playing as a team.

All teams need coaching on new competencies like conflict resolution, challenging each other's behavior, staying focused on the goal, compromising, negotiating, listening even when they don't want to hear, challenging themselves to think outside their own world view, balancing taking care of each other's feelings with staying true to the mandate, and overcoming their own fears of change.

That's an enormous challenge and unfortunately, this is not an exhaustive list. You can tackle this in several ways. One is to talk with the group about how to handle the pitfalls outlined and create a contract among themselves. Secondly, get formal training in some of the critical skills.

Involvement groups can be a very powerful way to increase the commitment of knowledge workers to the company and, in addition, to produce valuable results but *how* the task group is set up and run is very important.

Tabling the Report

Once the recommendations are ready, the team leader (with the whole team present if possible) should present the findings to the executive committee. This recognizes the work invested and allows detailed questioning of the thinking behind the recommendations so the executive group can understand the implications.

Sometimes, executive groups can't accept the recommendations of an involvement group. This can happen for any number of reasons. The executive group might disagree with a fundamental assumption (*we will be on target in our revenue plans this year*) or despite the best efforts of the challenge function, the employee group hasn't really followed the terms of reference. If this happens, you need to do three things: talk to the team, communicate to the rest of the company, and do damage control.

In talking to the team, the executive in charge should explore if there is any way to adjust the group's recommendations, change their spin, or otherwise keep the core intact. If the team hadn't considered all the relevant aspects, they might be asked to go back to the drawing board. If the decision can't wait, the executive in charge should explain why he must take it now. In any case, he should acknowledge the hard work, the disappointment the team feels, and his confidence both in them and in the process.

If the recommendations can't be largely accepted for whatever reason, make sure you're completely open with all employees. Without blaming, explain what happened, and why (see boxed scenario on the next page for an example).

> *The team has worked hard and I thank them for that. However, the task group thought X and the executive group thought Y. While both are viable, after a lengthy debate that included the task group, it was decided to go with Y.*
>
> *I know this is disappointing for the team, but even though their recommendations were not adopted, their work contributed to the debate by raising issues we might not have thought of. This shows the process is of real value and that we shouldn't be deterred by this one outcome. I know we'll all benefit from the continued reliance on employee teams to grapple with the tough issues facing us.*

Whatever you do, don't quietly bury the recommendations. Even if they aren't viable, employees (who don't know that) will interpret it as management ignoring what it doesn't want to hear. If you must reject the recommendations, explain why.

If rejection needs to happen, you must do damage control. You can ask the employee team how to change the process so recommendations are more likely to be accepted. You might also use communication vehicles such as the company newsletter to acknowledge that confidence in management has taken a hit and ask employees to stick with the process as the kinks get ironed out.

As you continue to use involvement teams, you'll probably build up some capital in the trust bank account and one rejection may be less critical. However, never assume it doesn't matter. It does, at any point. On the other hand, I would never urge you to take a major decision that doesn't sit right. Better to do damage *control* than damage.

Glitches in the Process

This process really does work and I have the scars to prove it, but having said that, there is no doubt that there are some glitches.

Will Involvement Ensure Commitment?

Although commitment is a central objective of this approach, you have to be realistic about how quickly or thoroughly it will evolve.

The involvement process must be systematic, that is, with a well-thought out plan of involvement, and systemic—one that includes as many people as possible. If you conduct enough successful employee groups, people will begin to trust the process and give you the commitment you seek.

It would be wonderful if one round of involvement activities produced huge gains in trust and commitment, an excitement about the future, and a wholehearted investment of intellectual capital. It isn't going to happen. It will take time.

Does This Process Produce Better Decisions?

I want to answer an unequivocal and resounding "Yes!" to this question, but the best I can do is a "Well, sometimes, usually, and probably over the longer-term." Employees, like managers, make mistakes, have to overcome their own control needs, have to push themselves to think strategically, and have to juggle complexities. While the problems will benefit from more minds being applied to their solutions, this process isn't a guarantee of better decisions. It will increase the likelihood that the decision, whatever it is, will be supported and implemented. In case that sounds like inadequate payoff for the rigors of involving employees, remember that the rightness of the idea or decision in no way determines its success. I can have a brilliant plan to revolutionize our company but unless I have the support of all the key players, it's not going to go anywhere. Being right is not enough. You also need the support of those who will implement the decision. So, keep these pseudo-equations in mind:

100% right X 0% support = 0 success
50% right X 100% support = some success

It's difficult to accept that you might have to go with a less than optimal solution if it has high support. However, in a learning environment, people often need to try out their preferred option first in order to take on the risk, threat, and personal change entailed in stepping up to the solution which will really do the trick. You can force the right decision through, but with no support, it will fail.

Summary

The tenor of the chapters about engagement have reflected the painful and frustrating fact that people cannot be talked into reality. They won't believe it nor commit to it unless they interact with it. Involving them is a way of giving them this opportunity. Involvement changes not merely how work is accomplished but how completely the heart and the brain are engaged in the company's business. It is the essence of releasing and using your intellectual capital. The next chapter will deal with an issue that is equally challenging—managing knowledge workers whose work you don't understand.

Main Points

- To demonstrate the employees' opinions count, the organization should start to involve them in the major decisions of the organization.

- The decisions need to be important ones with many ramifications and which affect more than one function.

- The executive group must decide whether these groups should be allowed to recommend or decide on the issue they are assigned.

- To run these involvement groups, terms of reference are needed as well as a process to pick team members.

- To help the process, a person should be appointed as a challenge function and all team members should be briefed on the complexities of the issue they are tackling and be trained on how to work in teams.

- If the executive group cannot accept the recommendation of the involvement group, they need to do damage control.

- Involvement will increase knowledge workers' commitment to the organization but it will take some time.

- Also, this process doesn't necessarily produce better decisions, but it does produce ones to which employees are much more committed.

Managing Knowledge You Don't Understand

It has always been a manager's job to get the best out of people, so tapping people's knowledge is a familiar role for all leaders. However, the information age produces a new wrinkle in *how* you tap it. Managers of computer programmers are particularly aware of this trend. Even a couple of years of managing rather than doing leaves you out of the loop. This is true in other fields as well. For example, managers of engineers and researchers find that even though they understand the broad lines of their staff's work, their ability to engage in detailed debates diminishes within a few years of assuming a management position. As the volume of knowledge grows year after year and specialization increases, more and more of us find ourselves in this position.

This has forced us to rethink our assumptions about supervision. In the industrial era, you were promoted to supervisor because you were the best worker and, the theory went, best able to train others and catch their mistakes. Supervisors, therefore, were super workers. This works pretty well when the increases in knowledge are steady but gradual and managers and supervisors can continue to acquire the knowledge needed to be super worker/ boss. However, the speed of new knowledge generation means that it is a losing battle.

Unfortunately, some managers are still trying. They respond to this proliferation of knowledge either by trying to acquire all the new knowledge themselves or by insisting that their subordinates explain everything fully enough so the manager could make an independent decision. Either way, they slow down the ability of their organizations to use the new knowledge quickly and effectively.

So how do you manage knowledge you don't understand? The answer is that you don't, at least not in the same way. The information age is forcing a divorce between the roles of super worker and boss. You can be one or the other but you can't be both.

While there is an important role for you as manager and leader, it's different from the one you're used to. Because you no longer have sufficient knowledge, you need to start moving the decision-making power to those who do. I know it seems irrational to give away more control if you are already feeling uncomfortable because you don't know the work well enough any more. It seems more natural to pull what you have closer in. After all, if you give away the decision making, what's left for you?

But we share decision making with more knowledgeable colleagues every day. We consult doctors on our medical treatment, mechanics on our cars, and teachers about the education of our children. Each of these professionals has more knowledge than we do about a topic on which we need to make a decision. So, actually we all have had experience in sharing decision making when we are managing knowledge we don't fully understand.

In addition, there is a growing trend among many large companies, such as Chrysler, Citibank, and Monsanto to reorganize under co-CEOs.[1] So sharing power is starting to be a fact of life even at the very top of the organization. Still, as we move that understanding into the place we work, the two questions posed above remain. How to share decision making without giving away the shop and whether this new role is enough for you. Let's examine each in turn.

Your New Role

Managers often feel uncomfortable about sharing decision making because they believe—as do many employees—that it means keeping

---

[1] Daniel McGinn, "Just Fine, Thanks," *Newsweek* (June 22, 1998).

their paws off everything and letting the employees make all the decisions. That's not true, as we'll discuss later, but your role does change. You need to move out of the super knowledge worker role and into one that combines the roles of teacher, scout, and keeper of the flame with that of manager.

Teacher

As we've already discussed, pushing down complexity helps people understand the context of their decisions, but you can't stop there. You need to continually ensure employees are asking the right questions. (What effect will that have on the selling price? Will customers buy it? How will it affect maintenance costs?) Your role is to help employees discover the choices and, without imposing a decision, challenge them to think through the options. You won't always agree with their conclusions, but you have an important role in helping them identify what they need to think about.

In addition, as with all teachers, you have the duty and the privilege of generating a sense of excitement in employees about the possibilities of their work, to call out the best of them. You can challenge them to be more than they think they can be, do more than they think they can achieve, be more creative than they thought was possible. This is done not through coercion or exhortation but by demonstrating in your actions and your words that you believe in them. You show that belief in a large way when you share decision making but you continue to demonstrate it by helping them to think through the parameters of a decision rather than deciding, allowing them to flounder but always with a hand outstretched to help, and praising the effort as well as the result. As with all the best teachers, you teach them how to fly and then step back and applaud the flight.

Scout

In addition to the role of teacher, you have an important role in keeping your ear to the ground. While your employees are busy doing the work, you need to be continually assessing the environment for both threats and opportunities. For example, if you're getting signals your company might acquire a product line similar to the one your unit is presently producing, your employees need you to spend time understanding the ramifications of that.

Continuing and even increasing your role as political scout will be invaluable in this fast-changing world.

Another role of scout is to represent the interests of your unit and your employees within the wider organization. This is a role that is familiar to most experienced managers but this new context suggests a slightly different spin on the task. In traditional management, the good manager was one who protected his turf and people. I remember one manager who boasted that nobody could kick any of his people's butts except him. And within the confines of the old role, this manager kept a bargain that was both fair and honorable. He protected his staff from criticism and attack from outside but, in exchange, was the arbiter of what was worthy of criticism within. However today's organizations need to be more permeable to influences outside our immediate sphere. Otherwise, we miss both opportunities and threats to our success. To be more open, the manager's role is no longer one of protector but of advocate. It is not about defending our unit or even our people at any cost, but about working toward solutions which allow all parties to win in the exchange. It is advocating for the unit and the people while recognizing the legitimate needs and aspirations of those outside it. So, this role of scout both brings information and intelligence back into the unit and helps the larger company understand and appreciate the contribution the unit makes.

Keeper of the Flame

It's not unusual for people with newfound authority to take off down one path without understanding the implications. For example, the employee may be so enthusiastic about the revenue-generating potential of her scheme, she may forget that a fundamental tenet of the company is building the capacity of customers to be self-sufficient. She wants to keep selling them fish rather than teaching them how to fish.

You will play a valuable role by keeping employees focused on the company's values and mission. You do this by asking the right questions as the teacher, bringing in relevant information as the scout, but also by challenging the employee's assumptions and even values. It is your role to say, "I can see the revenue potential in your idea but it doesn't transfer that skill into the organization. It's not who we are as a company." Needless to say, the employee won't have seen the idea in that light or she wouldn't have suggested it. So, you need to revert back to your teacher role to help her to understand how she can incorporate the values of the organization into her work. This understanding helps her make a better contribution.

There may be times when you have to say no if a fundamental principle of the organization is being violated. If you must, explain your reasoning very carefully so the employee can see the mission and values of the company in action. She may not like the decision, but it can be an important moment in her understanding of how she is expected to operate.

Some managers may fear that playing this role will alienate their knowledge workers who have gotten the reputation of quitting if everything doesn't go their way. But, if respectfully done, this role of keeper of the flame has the opposite effect. By helping the employee understand how the company's values apply to a client, you implicitly assure her that she will be treated the same way (e.g., we transfer knowledge to clients, we transfer knowledge to employees). In addition, you help create a sense of belonging to a larger whole. This comfort and belonging are important aspects of feeling committed to an organization even for notoriously fickle knowledge workers.

Manager

In addition to all of these roles, you still have most of what you've always done as a manager. In most organizations, you still do employee performance assessments, budgets, shift schedules, hiring, and so on. However, the *way* you do it may differ because of your other roles. For example, you might ask others to become involved in working out the budget for the unit—not just the number crunching but the thought process and objectives underlying it. It has become fairly common practice to ask employees to interview prospective hires to ensure that there is a fit with the work group. This is a way of sharing power that pays off both in better working relationships and in demonstrating that employees' opinions count.

So, your role is a formidable one. It is manager, teacher, scout, and keeper of the flame. As Rosabeth Moss Kanter, former editor of *Harvard Business Review*, points out, you must solve the problem of giving guidance and coherence to your unit's work in light of complex activities, diverse people, and the need for speed and innovation. Rather than a lesser role, the job of a manager is becoming more complex than ever. And, as we discussed earlier in the chapter, an important aspect of this new role is to share decision-making power with employees. It is the way you can manage knowledge you don't understand and also fulfill this new role of the manager.

Sharing Decision Making

Personal threat aside, managers have a legitimate concern that employees can't handle the kind of decisions managers make. While employees have more technical knowledge, they lack the business savvy, political acumen, experience, and judgment the manager has built up over the years. It is true that employees sometimes lack those qualities and that these qualities, when applied to a decision, make it a better one. So how can you share decision-making power?

This answer to this dilemma is twofold: One is to push down complexity—that is, use your experience and savvy to help employees understand the complexities of the business world we live in. It is a transfer of knowledge so employees can infuse their decisions with your experience. We've covered *how* to do that in Chapter 3. If you do it regularly, employees will be better equipped to make wise decisions.

But beyond that, it's important to recognize that sharing decision making isn't the same as giving it all away. If it made business sense for all decisions to be in the hands of employees, there'd be no need for managers. There is still a role for a person who integrates work across a multitude of workers and who pays attention to the politics and stickhandling which continues to be a vital part of transforming brainpower into wealth. The rest of the chapter will be devoted to how to share your decision-making power.

Your Decisions and Theirs

You probably already give some decision-making power to your people. How to organize their time, who to consult on projects. These are important to continue but the sharing needed to attract and keep knowledge workers goes beyond what is typical. For knowledge workers to stay with an organization and feel committed to its goals, they must believe that they have some ability to influence what happens both in their immediate environment and in the larger company. Thus, it is almost always true that you will need to consider how to expand your power sharing beyond what you're comfortable with or have gotten used to.

That's not to say that you should give away the shop, and there will always be some powers you retain in order to help you do the roles outlined above. However, these roles should not be the reason for retaining power but for giving it away. Teachers have their greatest impact when pupils choose to learn; scouts are most influential when people are willing to listen; and keepers of the flame can lead only when others are willing to follow. Sharing decision-making power will help you accomplish your new role better.

Having said that, we need to get practical about exactly how to share it so it has the desired effect on your knowledge workers but is also good for the company. There are various areas in which you can choose to share power:

- *Technical Decisions.* Decisions about the work itself. It might be the content of a new policy, the features of a new product, or difficult customer issues. These types of decisions are most sensitive to new knowledge. For example, an employee might see a feature in another product that would give yours a competitive edge if introduced.

- *Administrative Decisions.* There are some decisions which don't move the unit's work forward but do keep it operating smoothly. Examples are granting vacation or time off, shift schedules, pay increments, recruiting new people, preparing and tracking budgets, and the like.

- *Managerial Decisions.* Some decisions are about setting the direction for the unit such as, moving new ideas up the line for approval or aligning the unit with the strategic direction. These are managerial decisions as are ones which deal with an individual employee's issues such as a performance problem or rewarding an outstanding contribution.

Generally speaking, the first types of decision to share are technical in nature, or specifically about working level questions such as the design of the product cover, the contents of the help manual, the help desk procedures. You might need to go even farther into things like changes to the features of a product or the design of the software.

Ceding these decisions is tough because, let's face it, they're the most fun to make and best reflect your own expertise. Giving them up is hard to do when you have an opinion even if you don't have the most up-to-date knowledge. But these decisions are also the ones most likely to suffer if you hold onto them when someone else has a better grasp of what needs to be done.

In addition and perhaps even more importantly, ceding these technical decisions is exactly what knowledge workers need to feel excited and committed to their jobs and to the organization. These technical decisions are the ones they want to control because they directly impact their ability to do what they care about most—working with and expanding their knowledge. By giving up some of these decisions, you increase the likelihood that they will find your organization an exciting, fulfilling, and challenging place to work.

Other types of decisions, administrative and managerial, generally stay with the manager, although some organizations have moved very far along in allowing workers to take these decisions. Some hospitals and other 24-hour operations let staff members collectively set shift schedules, while other companies allow the staff to pick the people who can join the unit. If you decide to give these types of decisions to employees, you give them a sense of control over the conditions of their work and in addition, demonstrate that you trust them to make important decisions. Both of these factors help employees to feel committed to and interested in the fate of the company. Transferring some of these decisions can have an added benefit. A good example is shift work schedules. Employees are typically disgruntled by shift allocation, no matter what process is used, and there is often some lingering suspicion that the supervisor favors one person over another. If employees are given this responsibility, they soon come to realize that it is not an easy job. Mary has a babysitting arrangement which means she has to leave at 3 p.m., no matter what. Alan is a single parent with a teenager he can't leave at home in the evenings. Bart has regular appointments with a physiotherapist and Judy has recently needed time off because she's been having a lot of trouble with her teeth. Once employees are required to juggle the demands of the work and the needs of employees, there is both a greater respect for the work of the supervisor and a greater tolerance for the inconveniences inherent in juggling work and personal needs. So, ceding this kind of decision-making power can have unexpected benefits. However, having said all of that, it's more typical to give decision-making power on the technical matters first before embarking on any others.

There are three points to remember when you're considering what kinds of decisions to give to employees:

1. ***It's not all or nothing.*** You might keep decision-making power even in a technical area if the consequence of error is too high. For example, if a faulty product design has already prompted significant lawsuits, its redesign might well be scrutinized and approved by senior people.

2. ***The decisions you cede need to make a difference.*** If you allow employees to order the office supplies but keep control of how much is spent, they'll see you're not serious about sharing decision making.

3. ***You need to help employees grow into the decisions.*** That is, you can help them understand how to make management decisions by taking into account all the factors—such as financial, human resource issues, strategy and politics—that you might consider.

Can I Teach Employees What I Know?

It's natural to assume your knowledge can't be transferred to somebody else and to believe deep down that nobody can do what you do as well as you do. At some level, that's true. Until your employees know the business environment and practice incorporating it into their decision making, they probably aren't going to be quite as astute as you. That's not a reason not to transfer the decision making, but it is a reason to do it in steps.

How to Transfer Decision Making

Once you know what decisions you want to give to employees, think about how to do it. A simple, "Well, it's yours now" won't cut it in any but the simplest decisions.

First, if the decisions are to be good ones, you must make a substantial effort to help employees understand the context in which they are being taken. This includes any factual information about market conditions and customer preferences as well as the politics, history, and strategic directions. Don't skip this step. It's counterproductive to share decision making with people who don't understand the business. Once you've completed this stage, you can use the following process to actually hand over a decision or series of decisions.

Table: 6.1

Methodology to Share Decision Making

STEPS	TIPS
1. Identify the decision or types of decisions	• Be specific (you'll be responsible for delivering a finished product by this date, with input from all the appropriate stakeholders). • Identify where you will intervene (when it's ready to go to marketing, I'd like to have the final go-ahead).
2. Teach "why"	• The consequence of error • The context • The politics • The market forces
3. Set parameters	• Expenditures can't exceed $X; VP has to agree; must be delivered by this date.
4. Incorporate a simple and agreed upon measure of success	• Emphasis on simple (product incorporates stakeholder opinion or reason given why opinion not incorporated). • State a time limit if appropriate (you'll make these decisions on your own for the next month and then we'll take stock).
5. Agree upon check-in times	• Let's meet once a week just for an update, not for decision making.
6. Build into employee's performance assessment	• This doesn't have to be the typical boss/subordinate review. It might also be peer to peer. • In addition, the assessment might go beyond your opinion of the work to extend to adherence to the mission/values.

While this seems a bit formal, you lessen the chance of misunderstanding if you do it. For example, if you say, "You can decide that" at a particular point in a project, the employee won't know whether you're saying, "You can decide that on this occasion only" or "You can decide that in perpetuity." Needless to say, it's going to make a difference if you get your wires crossed.

Another advantage of being a little more formal is that the discussions of measurement and feedback (check-ins) emphasize that sharing decision making is an earned right with both responsibilities and perks. This is a message that's useful to send. In fact, you might want to use the list below to discuss with employees what sharing decision making does and doesn't mean.

Table: 6.2

SHARED DECISION MAKING	
Is[2]	Isn't
• Working independently but as part of a team, toward common objectives	• Throwing out the rule book
	• Freedom to define the company's objectives
• Understanding the parameters and constraints of the decision	• Bypassing everyone who will say no
• Weighing the impact of decisions on all affected stakeholders	• Doing the fun parts of someone else's job
	• Freedom to redefine unilaterally the outputs needed from your job
• More trade-offs not fewer	
• An earned privilege	

Managing Risk

Some part of you probably feels a bit queasy as you think of all the possibilities if you share decision making. Employees could spend scarce resources on frivolous things and dashing after pipe dreams. The risk of mistakes does rise as people get more authority and freedom to act. When things go wrong, the knee-jerk reaction is to rescind decision-making power. Sometimes that's the right thing to do, but more often the fault is ours as managers. We likely haven't instilled a way to think about making decisions which is helpful to employees.

When a mistake has been made, you need to deal with it in a way that both rectifies the mistake and encourages people to continue to learn and grow. To avoid or minimize situations where things go wrong, provide employees with a methodology such as the one on the next page to assess the risk of their decisions.

---

[2] Adapted from Anita Ross (VP Human Resources, IBM Canada) May 15, 1991, APEX Roundtable.

Figure: 6.1

Risk Guidelines

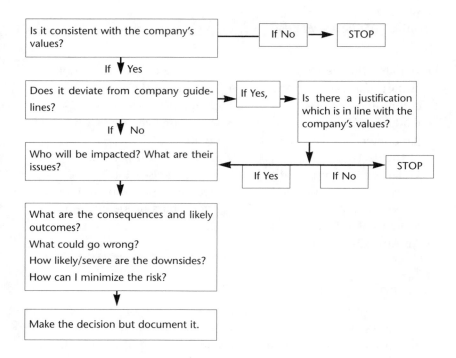

You can and should use this chart when discussing how to make a decision. It will be particularly helpful in the early stages of the process both to assure you that the right things are being considered but also as an opportunity to teach employees what they need to pay attention to.

Pitfalls

Sharing power has benefits in making the work more exciting for employees, increasing their commitment to the organization and even, occasionally, lightening the manager's workload. Yet, while it is very worthwhile for all of those reasons, it's not without its pitfalls. Here are several common ones:

- Advising Too Much
- Giving Employees the Benefit of the Doubt
- Bad Initial Decisions
- People Refusing Decision Making

Advising Too Much

You *want* to have your people come to you for advice even if they make the decision. Doing so recognizes your value-added. But *how* you respond will make a difference—whether you encourage people to think for themselves or they believe everything you're saying is just window dressing.

Here's one way:

PERSON	CONVERSATION
Employee:	*Phil, I just wanted to run my thinking past you about the Bettam contract.*
You:	*Sure, Alice. What's up?*
Employee:	*Well, Bettam wants permission to distribute the decision-making software to other companies.*
You:	*No way. Tell them that we own the intellectual property of the software.*
Employee:	*But it's to their sister companies.*
You:	*Nope. We licensed just to Bettam. I mean, I don't mind if we negotiate a lesser fee or even a volume discount, but I don't want to set a precedent.*

Well, you've solved the problem and you may even be right, but think about Alice. She thought she was asking for advice and you gave her an order. So what's she thinking now? "That's the last time I'll ask him. It's *my* decision. Next time, I'll just make it on my own." You've won the battle but lost the war. It was probably more efficient to make the decision yourself and certainly more comfortable, but you've cut the employee off from your wisdom in the longer term and undermined her confidence to boot.

Instead, try:

Employee:	*Phil, I just wanted to run my thinking past you about the Bettam contract.*
You:	*Sure, Alice. What's up?*
Employee:	*Bettam wants permission to reproduce and distribute the decision-making software.*
You:	*Really? How come?*
Employee:	*They want to use it in all their subsidiaries.*
You:	*Un-huh. And what do you think?*
Employee:	*I know it's not typical, but Bettam's such a big customer.*
You:	*True. So you think it would be good for us?*
Employee:	*Well, we don't want to lose Bettam's business over this, but some of those subsidiaries are pretty big themselves... We're losing the chance to sell into them.*
You:	*Good point. So what would be good for Bettam and good for us?*
Employee:	*I don't know. Maybe we need to give in on this one.*
You:	*Well, I'd really like a way that works for both of us. Can you think of any?*
Employee:	*What about a time limit on the agreement? Maybe a year or so?*
You:	*Yes, that's an option. Or maybe some kind of licensing agreement. I know Marge did that with one of her products. Why don't you talk to her?*
Employee:	*Good idea. I'll do that.*

It took longer to conclude this conversation than the first. No doubt the first was more efficient, but was it more effective over the long-term? I don't think so. Approaching things this way allows the employee to learn from you *how* to think about an issue which affects her decision. Even if the answer is self-evident, you help Alice most by sitting on your hands so she can work through the logic under your guidance. By doing this, you up the chances she'll continue to consult you. And then you'll have achieved what you wanted: shared decision making while still contributing your experience and acumen.

Giving Employees the Benefit of the Doubt

Managers sometimes have the fantasy that if they share power, people will take risks but never fail, will speak their minds but never argue with the boss, and will innovate but always go in the direction you want.

It isn't going to happen. Employees will make decisions differently from you. You need to make a distinction between having thought through the problem and giving the answer you agree with. It is quite reasonable to require that the employee has done the first but it is not to expect the latter. As long as an employee has seriously considered all the angles, you may have to go ahead with a proposal even if it's not exactly what you would have done. Needless to say, I'm not talking about a major mistake. I am talking about giving the employee the benefit of the doubt. Who knows, you might be wrong!

Bad Initial Decisions

The first few times an employee either makes a decision (or, if you're lucky, consults you), there may be an automatic reaction. With your greater experience, the ramifications may be obvious. What about the union? How much time will be saved? What about breakdowns? Wouldn't that unfairly advantage those who got to the office first? Such questions point out where an employee's decision thinking is weak, but there is a substantial difference between firing off objections and helping her identify where her thinking needs more development. Rather than a litany of questions, try another approach.

You:	*So, Pat, I see the memo went out asking for volunteers for your task group. Any responses yet?*
Employee:	*No, not yet, but they have until Friday.*
You:	*Oh, right. Are the unions going to send anyone in particular?*
Employee:	*The unions?*

cont'd

You:	*Remember that memo they sent a while back? They wanted to be involved in any process improvement initiatives.*
Employee:	*Oh. I forgot.*
You:	*Well, it might make a difference. What do you think you can do?*
Employee:	*How about if I walked over to the steward—it's Al, isn't it—and explained the process?*
You:	*I think that would work, but you might want to stress that you need his help. You know Al—he can get on his high horse pretty quickly. If he thinks you need him, he's less likely to be upset.*
Employee:	*Thanks. Good idea.*

It's nothing profound, is it? Except that there's a world of difference—one is guidance, the other humiliation. Employees need your help to make good corporate decisions, most particularly in the beginning. So ask the questions by all means, but do it in a way that helps the employee build her skill in wielding power.

People Refusing Decision Making

While some employees need coaching on moving into decision making slowly, others will need to be encouraged to take any at all. Either because of natural inclination, or a fear drummed into them by other bosses, these people fear failure more than they desire responsibility.

Sometimes, you can't get people to change their minds, but other times, it works to encourage them to take decisions in a more circumscribed area. As they gain confidence, you can expand the tasks. In most cases, it's possible to help employees take on more responsibility in their jobs even if they are initially reluctant to do so.

Is This Role Enough For You?

Sharing decision making has pretty obvious benefits to the company—more knowledgeable decisions, faster ones, happier employees. You increase the likelihood that knowledge workers will stay with the company, and it is a way to better use the company's intellectual capital. But doing all of this leaves a question hanging: What about me? Is it worthwhile for me? You're not alone in feeling that way. In a study on power sharing, 72 per cent of supervisors saw the programs as good for the company, 60 per cent good for employees, and 31 per cent good for themselves.

With a big piece of your job gone, will the new role be as satisfying or as exciting? Or are you going to be left with a "post-office" job, where the employees have all the fun stuff and the executives all the important stuff? I'm very sympathetic to the change required by managers. After all, you've sweated and sacrificed for years to get to a spot where you had the right to make the decisions, and now you're supposed to give them away?

Your role, while different, is no less important. In fact, you're needed more than ever. You are the organizational glue that holds all of these separate pieces together. You provide the context and meaning which allow people to contribute meaningfully to the whole. Without you, there are just separate pieces of knowledge, spinning off into the ether. You are coach, maker of meaning, political scout, enforcer of culture, influencer, and inspirer. Oh yes, and manager too, with some of the decision making and managing responsibilities you've always had.

Is decision sharing needed? Absolutely. But even so, will this new role be enough for you? I can't answer that for you. Only you can. But before you do, give it a try and not just once or twice. Like any complex skill, it takes a while to get good at it and until you are, you often can't tell whether you like it.

I think you'll find the new role has as many rewards as the old one. They'll be different and found in odd corners where you might least expect them. There is undoubtedly some excitement in fighting fires, but there is equal, if quieter, satisfaction in knowing that the thanks you're getting from your employees is more than pro forma; it is an expression of how much you are helping them to grow and thrive. You may give away some of the fun technical decisions but the compensation is knowing that you've helped the timid become confident and the unskilled become astute.

So it is a valuable role and can be a satisfying one but it requires that you change your mind-set about what a manager is and what you are valued for. Unless you can make that personal change, then you will always be longing for the good old days when you jumped on the fire truck yourself and saved the day. That you've nurtured and trained others to put out the fires or even avoid them is never going to feel as good if you're holding onto the industrial age view of managing.

Summary

Managing knowledge you don't understand requires rethinking what supervision and management means to you and the extent to which you can share your power with those whose knowledge is greater than yours. Although we've all had that experience in our daily lives, there are still questions about how to do this so the company benefits and whether, having done it, it leaves a job which is satisfying for you. It can be satisfying if you take on the new roles that are needed in addition to that of manager. They are teacher, scout, and keeper of the flame.

Main Points

- Managers have new roles in addition to that of manager: those of teacher, scout, and keeper of the flame.
- Managers increasingly have to manage knowledge they don't understand.
- Rather than attempt to master all the new knowledge, managers need to cede some decision-making power to the workers who have the new knowledge.
- These decisions will be primarily in the technical area but may also be administrative and managerial.

CHAPTER 7

&

Encouraging People To Learn

Leveraging what your employees know is a critical success factor in today's world, but as knowledge grows, proliferates, and specializes, making use of your employees' present knowledge base is not enough. To continue to create wealth with knowledge, the people themselves must be up-to-date. Without a continual replenishment of the well of knowledge, it will eventually run dry. Executives today seem to have realized that their human capital must be constantly learning to meet today's challenges but as the dialogue below illustrates, they are not always clear what that means.

"We're a learning organization," says the executive who called me in.

"And what makes you that?" I ask innocently.

"We've arranged with the community college to hold their classes right in our facility," he replies.

"That's an excellent initiative," I agree. *"What else makes you a learning organization?"*

The executive pauses. *"People can use their lunch hours and after work to attend the classes. They don't have to go across town to learn."*

"Yes, that's great. Anything else?"

After a few more attempts, the conversation dies.

Organizations sometimes mistake *announcing* they're a learning organization with *being* one. A learning program needs to go beyond piping in a few courses from the local university. This chapter will deal with setting up the kind of learning program that will make a difference.

So what is a learning program? Well, one part is of course training. It will be an important part of any learning program, usually its most visible and expensive aspect. But to more completely address the needs of employees, there are three components to a learning program:

- Formal Training and Development Programs
- Encouraging Informal Learning
- Rewarding Learning

Formal Training and Development Programs

These programs are familiar to almost everyone. They are the training courses regularly offered by the internal training department or advertised by a brochure that lands on your desk. It can be an individual course or a well-orchestrated and interlocking series of offerings. The common characteristic is pulling people together for some period of time to receive the same body of knowledge, skills, or understandings. But it's important not to confuse training and learning.

The Difference between Training and Learning

They aren't the same. I can take a training course, but it doesn't mean I learned. I may resist the ideas being taught (e.g., power-sharing), can't relate them to what I do, or already have the skills. Just because I've taken a conflict resolution course doesn't necessarily mean I'll be easier to get along with. Unless knowledge workers actually apply the lessons of the training, it isn't learning. So formal training doesn't always result in learning.

Nor does learning come only from training. The US Department of Labor and the Center for Workforce Development in Newton, Massachusetts released an important study which showed that 70 per cent of workplace learning is informal. When you think about it, we've always known that intuitively. I learn how to plan on a training course, but I learn how to maneuver through planning politics on the job.

No matter how expensive or well run, a training program doesn't ensure you have a learning organization. Knowledge workers need to learn, not simply be trained. Since 70 per cent of learning is informal, it makes sense to put effort into setting up processes to encourage that type of learning. That's not to say that you need to expend 70 per cent of your money or effort there but a greater focus on it is critical to creating a learning environment.

Formal Training is Important

I'm not advocating that organizations do away with or even substantially minimize formal training programs. Not at all. I have often found, as I'm sure you have, that a course has provided insights I might have eventually gotten but it allowed me to learn them faster and more holistically.

For example, I went on a training course specifically for newly appointed senior managers. Larry, the retired executive giving the course, asked us to work in small groups to solve a problem he had encountered. My group must have been suffering from training overload or something because we came up with a frivolous answer entailing lifetime pay-offs for several people. We merrily presented this to the class and got quite a laugh. But not from Larry. He tore a strip off us. He lectured us on our responsibility to ourselves and to those who had placed their trust in us and on our responsibility to fulfill that trust no matter how difficult or personally embarrassing it was.

Our group went home with our tails between our legs but the lesson is with me to this day and shapes how I see my role in any organization. Without the course, I suppose I would have learned it eventually. With it, the issue was brought into such sharp relief that the learning has been a life-long benefit. So I don't advocate dispensing with formal training but it's not the be-all and end-all. It's just one of a range of tools you need to transform your organization into a learning one.

To ensure that this tool is used effectively, consider the following for your training program:

Link Your Training Program to Your Strategic Priorities

It's surprising how often organizations forget to take a hard look at whether the training actually helps them reach their strategic objectives.

Organizational training should aim to change behavior, otherwise why are you doing it? Formal training is one of the most expensive ways you can do it, so while that's not a reason for *not* doing it, it is a compelling one for ensuring that the money is well spent.

To do that, you need to link training to the company's strategic direction. If it is to become a leading edge, low-cost provider in electronics repair, for example, technical training related to electronics repair would be part of the training as would courses on managing inventory, customer service, and process improvement.

The danger is that almost anything can be justified, if not as a present need, then as a future one. Take a basket-weaving course—it increases manual dexterity, hand-eye coordination, and relieves stress. See what I mean? You can justify almost anything, so your training people needed to be fairly focused about what is useful to your strategic direction.

Having said that, however, you should leave the definition of "useful" a little loose. I'll discuss why and a way to do that in the section on individual learning plans below.

Mandatory Training

When an organization starts linking training to its strategic direction, almost invariably, there is a cry, "But everybody should take this training." And sometimes, that's true. If a major issue is infighting, you might want to make a course on conflict resolution mandatory. The advantages are that the training:

- *Provides new options for behavior.* People sometimes really don't know or are not skilled at using alternatives to yelling or pushing conflict underground. Training usually expands the range of responses a person has.

- *Identifies officially sanctioned behaviors*. Training can send a message about how you want people to act. In the case we're talking about, a mandatory course on conflict resolution signals the intent of senior management to move to new ways of relating. Of course, it means nothing if you don't insist that these behaviors are actually used (see Chapter 13) but the training is still an important signal.

- *Provides a shared vocabulary*. The substantial benefit to an organization of shared vocabulary should not be underestimated. If you want everyone to go in the same direction, you've got to have common agreement on what "turn right" or "get better" means. If you don't, you lower the chances that people will act in concert.

On the other hand, mandatory training has some definite downsides:

- *It's expensive.*
- *It's untargeted.* If I'm already skillful at resolving conflict, I may not get much out of the course.
- *It usually needs some kind of monitoring system* to ensure that people attend the program, otherwise, those who need it most are most likely to be "too busy" to attend.
- *It can push out (through lack of funds) more urgently needed individual training.* You can usually handle this by making sure that mandatory courses are few in number and that there is money left in the training budget for individual needs.

So, mandatory training can be a powerful way to move the organization in the same direction but it's one that needs to be undertaken with a full awareness of the costs it imposes on the organization.

An Individual Learning Plan

Companies with a regular performance evaluation system usually also include training needs. You might wish to expand that into an individual learning plan that helps the individual map out the experiences and training he needs to continue to be successful. The organization can help in some areas (e.g., classroom training on a piece of software) and the employee should take responsibility for others (e.g., doing his best even on a boring project). The plan allows everyone not only to understand what he needs but also to start taking responsibility for his own learning.

Earlier, I warned against funding training unrelated to the strategic direction but then encouraged you to be flexible about that interpretation. It is at the individual level that this seeming paradox can be resolved. If the training department's doing its job, skills critical to the strategic direction have been identified and a program is in place to address them. However, there are invariably individual wishes/needs which aren't linked to the strategic direction but which are nevertheless important to the employee. Here a tenuous link to the strategic direction may be OK and possibly even positive. By allowing some latitude in what's considered appropriate to fund at the individual level, you may allow for the fact that different people make intellectual capital from different things. This isn't to say that it's carte blanche. Basket weaving may still not be acceptable, but it is possible to entertain requests that cannot be linked in a straight line to a strategic direction.

Alternatives to Classroom Training

In planning formal classroom training, training professionals should be encouraged to consider whether the need can be met through informal methods (discussed in the next section) or by any one of the following formal, nonclassroom, methods:

- *Checklists.* These lists capture the essential steps in a process. Airline pilots use them to ensure that they've covered all the safety requirements before taxiing down the runway.

- *Software.* Commercially available software for tasks such as letter writing and other skills are available. This kind of training has the benefit of avoiding travel costs.

- *Changes in workflow.* Process reengineering has shown us that sometimes the answer to a problem like insufficient production is not teaching people to manage their time better but of simplifying the work process so that the same result can be obtained with fewer steps.

- *Culture change.* Managers often try to solve organizational culture problems with training. There may be a great deal of conflict among staff. A manager's response may be to send everyone on training rather than note that responsibilities are unclear, she assigns work arbitrarily, and *who* you know determines whether you're *in* the know. Training when you really need to change the culture won't work.

- *Reading materials.* This one is often ignored. Trade journals and other sources, both electronic (such as the Internet) and written, can often be an excellent source of learning and is especially appropriate for those employees who just need to be kept current.

Some of these items (like culture change) are substantially harder to tackle than funding a training program but may be more effective. Others (like checklists) are often cheaper than formal training and just as effective.

Encouraging Informal Learning

You know from your own experience that some of your best learning has been when someone took the time to introduce you to a new skill or helped you get better acquainted with an old one. Or when a bunch of you have tossed around a few ideas over coffee. The opportunity to learn how to work easier, faster, or more creatively almost always occurs informally.

Speed and creativity are two essential characteristics for knowledge workers, so in order to both leverage their intellectual capital and continue to be competitive, making use of the informal learning in an organization is critical to successful management of knowledge workers.

However, informal learning is harder both to identify and to mold to your strategic direction. By its very nature, it doesn't occur in neat time slots or locations where you can grab it and leverage it. And most attempts to formalize it defeat the purpose. So it's understandable that most companies' learning activities have been restricted to training programs. However, while you can't formalize *what* learning takes place, you can set up conditions which encourage it. In this section, I'll cover several ways to do that, including establishing mentoring programs, conference attendance, on-the-job training, and learning events.

Mentoring Programs

The intent of a mentoring program is to link senior people in the organization with more junior ones for occasional one-on-one coaching on the premise that the former can help the latter both understand the operations of the business and be successful. These programs seem to be regaining popularity as organizations begin to realize that the projected retirement of baby boomers from senior jobs will happen faster than the next generation will be ready to take their places. Organizations are looking for ways to fast track the upcoming group and a mentoring program can be a way to pass on experience from one organizational generation to the next.

Mentoring programs can also foster informal learning between peers. For example, Careerware at ISM/IBM Global Services assigns a new employee to a "buddy" who helps the new employee find the cafeteria, fill out the right forms, and figure out who to go to when there's a problem. Most of my examples are management mentoring programs, as they are usually the first to be launched, but these can be readily applied to a peer-to-peer environment.

Many organizations start mentoring programs, only to run into trouble or out of steam, but when they work, they are so successful in encouraging employees to share knowledge, that it's worth spending some time figuring why they often don't work.

Why Mentoring Programs Don't Work

A mentoring program can falter either because there were some inherent design or structural problems or because of the attitudes of the people participating. Let's talk about both.

Structural Issues

- *The mentor is too senior in the organization.* I have been in organizations where a wet-behind-the-ears employee has been assigned or has chosen the most senior person in the organization as his mentor. The relationship never worked. The two do not speak the same language.The executive's knowledge and experience are too advanced to be of use to the new employee, who needs help with applying his book learning to the business world or getting a seat on a project team—things that the executive did so long ago he probably can't remember how to do them. In setting up the program, include guidelines on how many levels above the learner the mentor can be. Junior people should be mentored by mid-level people and they, in turn, by senior ones.

- *The mentor doesn't have the time to mentor.* Mentors need to know how much time mentoring could take. If the mentor's time is limited, suggest specifying how much contact time is acceptable so the mentor isn't inundated with questions the junior person might get answered in another way (e.g., how to arrange for a parking pass, how to get on a specialized training course) if she knew her time with her mentor was limited.

- *The mentor doesn't know how to pass on his/her knowledge.* If you've been working for any length of time, many important skills, like how to run a meeting or how to cajole difficult people, are second nature to you, you do them practically automatically. A training or coaching course can help mentors understand how to articulate their learning so they can discuss not just what they do but how and why they do it. This will increase the chance that knowledge transfer will actually happen.

- *The mentor is used as the only source of learning.* Invaluable though informal training is, remember, it's only 70 per cent of what the trainee needs. Mentoring needs to be supplemented with activities such as skill-building courses.

- *The learner isn't given the time to learn.* It's not enough to urge the learner to take the time to learn. The world is moving so fast that even new employees are up to their eyeballs in work from the moment they start. The program should require a series of meetings within a set period of time. There will be some grumbling on both sides, but doing this carves out time in which both parties must pay attention to the informal learning they want to happen. However, these shouldn't be required forever. If the relationship works, both mentor and learner will make the time. If it doesn't, the sooner you kill it off, the faster everyone can get onto something that does.

- *The learner doesn't understand what he can get from mentoring.* The point of being mentored is to learn things you don't know. It's not that much of a stretch to realize that the learner may not know he doesn't know. In the example above, the learner may think the mentor is a buddy, available to confer on how to send a parcel FedEx or what to wear to the Christmas party. He may not be able to distinguish between sending that package and developing the interpersonal skills so people will want to help him do it. A mentor shouldn't be involved with the former, but the latter might be grist for the mill. The learners may also need some coaching on making the most effective use of a mentor.

- *The learner is not temperamentally suited to the mentor's style or personal values.* If the mentor is a take-the-barricade-and-die-gloriously type while the learner is more a let's-see-how-we-can-compromise type, it's going to be a problem. The learner won't find the mentor's advice useful and the mentor will think he's wasting his time. This can usually be addressed by matching parties on some kind of personality inventory (there are lots that are neither intimidating nor difficult to administer). In addition, the two should of course have a chance to meet face-to-face to decide whether there's enough chemistry to make the relationship a possibility.

- *The learner is in the mentor's organization.* I have found that this doesn't work. If the mentor is the learner's boss, it will be difficult to separate the coaching/helping part from the fix-it/action part. Similarly, unless you have a particularly open and trusting environment, the supervisor of the learner will feel just a little nervous if the learner's mentor is his boss or boss' boss. It's going to be hard to believe that the supervisor isn't going to be discussed in some way since the topics of conversation will of course be problems at work. By and large, I'd advocate learners picking mentors outside their reporting line.

The Attitude Issues
While the issues discussed above are challenges, they are not as difficult as the attitude ones. The problems may not be many, but unresolved, they can sink the best-intentioned initiative.

- *The mentor doesn't embody the values of the organization.* If the mentor isn't aligned with the organization's values, it's like giving Mr. Hyde (of Jekyll and Hyde fame) a license to clone. The evil Mr. Hyde will urge the learner to handle problems in ways not aligned with what the organization wants to embody. "Hey, you've gotta grab the credit. If you don't, somebody else will."

    Unfortunately, it's often hard to know whether there's a problem since few people say things like, "I believe manipulation and coercion are the new management waves." However, if the mentors are volunteers (and don't feel otherwise coerced), there will be some self-selection. You have to feel good about an organization to be willing to mentor its employees and that increases the chances you're aligned with its values.

    But that isn't always going to be the case and there should be an escape hatch. Learners should have some private way (e.g., speaking privately to the person running the whole mentor program) to signal when things are out of whack. There should be a way built into the program to ease people out of relationships that don't work and drop the mentor from the list. One way might be to make it the norm to change mentors occasionally as the learner's interests and needs change.

- *The learner sees this as a fast track rather than a learning experience.* I have known learners who viewed the program as their ticket to the top and chose their mentor entirely based on whether the next big promotion was within the mentor's control (another reason for not having mentors and learners within the same reporting line). While one certainly hopes that the mentoring program produces promotable people, going into it for that reason alone is in opposition to its spirit of learning and discovery. You should set the expectations with the learners quite firmly from the start. Even if the intent of the program is to fast track, learners need to understand that promotion is a possible but not guaranteed outcome.

You can help this process by ensuring that the match is made based on what the learner needs to learn rather than who can promote her. Also, tracking whether she has learned (usually through her own, the supervisor's, and the mentor's assessment) is another way to focus on the learning and not on the promotion.

What Works in a Mentoring Program

- Participants are trained on how to mentor and be mentored.
- Considerable effort is placed on matching the right people.
- An escape hatch is available, the use of which is not a career limiting move.
- Participation is truly voluntary.
- The initial phases of the mentoring are somewhat structured.
- It is one of a variety of learning experiences for the learner.
- Promotions out of the program are available but not a prominent part of the experience.
- What and whether there has been learning is tracked.

As you can see, there are pitfalls to setting up a mentoring program. On the other hand, there are many benefits, the strongest of which is that you are putting the organization's focus on learning in the area where learning actually happens—informally.

Conference Attendance

I heard of one organization whose senior executives were up in arms when they found out 40 of their employees had attended the same conference. "Why couldn't one have gone and taken notes?" they demanded. At some level, the reaction is understandable. As money gets tighter and tighter and people's time more and more valuable, organizations are increasingly less willing to allow people to attend conferences which are often seen as boondoggles to exotic locations with attractive extracurricular activities.

I don't know whether 40 were too many or too few. If great learning was available, firsthand connection of that many might have been worth the investment. If it was marginal learning, one wonders why anyone was sent at all. When a conference is good, it is a hotbed for informal learning, since people can learn as much talking to likeminded colleagues over coffee as they do during the sessions. In addition, conferences can be one of the few opportunities to acquire knowledge that doesn't already reside in your organization.

It's not always possible to know beforehand whether the conference is going to be any good, but if you've been in your industry long enough, you know who does the most worthwhile conferences. Often, if you know people on the organizing committee, you can get a sense of its likely worth. As an organization, you can identify those conferences that have given good value in the past. That can be a guide for managers internally when they're looking for a place to develop staff.

So while conferences can be an expensive outlay of time and money, you need to ask yourself whether you need the knowledge likely to be acquired even if the acquisition is in Hawaii and there's a hula night. It still might be worth it.

On-the-Job-Training (OJT)

OJT is one of the best ways to transmit learning and usually one of the poorest managed. No one ever feels they have the time to do it. The most people get coming onto a job might be a manual tossed at them with "Here. Read this. Ask me if you have any questions." Or worse, they're just tossed into the deep end to sink or swim.

Applying more rigor to the OJT process can have substantial benefits. Checklists of what people need to know once they've joined the unit are very helpful. What kind of equipment they must learn to operate, from whom to get the training, what kind of certification is needed, will allow employees to take more responsibility for their own learning. HR can help identify the skills needed and link them to the location of the training, coaching, reading, and the like that will fulfill that need. They can also help the manager assess when the employee is up to speed.

While it's unlikely OJT will ever have the rigor and neatness of formal training, an organization can help managers to ensure that OJT happens as efficiently and effectively as possible.

Learning Together

Learning is a social activity. We all have burned the solitary midnight oil in our college days or even last week. But for the learning to benefit the whole organization, it has to get out of my head and into others'. The most effective, and sometimes the most efficient, way to do that is to set up activities during which people learn together. That's one of the reasons formal training can be so valuable.

To enhance the opportunities to learn together, consider scheduling formal training for intact work groups. Typically, this isn't done since it affects the unit's ability to keep the operation going. That is a compelling reason to avoid it, but if you can, having intact work teams learning the same thing at the same time can be very powerful.

A small consulting firm, Intersol,[1] takes one week every year to train all its consultants together. Now, there are only about a dozen, but it completely cleans the shop of revenue-generating people. The benefits are substantial. First, it allows an immediate transfer of a common knowledge/skills base into the organization. In addition, it helps work units apply that common base to their business immediately. I think we've all been on a course where an idea is raised that has major potential for our business. We bounce back to work ready to apply this new learning only to find that we have to spend considerable time trying to generate the kind of enthusiasm in our colleagues we felt when we first understood the implications. Events where intact work groups learn together can spark everyone at the same time.

For operational and other reasons,[2] it may not always work to set up learning for intact work groups, but if you can, you may be surprised at the speed with which the new knowledge is acted upon.

---

[1] I am associated with this firm at the time of writing, just so I'm upfront about this.
[2] Sometimes, you actually want to have a cross-section of the organization learning together.

Structural Capital

The gurus of intellectual capital will hate the fact that I've stuck structural capital in as a subset of a subset in one chapter. The building and maintaining of structural capital is a complex issue in and of itself, but for my purposes, databases, computer-networking capacities, and other structural capital fit in this section. Mechanisms to connect with others in the organization are important to encourage informal learning, but structural capital like databases, networks, processes, and procedures are just ways to help the learning go faster—not necessarily better but certainly faster. They are valuable for that reason alone, but even if you don't have everyone networked every waking moment or a database that shows everybody's skills down to Grade Three Championship Softball, you can still encourage people to connect and learn together. If you've got a networking system, so much the better. Structural capital is a tool to be used in the service of sharing knowledge, and it should neither drive informal learning nor be a substitute for it.

We've talked about mentoring, conference attendance, OJT, learning together, and structural capital as ways to learn informally. It's not an exhaustive list but I think you're getting a flavor for how the company might encourage it. Remembering that 70 per cent of learning happens informally encourages you to put the focus of your learning program there.

Rewarding Learning

The third component of a learning program is rewarding learning. Rewarding learning can be in the form of providing time (remember, knowledge workers find it rewarding simply to be able to expand their knowledge) or actual monetary awards. We'll discuss both.

Personal Versus Organizational Time

It's pretty standard practice to pay for training that is directly related to the job, but should organizations pay for, in funding and/or time, all learning? For example, do you pay for a person to get a college degree if she doesn't need it to perform her present functions? The automatic response might be "no," but the National Center on the Educational Quality of the Workforce has shown that a 10 per cent increase in workforce education level led to an 8.6 per cent gain in total factor productivity, while a 10 per cent rise in the value of capital equipment increased productivity only 3.4 per cent.[3] So it's possible it's worth paying for this employee's education, but even if you fund it, do you also have her do it on company time? You probably need to have a cutoff between what the company will actively support and what investment the employee needs to make herself.

There are similar issues raised with informal learning. One way to encourage continuous learning are regular discussion groups. These are often held at lunchtime to have least impact on the operations. However, in unionized shops, the question often comes up— do people get equivalent time off for giving up their lunch hours?

All of these are legitimate questions and revolve around the line between the company's and the employees' responsibility for learning. I'm not sure there is a right answer and it may change over time. It may be a question that you could ask a group of employees to recommend guidelines on how to balance the need to encourage learning with staying focused on creating wealth today.

Paying for Learning

Some organizations have tried to incorporate learning into the pay system by rewarding how much you know. For example, you'd get an increase in your pay every time you took a course that helped the organization. This is separate from promotion or bonus payments. It is trying to link learning to a tangible reward. I wonder about the efficacy of this approach. I think learning and wanting to learn are natural tendencies in human beings that have sometimes been drummed out either by the school system or by the way work has been structured. The human thirst for learning is alive and well as can be demonstrated by the way people tackle their hobbies. Many invest a great deal of time and effort in learning about and practicing a hobby whether it be golf, cars, or knitting. They are very open to learning and applying the new learning, and they don't have to be paid to do it.

There is a possibility that a pay-for-learning approach might work well in an organization or industry that has typically seen

---

[3] Thomas A. Stewart, "How a Little Company Won Big by Betting on Brainpower," *Fortune* (September 4, 1995): 121.

workers as a pair of hands unlinked to a brain or a heart. When people have gotten used to just doing what they're told and a transition to a knowledge worker mentality is desired, it is possible that paying them will invite engagement of their brains and hearts in the service of the organization.[4]

But overall, the trick is not paying people to learn but rewarding them when they *use* their knowledge. And I'm not sure you can set up a money-based reward system to do that. I think that the rewards an organization can give for knowledge use are largely intangible and based on some of the techniques in this book like encouraging communities of practice and sharing decision making.

Restricting Learning

A large consulting firm has decided that it won't let any of its employees go on SAP training because as soon as they've acquired the skill they go off to a competitor. Management is preventing its people from acquiring the skills they need to create wealth, but the manager who made that decision wouldn't agree.

He'd say: *"They just leave us! Why should I train people for my competitors?"*

To which I would reply: *"Don't they need SAP to be value-added?"*

"Well, yes, but they don't stay around long enough to do it!"

"So, they can't be value-added to their clients unless they have the skills, but if they do, they don't stay."

"Right," replies the beleaguered manager. *"So, the only answer is not to give them the training."*

Wrong, wrong, wrong. This company is not addressing the real issue—that of creating an environment in which people want to stay. Not just stay reluctantly and with a Monday morning headache, but with enthusiasm and commitment, eager to share their intellectual capital. The answer is not to dumb down your employees. That has never been the right answer and it's certainly not now when the knowledge and brainpower of your employees

---

[4] Although it will largely be in the realm of the formal learning.

are all you have to sell. Creating an environment where people want to invest their intellectual capital is undoubtedly harder than making a rule that prevents them from getting it in the first place. What's more, this kind of rule is simple, efficient, easy to understand, and easy to manage. There is just one problem. It doesn't work.

Summary

When knowledge is the coin of the realm, organizations must focus attention on steadily increasing the company's collective knowledge base. A training program is a necessary but not sufficient condition for a learning organization. Mechanisms to encourage informal learning and to reward its use also need to be considered. This chapter has concentrated on instituting a learning program to develop a highly knowledgeable workforce. The next section will deal with equally important human management challenges that arise as organizations try to use their structural capital effectively.

Main Points

- Training isn't learning.
- Formal training should:
  - link to strategic priorities
  - include individual learning plans
  - consider other options than classroom training
- 70 per cent of workplace learning is informal. A learning program should foster informal learning by activities like:
  - mentoring program
  - conference attendance
  - on-the-job training
  - learning together events
  - the right structural capital

- Rewarding learning is important but:
  - The balance between time the organization invests in a person's development and his own investment should be considered.
  - Rewards should be focused on how effectively the learning is used rather than the act of learning.

Section Two

The Human Side of Structural Capital

As discussed earlier, an important way to leverage your organization's intellectual capital is to have the appropriate structural capital in place to allow your human capital to connect and build knowledge. This can be computer systems and networks, but it can also be as simple as an up-to-date company telephone directory and meeting spaces for employees. However, as we also saw, there are several management challenges in using your structural capital to the fullest. Leveraging structural capital requires:

Freeing the Flow of Information. Companies need to communicate often and about hitherto confidential information. Chapter 8 will show you how to do that.

The Free Movement of People and Knowledge. Once you've got the information flowing, people can use their knowledge to help create wealth, but only if they and their knowledge are free to move around (Chapter 9).

Sharing and Learning. You can have all the channels open but unless employees are willing to fill them both by sharing their knowledge and learning from others, you can't create wealth. Chapter 10 will deal with this issue with respect to individual employees and Chapter 11 will talk about encouraging the team behavior necessary to share with and learn from others.

Rewarding Knowledge. If you don't reward these new behaviors, they're unlikely to be maintained. Chapter 12 will deal with how the company and the manager can do that in ways beyond money.

Being Willing to Change. Both managers and employees have to be willing to make some personal change to leverage the intellectual capital in the organization. This is a process in and of itself and Chapter 13 will discuss it.

CHAPTER 8

৪৫

Freeing the Flow
of Information

Why do you need to free up the flow of information in an organization? Why expend the time and energy letting people know what's happening ASAP when they'll find out when they need to? Does it really make any difference to tapping intellectual capital? To answer these questions, we need to think about the role you want and need employees to play in this world of brain as opposed to brawn power.

In a world where you cannot command innovation and contribution, you have to create the conditions where the employee will want to do both. A base requirement for that is they understand what needs to be done to further the company's goals. The right kind of communication helps this.

In fact, when the CEO of Anheuser-Busch (America's dominant brewer) was asked how to ensure that innovative new strategies emerge in his company, he said, "You're going to laugh at this—it sounds so simple—but the key is communicate, communicate, communicate, at every level in the organization, and to start at the lowest level possible."[1] Similarly, the chief learning officer at Sears, Anthony Rucci, maintains that his function is primarily to give people the information they need to have an enlightened opinion about how to do their job better.[2] In addition, poor communication was

---

[1] Gary Hamel, "Turning Your Business Upside Down," *Fortune* (June 23, 1997).
[2] Sherman Stratford, "Bringing Sears into the New World," *Fortune* (October 13, 1997).

found to be the reason for a generally low level of trust between managers and employees in a recent study conducted by the consulting firm, Watson Wyatt Worldwide.[3]

Finally, and pragmatically, information gets out anyhow. There are very few times when even the biggest, open-a-vein-and-swear-secrecy kind of thing doesn't generate rumors. Communicating early and often can help you spin the information in the direction you want it to go. For example, if a merger is being negotiated, the earlier you get to people, the less you have a workforce fearing takeover and the more you can encourage it to see opportunities opening up. Putting your own spin on the news doesn't have to be —and shouldn't be—manipulative or underhanded. It is simply making sure that your side of the story is also available. It is not distorting the news but making sure that the advantages as well as the disadvantages are understood.

So communication is important if you want to create an environment in which people will contribute their intellectual capital to the company's stores. However, communication is used to mean a variety of things like "tell me what's happening," "ask my opinion," "let me influence the decision," or even just, "include me." Just so we don't get confused here, when I talk about communication, I mean primarily the organization's ability to get its message out to its employees. In previous chapters I've covered the other needs such as involvement and consultation often lumped under communication.

What to Communicate

There are a broad range of issues which are helpful to communicate. These include:

- Mission and values
- Misperceptions/misunderstandings of how decisions taken relate to the mission
- Major decisions and the reasoning
- Major changes in direction
- Rumors and discrepancies

---

[3] "Trust Levels Poor in Canadian Companies," *The Training Report* (July 1998).

These are pretty standard but what and when you need to communicate may differ from what you expect. Typically, management sends out a newsletter to cover issues such as major decisions or changes in direction, but employees still complain these are too little, too late. And truthfully, a newsletter alone—while a valiant effort—doesn't come close to filling the need for specific and current information employees have.

The complaints arise because newsletters are typically after the fact, sanitized to put on the best possible face, and don't help employees relate the news to their own situation. If you are going to help people to understand how they can contribute, you need to address all three.

- *After the fact.* Most employees find out a decision was in the offing only when it's a done deal. It may be a good decision and may not have required employee input but announcing it after the fact still doesn't promote good communication. Before a big decision, you should be talking about why the decision is necessary and what factors the company will use to make it. This allows people to think it through and understand how it relates to their work. Good communication is not only after the fact but before and during.

- *Sanitized.* This may sound contradictory since I earlier encouraged you to communicate so you could put your own spin on the news, but sanitation and spin are different. Sanitation occurs when a company announces a new initiative that will cause pain, disruption, anxiety, and loss, by maintaining in its communication that it will not cause pain, disruption, anxiety, and loss or worse, that the pain, disruption, anxiety, and loss employees are experiencing is actually joy, hope, and great expectations. That's sanitation. Spin acknowledges the difficulties inherent in the move and adds those things that are also opportunities. It is inviting people to see that the future is neither all pain (which they fear) nor all hope (which management is prone to) but somewhere in between.

- *Unrelated to their work.* I have been guilty of this. In a major revamp of an organization, we regularly communicated the organizational models we were considering. The feedback was, "Quit with the theory and tell us what's happening." Since the model we chose would determine the kind of work people would do and even whether they had jobs, we just assumed that they weren't "getting it." Because the implications were self-evident to the decision makers who were living it, doesn't mean it translated well to those who weren't. We should have spent more words on relating the models to their jobs and helped individual managers customize the meaning.

So you need to use communication to transmit major decisions and changes in direction, to deal with rumors and misperceptions. Which leads naturally to the question of how much employees need to know.

How Much Do Employees Need to Know?

Even if managers accept that people's communication needs are great, there's always a question of how much they actually need to know. Is it wide-ranging knowledge of the company or just enough to do their jobs? Even if the former, is it management's responsibility to provide it? And is provision enough or is there a responsibility to ensure they understand it?

For example, should you share profit and loss information with your employees and if so, how completely? There are companies where that is *the* closely guarded secret, right up there with your uncle Ted's unfortunate interest in rutabaga. In others, it's common knowledge. In the first company, "just enough" seems to be the byword; in the second, it's "we're all in this together." Frankly, my bent is to tell people everything you possibly can, short of invading privacy. When I say everything, I mean everything—plans, scenarios, possibilities, hopes, dreams. There are usually objections to this sweeping statement:

- *We can't spend all our time communicating. We've got a business to run.* This is true, but actually, once you set up a communications plan, it probably isn't going to take all that much time. Part of the plan will be a regular production and distribution process so that the means by which people get the communication is set. All you have to do is fill in the news itself. Once you've put these processes in place, the time you need to actually communicate can be surprisingly short. In return for this effort, you can have a news vehicle people read and believe is credible.

And remember, the business will only run if the knowledge workers inside it are on board. They won't be if they don't know what's going on.

- *We can't release that. It'll give away our plans to competitors.* There are some times, such as the first moves of a merger, when making these overtures public would be like a first kiss with a spectator gallery. But many excellent organizations have opened up about previously secret information. The confidence demonstrated in their employees by a virtually full disclosure was returned in kind when the confidential information remained within the company. In any case, if this full disclosure of financial information seems too much (and it may well be), one option is to explain the logic behind the numbers although not necessarily the numbers. This may be all front-line people need to understand and buy-in.

- *Even if we release the information, employees won't understand it. It's useless to them.* If the information is crucial—that is, it is going to rule employees' lives for the foreseeable future—you have a responsibility either to put the information in an accessible form or to take the time to explain what it means.

Naturally and realistically, communicating "everything" has to be tempered by limits of time, effort, money, and the like. But it frees up communication in a surprising way when the discussion is not *whether* something should be communicated, but why certain pieces should *not* be (and my grand statement aside, there probably are times when this is the case). This is an issue that you need to discuss with your management team.

In addition, the communication must be a corporate-wide imperative. Some managers have always communicated with their staff; others have not. For communication to be an effective tool to engage your intellectual capital, it must move out of the realm of optional personal preference to a managerial requirement. One way to do this is to produce a corporate communications plan that will both lay out what is required and track progress.

A Communications Plan Responds To the Need

When employees complain that newsletters are too late and too vague, more often than we would wish, managers shrug their shoulders, effectively saying: "Hey, that's all the time/energy/money we can put into communication right now. If it's not enough, you'll just have to make do. I've got more important things to worry about."

There's a lot of truth to that statement. These days, everyone is running just as fast as they can. You're busy doing rather than communicating about doing. For another, things may be in flux. You may feel you can't communicate yet because crucial decisions haven't been made about a new direction or a new way of approaching your present markets. Regardless of the reasons, employees still feel frustrated and they can't or won't invest their intellectual capital in a company where they feel shut out.

While competing pressures will undoubtedly pull you in opposite directions, the company nevertheless needs a way to communicate in a timely way with employees. A rigorous communications plan is a critical and usually underused method of drawing people into the heart of the organization.

Without a plan, communication just doesn't get done. No one ever seems to have the time to do it (much less properly) unless someone is accountable. In addition, many a new direction is jeopardized by confusing and inconsistent messages. Employees can't adapt if they're getting different messages about what they're supposed to adapt to. While I know managers don't jump out of bed, thinking, "Great! Who can I confuse today?," allowing everyone to communicate about a new direction without an agreed-upon approach has the same net effect as if they were. To avoid this, you need to have a well-thought out, well-implemented plan.

Structure Of a Communications Plan

What you need to communicate can often change rapidly. Say a large contract that the company needs to justify its strategic direction hangs in the balance. If the contract is won, you can announce the next steps in the strategic rollout. If it's lost, you might need to communicate a pulling back to rethink the direction.

It's normal to have difficulty determining communication requirements over the longer term but it is possible over the short term. In the example above, people need to know that the contract was being bid on and why it is important. You tell them that as well as when they'll know the outcome. If things are a bit hazy beyond that, you can simply state that or talk about tentative plans.

You can put together the components of a communication plan in enough detail to get your minds around what should be done and who should do it in a general sense (or based on the very short term). Then, as events arise, you can concentrate on the content of the communication and *not* on principles or mechanics.

So let's look at each component of this plan. The table below shows the categories of information needed in the plan as well as an example for one communication "event." The rest of the chapter will cover how to build a plan based on these categories:

- What
- With whom
- Audience needs
- How
- Who
- When
- Action expected

Table: 8.1

What	With Whom	Audience Needs	How	Who	When	Action Expected
Communication of transition plan	direct reports	What am I expected to do?	meeting	Joe	May 26	knowledge, involvement, commitment
	staff	How does this affect me?	memo	Ellen	May 27	knowledge, involvement
	other stakeholders	Is this related to my work?	memo	Mike	May 27	knowledge

What to Communicate

The actual content of the message will be determined by events you may not be able to foresee right at the moment. So to come to agreement on what to communicate, have a discussion at the management table on what the company wants to get out of the communication (the objective) and therefore the messages you want to send.

In Table 8.2 below, I've illustrated some possible objectives and the corresponding messages you'd want to deliver.

Table: 8.2

Objective	Message
• provide information to employees to do their jobs	• help us innovate
• contextualize what is happening so employees understand the changes	• be prepared for change and to change
• provide information to facilitate individual learning	• take charge of your own career • understand your options
• contribute to (enhance) cultural change	• we don't have all the answers
• inspire, motivate	• we will support your growth
• help achieve strategic goals by maintaining commitment	• we need your help

If the main objective for your communications is to provide context for employees, the message you want to send is something like "be prepared for change and to change." This message would be embodied in all communications, without respect to the content. By choosing an objective and corresponding messages, the executive committee can shape their communication themes even if the exact content has yet to be determined.

During the discussion of objectives and messages, you will undoubtedly get someone who says, "They're all good. Let's just do all of them." Trying to accomplish them all isn't realistic. If you do, you'll have an unfocused, all-things-to-all-people approach that will confuse the very people it's intended to help. It's possible to have more than one objective, but the executive committee needs to spend some time thinking through the consequences of one choice or other.

The messages and objectives are particularly useful for aligning all your communication. You probably already have a number of newsletters operating. They should continue to convey information to their specific audiences, provided the underlying messages and objectives harmonize. If all the other communication is saying: "Yes, this is tough, but we'll get through," and the finance newsletter is implicitly saying: "We're going under and here are some job leads," you'll confuse everyone. Aligning the messages and objectives of disparate communication vehicles is important to avoid these variants.

With Whom to Communicate

Obviously, employees are the primary audience but are there any subsets within the employee group which are different enough to warrant separate consideration? Geography, regional/headquarters functions, management level, or professional work (scientists/engineers or shop floor people) may make a difference. You may provide the same information but with a different explanation. Changes in headquarters may be ho-hum for the regional offices unless you explain why it matters to them.

Don't choose too many subsets. It makes the communication task that much more difficult. In any case, people often like to know everything that's going around. So initially at least, you may not need to make too many distinctions.

Just a word about the media. Media coverage can also affect internal communication. In particular, never, ever, ever allow employees to find out about a major change in their company through newspaper headlines. This generates tremendous resentment. The message you send is that the company cares more about its public, its stockholders, and the business press, than it does about its employees.

I know some issues have to be very hush-hush until the moment they're released. OK, so if you're going to release material to the press for publication the next day, brief staff at 4 p.m. on the day before. At the very least, schedule some kind of communication on the morning the news will break. Skipping this step can cause great damage to your communication efforts and perhaps to that new direction you've just announced.

Audience Needs

When people receive communications, they have some needs that have to be fulfilled if they are to find the communication satisfying and credible. Examples of these communication principles are outlined below. Since they seem like motherhood, I've also included the challenges that may arise if you adhere to any one of them:

Table: 8.3

The Principle *Communication* *will be:*	The Challenge
• positive, fact-based	• If the news is bad, what do you do? • What if you don't have all the facts people need?
• in context for the audience	• How do you address the appropriate level of understanding of the complexity of the situation?
• delivered in a timely manner	• Does "timely" mean "gets there when promised" or "has the most up-to-date information?" If the latter, how do you ensure that you can get access to the latest breaking news, get it verified, and out to the audience as quickly as they need it?
• delivered simultaneously	• Can you ensure that all parts of the organization (i.e., without respect to geography or hierarchy) get the information at the same time? • Do you always want that to happen?
• implemented proactively	• Do you report on past events or on things that are coming up? What do employees need?

The executive group should spend some time discussing the principles chosen. Doing this will allow them to identify what trade-offs will be required among the principles. For example, sometimes you don't have the whole story and a partial telling may be misleading, but if you wait until you have everything, the news will no longer be timely. You'll need to make the trade-off and let people know which you opted for. If you opt for timely over accurate (which I would usually do), your communication might look something like:

> *Right now, it looks like Division B won't have any layoffs. However, this isn't confirmed and can't be until [date]. We know that Division A will have 200 layoffs, starting January 1 and Division C will close the plant in Washburn and scale down operations in Putney. The extent of the scaledown in Putney hasn't been determined yet, but we know it will be substantial. We should be able to communicate the extent by [date].*

This communication doesn't feel very satisfying and yet employees much prefer such incomplete information as soon as it is available to silence. In any case, identifying the principles makes it easier to move quickly. You can avoid long discussions about whether this is really what we want to do and whether we shouldn't wait until things are clearer. Have the discussion up front and work through your views before people are clamoring for the latest.

How to Communicate

Typical communication vehicles are one-way (static) or two-way (dialogue). This section will deal with static communication and the next step will talk about two-way.

"Static" is any communication that has a minimal ability to interact. Common static media would be newsletters, bulletins, e-mail, voice mail, and memos. These set messages are important aspects of the communication effort, although they need to be used in conjunction with the dialogue vehicles—conversations—and are not a substitute for them. This section will focus on newsletters but the comments are applicable to all types of static communication.

We've already discussed the specialty newsletters that need alignment to the communications plan. If you don't have a newsletter or are just starting one up, here are some issues to consider.

Table: 8.4

Newsletters	
• How Often Will It Be Issued?	• Pick a regular time, otherwise it won't get done. When you have least time to do it, people need it the most—an inflexible schedule will force you to pay attention. • Regularity of publication will encourage it to be seen as a reliable and timely source.
• Contents	• Broad directions, big picture discussions at the strategic level. • Report about what's going to happen as well as what's happened. People will feel more connected if they're reading about whether things evolved the way it was hoped rather than hearing about the decisions after the fact.
• Reading Level	• If it's too high, the message is not going to get through, no matter how beautifully worded or factually correct it is. • Explain issues in as simple (although not simplistic) a manner as you can.
• Length	• A one-page maximum focuses the message and increases the likelihood it will be read.
• Distribution Method	• If you want the newsletter to be the preferred source of information, prompt delivery will make a difference. Make sure your distribution methods are efficient.

Who Will Do the Communicating?

Often, you will want to communicate major events in person. This is preferable to newsletters or other vehicles since it allows for give and take, but who does the communicating is a perfect example of Marshall McLuhan's aphorism about the medium being the message. The message you send goes beyond the content itself to who delivers it. So choosing the communicator is as much a part of the communication effort as the facts being communicated. There are many possible communicators. Let me point out some and when you might want to use them:

Table: 8.5

Description	Why/When You Might Want to Use Them:	Why/When You Might Want to Think Again:	What You Need to Do if You Use this Approach:
The normal management hierarchy	• if local flavor important • if consistent message is not critical • for ease of administration • if you want to show all management is behind the content	• if many key managers not yet committed • if many key managers not good communicators	• train the managers on communication techniques • provide managers with main points of the message to be conveyed • monitor the distribution of the message to ensure full deployment
CEO	• to say "this is important, pay attention" • if you need news to come straight from horse's mouth • to match importance of messenger to message • consistent message is required	• if CEO credibility, conviction, speaking talent or knowledge is shaky • if it lets other senior managers off the hook • if getting out message quickly is paramount • if everyone must hear the message	• speaking notes, coaching, overhead slides • possible difficult questions and suggested answers

Table: 8.5 cont'd

Description	Why/When You Might Want to Use Them:	Why/When You Might Want to Think Again:	What You Need to Do if You Use this Approach:
Supervisors	• when the change needs to happen throughout the organization • when their lack of support will jettison the initiative • when you want the message to be "pay attention, this is about *you*."	• if many or key supervisors don't understand or are not committed • if many or key supervisors are not good communicators • if the message is largely a strategic one	• increase face-to-face contact with senior managers • do special briefings • "heads up" announcements, to cue when to communicate with staff • train supervisors on communication techniques • provide the main lines of the message • monitor for full deployment
Key Communicators • not management but opinion leaders	• if credibility of communicators is critical • to provide a mechanism for feedback	• if managers may feel out of the loop • if a big picture perspective is important • if consistency of message is critical	• similar to what you would do with supervisors

As you can see, there are many possible communicators and more than one channel is very useful to get out important information. Using a variety increases the chances you'll hit everyone. Also, some people retain information better in print, others verbally. Finally, a consistent message coming from several sources reinforces its credibility. Organizations often get into trouble because they rely on only one (usually the normal hierarchy). If there's a blockage in the system, nothing gets through. Using multiple channels minimizes this problem.

Multiple channels can be a challenge for consistency. More than one messenger can give different messages. However, if you have reached agreement on previous steps like the communication principles and consistently provide your communicators with support materials containing the messages you want conveyed, it doesn't have to be an insurmountable issue. And even if it does take some effort to ensure that there is alignment among messengers, you will find that that effort is outweighed by the advantage of having the same message come to employees from a variety of sources. When the message is repeated, more people hear and understand it.

When/How Often to Communicate

A regular communication pattern will encourage the perception that you are including people in the company's life. Thus, you might want to have a regularly issued newsletter, CEO briefings, staff meetings, or distribution of news to your key communicators. Once you've set up the mechanisms, you can use them for the fast-breaking news that needs quick distribution.

The Action Expected

Communicators don't often think about what action they expect to occur when they send the communication. They don't pose the question: What do I want the recipient to do or feel differently from what she is doing or feeling now? You must want something or why bother communicating? Unless you know, you'll get a range of reactions all the way from this is important to me to this is file 13 stuff.

The desired action may be quite minor. For example, if you're keeping people up to date on the merger, the only action might be to keep it in mind. However, at other times the communication needs people to start moving in a new direction or to check out rumors before they pass them on. You need to be clear every time what you want people to do differently once they've read the communication.

Summary

A free flow of information is critical to both encouraging knowledge workers to feel committed to the company but also ensures that the knowledge work is as market-driven as possible. However, since no one ever has enough time to communicate well, it's important to have a communication plan which will set up channels of distribution and production. Once the processes are in place, it will be easier to communicate both quickly and well. Communicating well takes some effort. However, its payoff will be worth it as you see the contribution it can make to committed employees who trust their managers, have the information they need to make good working-level decisions, and are willing to work with the company to create intellectual capital.

Just as it is important to free up the flow of information in an organization, so it is important to free up the flow of people. Why that is the case and how to do it will be covered in the next chapter.

Main Points

- Organizations need a free flow of information both for new knowledge to be transmitted easily through the organization and for knowledge workers to believe that they are in the know.

- Employees should be told as much as possible, including financial and other confidential information that has hitherto been keep secret.

- A communications plan should cover what to communicate, with whom, audience communication needs, how to communicate, who will do it, when, and the action expected from the recipient of the communication.

The Free Movement Of People And Knowledge

Let's imagine a common scenario in managing intellectual capital. A skills directory—a listing of the skills of all employees—has been loaded on-line. A product manager who is your peer (let's call her Tina) uses the directory to find who can help her market her product on the Internet, and the name of your employee Fred, pops out. Tina contacts Fred, and asks him for help. You find out when Fred mentions it. He's pretty pleased because Tina's product has lots of possibilities.

But while he's feeling pleased, you're wondering how can you accomplish your goals if people swoop in and grab your resources. And a valuable one at that. You may feel you have to take steps to prevent Fred from working with Tina or at least keep the intrusions to a minimum.

If you do, the organization can't use Fred's skills to maximum benefit. Tina knows Fred has the knowledge but she can't access it; therefore, the spread of knowledge is inhibited, and the money invested in creating this bit of structural capital is wasted because it can't create wealth. A critical part of using intellectual capital successfully requires sharing people and knowledge more freely than is customary, but it won't work if the manager's needs aren't met as well as the organization's. This chapter is about balancing those two needs.

Meeting the Manager's Needs

Although you play it cool when you first hear about Tina's request, what things come to mind?

- I Need to Accomplish My Work Goals
- That's My Mandate
- I'm Losing Control

Let's talk about how to deal with each one.

I Need to Accomplish My Work Goals

Your headcount is determined by the work goals of your unit, and unless you're in a really unusual organization, you never have enough people for the work. But if you truly believe in encouraging a freeflow of knowledge, you may be able to do something. If you talk to Fred about accomplishing the goals you've set with him, he might say one of several things:

- *I can do it on time and on budget plus do the other project.* Well, no contest. You give Fred your blessing and off he goes. However, there is a little niggle. If he's got extra time, why can't he use it for the unit and not for Tina? And, even more importantly, if your boss knows you loan out people, won't she begin to wonder whether you need all of them? These are both good and realistic questions.

    You could say, "Well, Fred, if you have all that much time, why don't you do one of those projects we never seem to get to? What about cataloguing all the initiatives, or documenting your lessons learned, or even giving me a hand with the budget plan for next year?" Fred's been asked to do an interesting project that will expand his skills and moreover, recognizes his value. And you want him to help you with your paperwork? Aren't you being just a trifle dog in the manger? If Fred wants to do it and you believe he can hit his targets on time, what's the problem?

    Is your main concern the second question, "What will my boss think?" If the organization institutes the suggestions I'll make later in the chapter, it won't be a problem. Your boss will welcome, or at least support, this sharing. But there's many a slip between pronouncement and fact. You may fear your boss will slap you with a catch-22: "I want you to share your people's intellectual capital, but I'll take away anything that looks like extra."

So what do you do? Of course, you need to proceed cautiously if you think your boss is so inclined. Try explaining why keeping the expertise you have together is important (see "Communities of Practice," on page 155 for ammunition) even if you loan it out frequently. However, that may not work. If not, you should be frank with Fred. Discuss the situation with him. You might say:

You:	*Sounds like a great project. You're sure you can do everything on your plate as well as Tina's project?*
Fred:	*Sure. I've lucked out recently. Both SCOM and the Lytech projects needed similar solutions. So I saved some time.*
You:	*Well, I want to give the go-ahead but to tell you the truth, I'm worried about the optics.*
Fred:	*Optics? What do you mean?*
You:	*Well, yesterday, Marge made a joke about how often our group shows up on other work teams. I'm concerned that she might be serious.*
Fred:	*Can't you just tell her Tina's project's a really good one?*
You:	*Of course. But I think she was talking more about the number of outside projects people are taking on.*
Fred:	*She doesn't think that's good?*
You:	*The jury seems to be out for her. I think we need to cool things a bit until I get a better read from her.*
Fred:	*You mean I can't do Tina's project?*
You:	*Could you put it off for a quarter? That might help.*
Fred:	*Sure, but Tina won't like it.*
You:	*I understand that, but it might be the best we can do.*

It's unfair that you have to worry about your back when you're trying to be a good corporate citizen. It may be the best you can do for now, and things might be different in three months (you might be past resource allocation time). What's most important is that you've communicated to Fred that you want him to share his expertise, but you need his help to make it work for everyone. Unless Fred is very difficult, he'll respond to that appeal.

- *I can do it if one of the assigned projects is slightly late.* This is obviously a judgment call. If you don't believe it will have an impact on your ability to deliver, you might agree. If it will, you need to have the following kind of conversation with Fred:

You:	*Putting off SCOM for a month? I don't know.*
Fred:	*I spoke with Roger at SCOM and he's OK with that.*
You:	*Really? Last time I talked to him, he couldn't get it fast enough.*
Fred:	*True, but he saw why it was necessary. After all, it's only a couple of weeks.*
You:	*Well, four. That's pretty significant.*
Fred:	*But Tina's project is important and really excellent to work on.*
You:	*SCOM is important too. In fact, it may be more critical because it enhances service to present customers. Tina's project is aimed at new customers.*
Fred:	*Well, that's important.*
You:	*Yes, but customer service is a top priority. We need to work the projects that help that first.*
Fred:	*I suppose. But I'd get to do the strategy part in Tina's project.*
You:	*I'm not suggesting you drop it. Can you put it off until after SCOM?*
Fred:	*Tina needs it now to hit the high-traffic season.*
You:	*I know it's not optimal, but I can't think of any other way. Can you?*
Fred:	*No, I guess not, but Tina's not going to be happy.*
You:	*You know it. If we need to, let's sit down and talk about it.*

It's important you're clear about how the decision is being made. You've based it on the company's mission and values. If you consistently make decisions this way, employees will eventually realize that the process is both fair and reasonable and that sometimes their intellectual capital is best used right where they are.

- *I can't do it unless I get relief from another project.* Fred can do SCOM or he can do Tina's project but not both. In either case, you need to use the same logic—what will move the strategic direction forward the most and is most consistent with the company's values. It is very likely that the difference between the two projects will be marginal. Both projects are probably worthwhile and both will contribute to the strategic direction. It is a judgment call as to which is more worthwhile and Fred may well disagree with your assessment if it isn't in line with his preferences. Even though Fred may be disappointed or disagree with your logic, if you show that you have given his preferences serious consideration and that your decision is based, not on personal whim, but on a true attempt to do what is best for the company, he will usually be able to accept the decision with good grace and turn his energies to doing a good job on the higher priority item. The way you handle this situation can help to ensure that Fred uses his intellectual capital for the present project, even if it isn't what he'd prefer.

That's My Mandate

There are two problems in this issue. One is whether helping a peer makes her look more successful than you. This is about the rewards system in the organization and we'll discuss that later. However, a problem also occurs if your group is responsible for a certain body of expertise. Say your group is the company's center for Internet commerce. It's what you're resourced for and your raison d'être. If people like Tina run around doing it, how does your group add value? Not only that, but what about the corporate Internet commerce priorities you're responsible for?

These are all excellent reasons for wanting Tina to quit it. However, Tina's arguments might be: "I need this now. You guys are too slow." Or "You're not doing it the way I need it to be done," Or "Nobody consulted me about the corporate priorities for Internet commerce." Or even "What's all this bull about intellectual capital? How come I can't get the expertise I need when I need it?" There is a way out of this dilemma.

I was once responsible for national delivery of a set of service products. Each regional office had resources at least equal to, and often greater than mine, and they didn't report to me. They were perfectly capable of developing what they needed on their own, thanks, and initially didn't see the need for a national presence. Our customers needed to receive the same level and quality of service no matter where they were, but when I tried to put all the regional priorities into a national queue, you can imagine the reaction. They all nodded politely and continued business as usual.

So, instead, I worked on turning regional priorities into national ones. If we heard of a regional project being undertaken, I'd offer to fund a couple of people from other regions (and one from HQ) to be added to that region's project team. Thus, the initiating region got the product it wanted when it wanted, but we simultaneously had a national product.

Eventually, regions saw the benefit of pooling their resources with ours and became actively involved in planning the national agenda. The regions came to see headquarters as a way to get expertise they lacked. It also meant I had access to many more resources than I might otherwise.

To get this to work, I had to rethink my role. Instead of setting national priorities and then trying to convince the regions to fall into line, I had to transform regional priorities into national ones. I had to find out where the parade was and grab the baton.

You can become the focus of expertise and share your resources out if you're willing to reconsider your role in the process. If you have to do it the old way (my priorities, my control), you may be out of luck. But if you can stay open to new configurations, you may be able to get it to work.

I'm Losing Control

In typical management, the manager decides who works on what and when. It is an ordered way to conduct business although people can waste a lot of time as approvals go up one side of the chain of command and come down the other. Much of the goodwill we've built up over the years with our work colleagues is spent on getting things done more quickly than if we followed all the rules. But those rules are still there when people step on our toes.

You could insist Tina and all other managers who want to use your staff ask your permission, allowing the use of your intellectual capital in an orderly way, and giving you some semblance of control over what's going on. That seems to make sense, but if you do it, how does this free up the flow of people in the organization? Isn't it just business as usual? You put Tina's project in the queue according to your view of its importance.

Because you don't know the product as well as Tina, or Internet commerce as well as Fred, you don't know if this project is more valuable than your priorities or even the corporate priorities. "But somebody's got to decide," you object. You're right, but why can't it be Fred and Tina jointly? "But," you continue, "If I do that, how will I deliver on my own unit's goals and how will I be sure that each employee is working on the important stuff?" These are both good questions. We've already dealt with the first one in accomplishing work goals, but what about the second?

If you've been helping the employee to understand how complex the environment is (Chapter 3) and how his work fits into the mission, you can probably trust him to make a good decision. You can help him recall the need to factor in strategic priorities by asking, "Where does it fit with where the company's going?" If he can give a credible answer, perhaps it makes sense for him to do it even if the decision might be different from one you would make.

Structural Ways to Encourage Free Movement of People

Individual managers can do some things to support the free movement of people but organizations need to do their bit also by creating slack in the system and rewarding managers who share resources.

Creating Slack in the System

To encourage free movement of people, an organization could make sure that it is slightly overstaffed. Does a cold shiver run up your spine to contemplate a less than 100 per cent use of resources? That does sound irrational and inefficient, doesn't it? And yet, there's 3M which allows its researchers to use 15 per cent of their time to work on projects of interest to them personally even if outside of the corporate objectives.[1] In addition, many excellent service organizations

---

[1] Marshall Loeb, "Ten Commandments for Managing Creative People," *Fortune* (January 16, 1995): 135.

have realized that no more than 75 per cent of a person's time should be locked in. Otherwise, everyone is running so fast it's not possible to take advantage of opportunities that present themselves for either extra service or new products.

You want people both to learn and come up with new ideas. You don't usually do either running flat out or racing to a deadline. You're *applying* learning but not actually learning. To learn or get creative, people need the time to sit back and think about what's happening or the chance to throw around an idea with a set of like-minded colleagues. If they don't have that, they don't learn or innovate well.

So, maybe we've gotten it all (or partly) wrong. Maybe it's not the sitting nose-to-the-computer work that is most productive for companies. Maybe staring off into space, doodling, schmoozing, and hanging out are equally useful. Maybe the best productivity comes not from minimizing chat time but increasing it. Think about that. Obviously, at some point you have to turn schmoozing into wealth, but building some slack into the system fosters that which is most valuable today—the brainpower of your organization thinking together.

So if you can, staff organizations at slightly overcapacity. If that isn't possible, designing floor plans for casual meetings, coffee rooms that invite hanging out, and even regular social events at work will also encourage people to learn together.

Reward Managers Who Share Resources

Organizations should reward managers who share their resources and still get the job done. Or at very least, try to avoid the fear, as in the scenario above, that your boss would take your resources away if you share them.

But how do you do that? Money is always an option and we'll discuss the pros and cons of monetary rewards as well as award programs in the next chapter. Other ways to signal the company's belief in sharing intellectual capital are assessing it in your performance evaluation system, promoting or handing out plum assignments at least in part because sharing was demonstrated, and "talking it up." The latter means making the link for people between Fiona's getting the coveted assignment and her willingness to help her peers. When you announce her appointment, you might say something like, "Needless to say, Fiona is an excellent all-around manager, but I want to highlight one particularly impressive thing. Fiona has recruited a great team of people and is always willing to have them help others out when needed. That's the kind of manager I want."

These steps will make a difference if people are worried that helping others will put them at a disadvantage. Of course, you can't expect immediate conversions to sharing and helping all over the organization, but if you are consistent in your reward of sharing resources, it will eventually become a part of "how we do business."

We Won't Pay for the Move if You Ask for it.

We've been talking largely about how to let people move between projects or bosses, but the same logic applies to relocations. A large multinational firm has a policy which boils down to: if you ask to be transferred, you pay for the move. This is true even if the destination office desperately needs your skills. So even if you're needed, you get penalized for wanting to go.

You can imagine the little dance that goes on between recruiting manager and potential transferee. It would go something like this:

Manager:	*Hi, Bill. How's the weather in Boston?*
Transferee:	*Snowing as usual. I was half an hour late today because of the storm. These winters are really getting to me.*
Manager:	*You should live here. It's 80 degrees today and sunny.*
Transferee:	*Sounds great. I'd love it.*
Manager:	*So, you want to move to Atlanta?*
Transferee:	*Well, I don't know. Are you asking?*
Manager:	*Depends. Do you want to come?*
Transferee:	*Do you want me to come?*
Manager:	*I asked you first.*
Transferee:	*I don't know . . . why do you ask?*

And so on. What a silly conversation! Human resources practices that inhibit the freer movement of people are not in the long-term interests of the company. If you need someone's knowledge in a specific spot, pay for the costs associated with that move.

The Free Movement of Knowledge

Freeing up the movement of people within the company is an important way to encourage the effective use of intellectual capital, but people don't have to physically move to share knowledge. Some of the best sharing happens with everyone staying right at his or her own computer. And some of the roadblocks to sharing are part of our everyday office life. Let's talk about some ways to encourage the free movement of knowledge.

Noncompetition Agreements

Some part of the whole intellectual capital movement has tried to retain the knowledge for the company even if the person leaves. Another attempt at this has been to lock people into strong noncompetition agreements. The logic seems to be that if we can make the penalties for leaving stringent enough, people won't. Or if they do, they won't take their knowledge with them.

These are charming but naive fantasies. Given that intellectual capital can only be invited and not commanded, how much are you getting from someone who's staying only because the penalties for leaving are too high? And when they leave, the belief they won't take what's in their heads is ludicrous. Of course, they can't take the patent, the new invention, or any other tangible products, but trying to prevent them from using their knowledge is unrealistic.

In any case, a noncompetition agreement is kind of like locking the barn door after the horse has escaped. You may have some limited success in preventing the departing employee from spreading your competitive advantage around, but all you've retained is the base of creation, the knowledge itself. In losing the employee, you've lost the ability to create wealth from that knowledge. And while you can eventually hire a replacement, this job market means that it will take a lot of time, a lot of lost opportunities, and a lot of getting up to speed before the replacement operates at the level of the person you lost. Whatever you might have gained by retaining the knowledge, you've lost in speed of integration.

So even if noncompetition agreements are a fact of life, the issue is not about the type of agreement, but how to keep both the person *and* the knowledge which create wealth. It is about creating an environment where people *want* to stay and contribute. One of the best ways to do that is to encourage a "community of practice" in your company.

Communities of Practice

A community of practice is a group of people who keep in touch based on their specialized interests. Researchers and engineers have always done it. Their professional associations are based on that premise, and other areas of specialized knowledge create communities of practice for themselves because they are a necessary part of knowledge work.

The community aspect of knowledge generation is very important as I experienced in my first job out of graduate school. My boss told me that he expected a big difference in our product innovation because of my psychology background, but whenever I brought up issues my training had taught me were important, the others in the unit looked at me like I was an alien. And in some ways, I was. I learned what Arie de Geus, former head of planning for Royal Dutch Shell Group, points out in his article on companies that have survived for centuries—"keeping a few innovators on hand is not enough to ensure institutional learning. The organization must encourage those people to interact with others."[2] The random hiring of specialized skills doesn't ensure learning any more than the random planting of flowers makes a garden. Experts need communities of practice so they can interact frequently and freely with others in their field and thus generate more and better knowledge.

Why is that? According to research done by the Palo Alto Institute for Research on Learning,[3] learning is primarily a social activity, despite the images we have of burning the midnight oil in university days. I ingest knowledge individually but when I try to *use* it, the most productive times come when I toss the idea around with like-minded colleagues. We learn by learning together. Knowledge is transferred and innovation generated. In addition, the act of learning together allows that which was private knowledge to become public and that which was tacit to become explicit. It is only when knowledge is both public and explicit that an organization can leverage it to its advantage.

So, knowing how important learning is for your organization and that learning is social, it makes sense to encourage communities of practice to get both. Communities of practice form without management support and often in the face of (inadvertent) management discouragement. For example, finance people are often assigned to

---

[2] Arie de Geus, "The Living Company," *Harvard Business Review* (March-April 1997): 57.
[3] Thomas A. Stewart, *Intellectual Capital: The New Wealth of Organizations* (New York: Doubleday, 1997), 95.

individual business units, but they have colleagues in other business units with whom they need to interact to increase their professional knowledge. Even though the management structure makes it more difficult to stay connected, they usually do, even if it's only the gang who meets more or less regularly for lunch. A community of practice includes, but is not limited to, the people in one company. In fact, it's more typical for people with specialized knowledge to relate across organizations.

So the good news is that these communities of practice form spontaneously, and that's very important, given they are a major way in which knowledge is transferred and innovation generated. However, before you put your feet up with the sense of a job well done, consider other characteristics of communities of practice as outlined by the Institute for Research on Learning. They:

- are voluntary
- have no specific deliverables
- cannot be created by fiat
- are responsible only to themselves

You need a community of practice's innovation and knowledge transfer but you can't determine its membership or participation, you can't require a particular output, and they don't report to you. So, the good news is that even if you do nothing, they'll happen. The bad news is that there are none of the usual organizational levers to get them to do what you need. In fact, Thomas Stewart, in his book on intellectual capital, states flatly that "Organizational learning depends on these often invisible groups, but they're virtually immune to management in a conventional sense—indeed, managing can kill them."[4]

What You Can Do to Foster a Community of Practice

So, without really intending to and simply by being themselves, managers can kill a community of practice, the wellspring of the new knowledge and knowledge transfer that all organizations need to prosper. Sounds pretty bleak, doesn't it? But while trying to direct a community of practice seems doomed to failure, you can and should do some things that will encourage (although not compel) it to produce useful results:

[4] Thomas A. Stewart, *Intellectual Capital: The New Wealth of Organizations* (New York: Doubleday, 1997), 97.

- *Bring in experts from other organizations to address your group.* Knowledge workers are usually very keen to know how someone else in their field has tackled the problems they face. If you fund the travel and other expenses of these experts, they will often be willing to share their knowledge with your people.

- *Encourage people from outside the company to participate in your unit's bull sessions regularly.* Rather than assuming that all group sessions are for the team only, open some of the brainstorming sessions to other members of the community of practice. It will help to stimulate the thinking and possibly bring in a new perspective. Naturally, issues of confidentiality and proprietary information need to be attended to, but there are usually large areas of knowledge that can be discussed freely even given these constraints.

- *Pay for memberships in relevant associations.* Associations are usually readymade communities of practice. By encouraging your employees to join, you increase the likelihood they can add to their store of knowledge.

- *Give employees a limited amount of time to work on association activities.* Having your employees actively involved in their community of practice will pay dividends. Allowing some work time to be devoted to association work (e.g., telephoning, conference organization) can have a useful payoff.

- *Fund/sponsor some association activities.* Funding doesn't always have to be in cash. You can loan a meeting room or arrange for them to buy meals for their conference under your company' umbrella agreement with a caterer. Sponsorship doesn't have to be costly.

- *Pay for the occasional lunch or coffee meeting.* When like-minded colleagues meet, even over lunch or coffee, work often gets discussed. While a blanket expense approval is probably inappropriate, allowing employees to claim the occasional meal when the conversation was primarily about work will encourage them to tap their community of practice for the knowledge your company needs.

- *Create a center of excellence in your own workplace.* In the next part, we'll focus on creating a center of excellence as an idea with potential to promote knowledge transfer and innovation.

Creating a Center of Excellence

A center of excellence is a workplace that considers itself to be the best in the company, country, or world class on some well-defined piece of knowledge. For example, one consulting firm I know believes that it has developed the most effective and efficient processes in the country to diagnose and resolve Y2K problems. In another company, the regional finance unit believes that it gives the best advice with the best response time of any other finance unit in the company. These centers of excellence have not necessarily gone out of their way to gather objective proof that they are the best. The more likely yardstick is their ability to bring in business that is exceptionally challenging and profitable, the satisfaction of their customers and the willingness of their knowledge workers to apply their intellectual capital to these leading-edge projects. They are also centers of excellence because they have that indefinable but nevertheless palpable air of excitement and purpose that differentiates them from other workplaces almost from the moment you walk in.

Creating a center of excellence creates all kinds of benefits. You retain valuable knowledge workers because you offer them what they want most—the opportunity to work on fascinating, challenging, and leading-edge "stuff," which not only needs but demands their innovation, intuition, and analysis. You may even solve your recruiting problem since, as people begin to know that yours is a great place to work, they'll come to you.

Equally important, creating a center of excellence increases the chances that the elusive community of practice that you can neither control nor direct, will take up residence in your unit. If your unit becomes the focal point for the local community of practice, that usually means a number of the community members are on your team. This increases the likelihood that the issues the community of practice will work on will be those you actually want addressed simply because your guys want to a chance to toss around solutions to problems they're presently struggling with.

So how do you create the workplace of choice? What do people need? Actually, the needs are not all that surprising. They are more autonomy in doing the work; involvement in work decisions; work on leading-edge projects; and having fun.

We've already talked about giving people more autonomy and involving them in work decisions (Chapters 5 and 6), so let's examine the other two—working on leading edge projects and having fun.

Working on Leading Edge Projects

High-tech workers regularly switch companies to do something new, but they are just the vanguard. Working on something new or leading edge is what excites a knowledge worker.[5] They crave learning and stretching. They want to be able to apply their knowledge and creativity to solve problems no one else can solve and experiment with solutions no one else has thought about yet.

Having work which is leading edge can pose a problem for managers. For one thing, you may have to rethink your unit strategy. If most of your business has been repeating the same solutions for different clients, you may need to think about how to migrate more of the business to more unique problems. In addition, while working with the newest technology may keep a knowledge worker happy, you need to trade off your ability to keep her on the job with the needs of the company. Sometimes, it really is best for the company to have a plain vanilla solution rather than the banana split the employee would have more fun whipping up.

Which brings me to the question, what do you do when some or all of your projects aren't leading edge and won't be in the foreseeable future? For example, programmers fixing the Y2K problem on legacy systems have a boring, repetitive, nonskill building job that is nevertheless crucial. How to you create a center of excellence then? How to you keep your knowledge workers?

It is possible to do and the Y2K problem provides an excellent example. Municipalities everywhere have to ensure that their emergency dispatch systems are working on January 1, 2000. If not, a fire cannot be reported, and even if it is, the fire engines can't respond because the computers believe they're overdue for maintenance. The City of Ottawa has used an innovative combination of monetary incentives (part of the annual bonus will only be paid out in 2000) and an emphasis on how important each line of code is, how it might literally be the difference between life and death. Although the task is boring, it is infused with a meaning which is so compelling that it can help to alleviate some of the problems inherent in the work. The success of their approach is already evident. Since they instituted this approach, they haven't lost one programmer where before the attrition rate was one a month. So, if you can't provide leading-edge work, make sure people understand the importance of

---

[5] By personality or upbringing, you'll get some knowledge workers who enjoy applying the same solutions or knowledge over and over again, but they're in the minority.

what they're doing. If you make meaning for people, it can be as motivating as being on the leading edge.

Having Fun

Of course, you know we're supposed to have fun. You know it because, having delivered the produce-or-die message, the high-muck-a-muck says, "Finally, it's imperative we all have fun." Not too much fun, of course. Nothing that takes away from *productive* time. You sort of get the feeling you should have fun in the same way people smoke now...in out-of-the-way places, furtively, and with a sense of guilt.

Centers of excellence are almost always fun places to be—not just exciting work environments—but actually fun. So, how do you do it? Barb MacCallum of Careerware, a career guidance software business, has developed some rules of thumb as she retains her programmers over long periods of time while scoring out-of-this-world customer and employee satisfaction stats.

- *Find a fun person and put him in charge of regular events.* Fun that builds connection needs to be worked at. While spontaneous TGIFs are fine, you should also give the fun person the task of coming up with some regular events that create a sense of fun and excitement in the office. Their exact nature will depend on the group (see below) but the employee should be allowed to do at least some of this arranging on company time. For example, if the employee in charge of fun is arranging a software treasure hunt or a Christmas in July picnic, he should be allowed to make the arrangements for the Christmas decorations, the food, the location, and so on, as part of his regular duties. Needless to say, you need the kind of person who will understand that these duties don't take precedence over regular work duties, although they might displace some of his lower priority ones.

- *Use the employees' standards of fun, not the manager's.* This came home to me when Barb had to introduce a no-necking-in-the-halls rule. At the time, I was managing a group of people close to retirement, and my main concern was keeping them productive until then. Forbidding kissing in the hallways just never came up. Sometimes, age really does make a difference. You might want to bow out of approving what kind of fun people have. Your tastes and your gang's may well be different.

- *It doesn't have to be big or expensive, but it does have to include everyone.* That means no golf days for the sales guys only. You don't have to make it elaborate, but it does have to be something everyone can participate in, and remember it's not just that they *can* participate but they *want* to. For example, holding an office golf tournament works only if everyone knows how to play golf or you've set up the rules so that even the duffers can have fun. Similarly, rock climbing might be a blast for the younger crowd but not to the more sedentary.

Teams and Communities of Practice Are Different

Teams and communities of practice may look similar on the surface but they are in fact very different. Teams have goals, deliverables, can be created or disbanded by management, and report to somebody. None of those things apply to communities of practice. Also, communities of practice often include people from outside the organization. So, people may be both team members and members of a community of practice, but their roles are quite different.

If you can create an environment which is always pushing the envelope, gives people a fair amount of autonomy, involves them in decisions which affect them, and makes it a fun place to work, you can create a center of excellence. If you do that, you're more likely to have it coincide with a community of practice which will draw people (even those outside your group) to help you to innovate and transfer knowledge.

Having Fun Gone Wild

Some management experts advocate keeping high demand knowledge workers by encouraging them to have the equivalent of nonstop fun, letting employees do what they want.

However, like overly permissive parents who let their kids run wild, overly permissive employers don't do workers any good in the long term. Yes, it might be fun in the short term, but does beer on tap and pizza on demand make people more committed? True commitment comes from control over and respect for your work, not whether you can bring your parrot to work and run around barefoot.

And if you are going to play a parent's role (which has its perils in a workplace), remember that the most valued ones are not those who let you stay out all night, but those who help you achieve something great, help you be more than you thought you could be, help you over the hard bits, and applaud your flight. So it is with workers. Achieving something greater than you thought you could is better than all the pizza in the world.

So having fun is important, but it's not enough. Having fun within the context of accomplishing important and respected work is the true way to retain knowledge workers.

Proprietary Information

For good knowledge transfer, the sources of knowledge need to be varied and the communities of practice need to include people from outside the organization. All this knowledge can be pooled and shared, and that's good if the knowledge transfer is coming *into* your organization. But what about transferring knowledge *out*? That's not so good, especially if it is proprietary or competitive knowledge.

This problem isn't a new one. Organizations long ago recognized they needed to contain the spread of knowledge in areas important to their competitive advantage, hence, patents, proprietary information, and confidentiality agreements. Patents and such work well only when there is a limited body of knowledge to protect. As knowledge grows, these processes are less and less effective. New knowledge, while a shy thing in some ways, is nevertheless relentless in others—there is a tendency for more and more people to know it. Also, knowledge doesn't do well boxed up. The next breakthrough is usually a combination of your proprietary knowledge and knowledge from some other source. If you don't let it out to play, you won't get the returns.

It's a conundrum. Knowledge isn't an asset unless it creates unique value, but if it's unique, you can't have it floating around generally available. The need to be first to market often means keeping your knowledge under wraps, but if you do, you restrict the movement that is necessary for further knowledge transfer and innovation in your community of practice. So how can you have the benefits of a community of practice and still retain proprietary or competitive knowledge? It can be done, but you may have to loosen up your definition of proprietary knowledge and who can know it.

I once ran a learning group for my company's clients. We often had presentations from individual companies even though many competed directly with each other in the marketplace. They had decided that learning together was more important than keeping their distance and dealt with this problem in interesting ways. For example, a big computer firm gave a presentation on how they improved quality. Knowing there were competitors in the room, the presenter told the group his overheads wouldn't be available and presented the financial information that proved the worth of his effort in ways that avoided actual figures. He shared his knowledge without giving away critical competitive information. You may object, "But the presenter was giving away a competitive advantage merely by showing how the company had improved its quality." True, and this is what I mean about how absolute you are in your definition of proprietary information. Some competitive information is going to be shared.

Research scientists trade proprietary information all the time. They discovered that if they didn't share meaningful information with their community of practice, they didn't get any back. If others cooperate and you don't reciprocate, you are eventually cut out of the circle of people learning together and fall behind. If you continue to keep your cards close to your chest, you'll eventually find yourself playing high-stakes poker in a bridge game. Thus, you need to engage in a quid pro quo.

So sharing even proprietary information may be necessary to get the benefits of learning and innovation in your organization, but how do you prevent it from going too far? As in our example, if people understand the company's mission and care about their relationship to it, you can probably trust them to draw the line so that critical information doesn't get into competitors' hands even as they share their knowledge.

This is an example of the need to change our attitudes and beliefs to fit the information age better. Knowledge and learning are the most important competitive advantage, but their generation is not in our hands; we need to find new ways to relate to them. One way is to accept that some proprietary information will be released in a knowledge exchange and that if the people doing the transfers care about the company and believe they are trusted, they will make the right decisions about how much they need to give away to get good information back.

Summary

While we all want our intellectual capital to be used to maximum benefit for the whole organization, some of the ways we operate can get in the way. Some of the stumbling blocks are the manager's and some the company's. In order to use structural capital effectively, we need to address issues such as control over the work being done, creating slack in the system, and rewarding managers who share resources. It also suggests that we need to rethink issues such as proprietary information and communities of practice. This chapter has focused on increasing the store of knowledge that knowledge workers have. The next chapter will help employees to share the knowledge they've acquired for the good of the organization.

Main Points

- Managers are reluctant to allow free movement of workers and knowledge because it might adversely affect the resources they control or might jeopardize their ability to deliver on their mandate.

- Organizations can encourage freer movement of knowledge and people by creating slack in the system and rewarding managers who share resources.

- Noncompetition agreements are of doubtful value for leveraging knowledge into wealth.

- Communities of practice transfer knowledge and innovation but cannot be controlled.

- Managers can foster communities of practice and create centers of excellence.

CHAPTER 10

∞

Sharing
and Learning

We often use the term knowledge—as in knowledge workers—as if it were synonymous with learning, since it's understood you can't use the knowledge you haven't learned. While that's true, it's not the whole truth. The distinction between the two becomes important as we talk about how to manage the specialized and proliferating knowledge in our organizations. Knowledge is a body of information, technique, and experience that coalesces around a particular subject. Learning is the capacity to take in that knowledge and integrate it into how you work and what you do.

Structural capital is best at capturing and making *knowledge* available. But while it makes *knowledge* available faster, it doesn't ensure that it is learned. Only the workers themselves can turn the knowledge into learning. So while building knowledge is critical to using intellectual capital, it is only truly effective if the learning is both "fast" and "deep." Let's talk about what both of those mean to your organization.

Fast Learning

Arie de Geus believes "the ability to learn faster than your competitors may be the only sustainable competitive advantage."[1] Royal

---

[1] Ann Walmsley, "The Brain Game," *Globe and Mail Report on Business* (April 1993): 38.

Dutch Shell is not only one of the oldest companies in the world but was also one of the few oil giants prepared for the Middle East oil crisis of the late seventies.

Knowledge pivotal to your business will probably eventually overcome the barriers erected against it and become part of the mainstream, how-we-do-things-around-here.[2] However, if it has to struggle to become established, it's more likely to succeed only when it has become standard knowledge or common practice in the industry. Knowledge which is adopted late doesn't create wealth but simply prevents you from losing more than you have to. For example, ATMs were a competitive advantage only when not all banks had them. Now they are ubiquitous and just the cost of doing business. To leverage your intellectual capital for competitive advantage, it's not just how much knowledge is floating around but it's how *fast* the learning is integrated into the business.

In fact, Hubert Saint-Onge, one of the world leaders in the field of intellectual capital, uses an interesting and powerful analogy. Drawing on his banking experience, he talks about the concept of "float." In banking terms, float is the amount of time between the deposit of money in an account to cover a cheque and the withdrawal of the funds to pay it. Similarly, there is a "technological float," between when a new technology is invented and when it impacts the marketplace. Better communication and production capabilities have shrunk this period enormously, although "organizational float" —the time it takes for an organization to react to a new development in the market place—hasn't changed to keep pace. He believes that organizations that cannot shrink their organizational float—that is, increase their speed of integration dramatically— will not survive this information age.

The need for speed changes the whole dynamic of how learning occurs in organizations. It's analogous to cars and horses. Cars are not just faster horses— their speed and versatility completely transformed our society. Being able to reach far-off points faster made suburbs possible and the dream of owning your own home a possibility. Our sense of community changed from one that was bounded by how far a horse could travel in a day to one that is still being defined today. The problems of the inner city are partly the result of the automobile allowing the more affluent to move away from where they worked.

---

[2] Although this isn't always true and the landscape is littered with companies who weren't able to shift to the new knowledge soon enough to stay in business.

Speed in and of itself, can radically alter not just where but how we live, and so it is with speed of learning in an organization. We're still not sure exactly what the changes will be, but they are almost sure to be profound. And they certainly start with trying to increase the speed of integration of learning in an organization.

Deep Learning

While learning needs to be fast, it also needs to be deep. There is a difference between deep knowledge and deep learning. Deep knowledge is a very profound understanding of a particular subject area and organizations certainly need people with this kind of depth in their particular fields. However, deep learning speaks more to the *way* we learn. It is about learning how to think together.

For example, I may believe that the more senior you are, the more likely you are to be right. So, I'll always defer to the most senior person in the room, and it might not even occur to me that I have an equally good or better solution. The easy solution for this particular problem is for the most senior person to say, "I think everyone has something important to contribute and I don't have all the right answers." That might work for that particular instance, but the corollary to my original assumption is that people more junior than me have little to offer. Thus, I cut myself off from the knowledge they have as well as from contributing my own. So, even if you could do an end-run around one assumption, there are plenty more where that came from.

In addition, assumptions are almost by definition, something we are not aware of. Only by learning in a way that encourages bringing them to the surface can I assess whether they get in the way. And it can make a significant difference. Remember the *Challenger* disaster? It all came down to a faulty O-ring which the scientists and engineers knew about before the tragedy. "Carefully defined procedures and check-points did not stop people from withholding their doubts and preventing or delaying productive debate about possible dangers; they were following 'official' protocols and unofficial face-saving rules."[3] Our assumptions about how we learn and share knowledge do make a difference.

---

[3] William N. Isaacs, "Dialogue, Collective Thinking and Organizational Thinking," *Organizational Dynamics* (1994), 28.

While learning new knowledge is important, so is continuing to deepen how you learn. Among other things, that means:

- Raising differences rather than smoothing over them.
- Suspending your view rather than defending it.
- Accepting rather than discounting how your own thought processes influence your experience.

Employees must be willing both to share what they know and learn from others quickly and deeply for structural capital to be used effectively. While these may seem easy and obvious, it turns out that getting it to happen is neither. Let us consider what gets in the way of employees learning from one another and how to deal with it.

How Do You Know if the Learning Isn't Getting Through?

On the surface, it seems there shouldn't be any time lag between understanding and acting. I see a red light and I stop. For such simple knowledge, the lag is fairly short and doesn't have to be managed in any kind of important way.

But we're talking about learning and sharing knowledge that might be threatening or disruptive. If I come up with a whole new way of manufacturing a product that requires people to move and think faster, its introduction will generate all kinds of fears and concerns. What if I can't think that fast? What about quality? Can we still do as good a job? Why should I bust my butt on this? This threat to my equilibrium is usually expressed is in one of three ways:

- It's Not True
- Even If True, It Doesn't Apply
- Even If It Applies, We Can Do It Better

It's Not True

That's always first out of the gate. It is a common response when, for example, managers see the results of an employee survey that aren't positive. Typically, their first reaction is to attack the data collection method, the motives of the person who collected the data, the questionnaire itself, how many people filled it out (too few—not a valid sample; too many—stuffing the ballot box), and so on. In the example cited above, it sounds like, "It won't work," "The unions will never go for it," "Are you bucking for a promotion?" Sometimes these complaints are legitimate but more often than not, they are a way to deny that new learning is required.

Even If True, It Doesn't Apply

Once people get past that stage, they may move into "OK, it's true but it doesn't have any implications for me." The usual objections are our market is different, our employees are different, our customers are different, our industry or sector is different, we face different problems. In our example, it would be "It might work in a small plant but not here," or "Our workers are too old/inexperienced/laid back for it to work here." And again, these may be true, but they're arguments for tailoring the learning to suit your environment. More often, they're used to discount the knowledge completely which means that we don't need to acquire it or change what we think and it's business as usual.

Even If It Applies, We Can Do It Better

Sometimes a new idea is so compelling that it's really not possible to use the other two reasons. A drug with impeccable research, a management method which has had spectacular results. If I decide I need to know this new stuff but my feelings or the reward system pushes me to avoid learning from the expert, I could still resist adopting it by saying something like, "I know this worked before but I think it would be much better if we completely revamped the whole idea before we tried it out." This is a less destructive but still inefficient way to handle new knowledge. If we had worlds enough and time, this might be a very valuable way to proceed. However, since success depends on speed of integration, this reinventing the wheel approach is not the way to go. There will be enough stumbling around when learning the new knowledge anyhow without also reinventing it.

Why Learning is Slow

In the face of threatening or disruptive knowledge, people go all the way from denying that there's anything to learn to learning it entirely on their own. And yet, it's in their long-term best interests as well as the company's to learn it quickly. Why do people act in what seems an ineffective and inefficient manner? Why all the resistance?

It comes from a phenomenon to which all of us are prey. Even economists, in the person of Michael Jensen of Harvard, don't believe people act strictly on logic and optimizing options all the time. About half of the time, they use PAM—a Pain Avoidance Model.[4] Intuitively, we know this is true. We avoid going to the dentist even if it will be better in the long-run if we do. We put off telling an employee his report stunk even when it would allow him more time to fix it. And we stick with the tried and true if using the new knowledge is more inconvenient, messy, and/or painful (which it almost always is).

So while we sometimes act rationally and logically, at other times we act in ways which avoid the pain of losing control, recognizing personal error, and/or changing one's theories of the world and of oneself.[5]

Interestingly, the people who have the most problem with this are often the smartest or most successful in your organization. In a classic *Harvard Business Review* article called "Teaching Smart People How to Learn," Chris Argyris points out that many smart people pride themselves on being experts, and because they're very heavily invested in their already acquired store of knowledge, they can be reluctant to learn from others. [6]

In addition, expert professionals have had little experience in learning from failure. In fact, they often set up their work to minimize it. They think of it as "building on their strengths" or "sticking with their knitting," but it can also result in a conservatism in learning choices. So when things go wrong (as they inevitably do) and they need to learn from the experience, they're not very good at it. They deny it happened, deflect criticism, blame others. "It wasn't me—it was the incompetents you make me work with." All ways to avoid the pain of considering that they might have made a mistake and/or have something to learn.

So learning can be slowed down because people avoid the pain of losing control or changing how they see their competence. Acquiring new knowledge because it is for the company's good is not a very

[4] Geoffrey Colvin, "The Most Valuable Quality in a Manager," *Fortune* (December 29, 1997): 279.
[5] Ibid.
[6] Chris Argyris, "Teaching Smart People How to Learn," Harvard Business Review (May-June 1991): 99.

compelling argument when faced with the disruption of changing how you see yourself and what you do.

Wait a minute. My guys love to learn. So do I.

You may be thinking, "What's the fuss? Why just last week we all went on a conflict resolution course and had a great time and learned something too." There are lots of occasions when learning is both easy and fun. That's great, but as with most of these events, it is up to you whether you use the knowledge.

Often the new knowledge needs to be integrated quickly to be a competitive advantage. For example, we need to change our distribution channels from print to the Internet. Our skills in working with printers and targeting audiences go out the window as we figure out how to draw people into our Web site.

If people can choose what they learn, or even whether to learn at all, their resistance to doing so is likely to be less. However, when the knowledge *must* be acquired, their resistance will likely be higher, and your work in convincing them that it is in their own best interest, is that much more of a challenge.

The Three Stages of Change

What can you do about avoiding this slowdown of learning in an organization? You can help learning occur in three stages which are easy to describe but not to implement: awareness, invitation, and requirement.

Table: 10.1

Stage 1: Awareness	Stage 2: Invitation	Stage 3: Requirement
• Explain why it's important • Explain what needs to be learned	• Train new behaviors • Coach • Change rewards systems	• Promote/reward those who learn from others • Sanction those who do not

Tips and Tasks

How do you get this change? You need to move quite methodically through the three stages. Let's use an example to demonstrate what you can do at each stage. You supervise a group of accountants who work with various business units of the organization. They all work pretty independently and have developed their own ways of doing things. However, you'd like to have them use a balanced scorecard approach [7] as a way to get the whole corporation to adopt it eventually. You have one person (George) who is an expert in balanced scorecards but everyone else uses a more traditional approach.

Stage 1: Awareness

Here are some of the things you could do in the awareness stage.

- **Link It to the Big Picture**
  In introducing the balanced scorecard idea, help people understand why it's good for the organization and them. George might give a short presentation on the process after people understand why it's important.

- **Talk It Up**
  Even if you do a presentation, don't expect everyone to jump on board. Most likely, they'll file it under "interesting and I must get to that one day," even if you've specifically said you'd like them to start using it.

  Keep talking it up by circulating articles on the topic, bringing in someone from an organization using the process, or even just asking, "Hey, is this an opportunity to use the balanced scorecard?"

- **Assign Your Expert to the Plum Projects**
  You may need to move George into projects that might have been traditionally the bailiwick of another accountant (Rose). He might lead the project or be a consultant to Rose. This may not sit well with her but you need to insist that, at minimum, George be at the table to offer his views.

---

[7] This is a financial reporting approach that includes more than financial indicators. Depending on how it's set up, it might include gauges of employee and customer satisfaction, for example.

- **Don't Make the Past Wrong**
  When you start to drive the scorecard idea, people may believe you're implying what they did in the past was wrong or inadequate. Address this specifically and repeatedly by saying things like, "We've been doing an excellent job, but we need to keep improving how we serve our clients. The balanced scorecard is one way."

- **Expect Accusations of Favoritism**
  Even if you do that, people may accuse you (or worse, think it but not tell you) of favoring George—he's either about to marry your sister or has something on you. This is a common way to deny that the new knowledge is useful. It's easier to impute negative motives to you and George than to change how I think. As John Kenneth Galbraith once said, "Faced with the choice between changing one's mind and proving there is no need to do so, almost everyone gets busy with the proof."

  Because it's more likely that people will think favoritism but not say it, be extra careful to pay attention to the good work other people are doing. Eventually, as people recognize the value of incorporating the new knowledge into their own work, the suspicions will die away, but don't let them deter you from encouraging adopting the new way.

Length of the Awareness Stage

There is no definitive answer to how long the awareness stage should last. The length of this or any other stage depends on how quickly people understand *why* they must change, how important the change is to the company, and how resistant people are to it. The only thing that is certain is that each stage almost always takes longer than the manager wants it to.

Managers often assume that they just need to explain the importance of sharing and learning once and awareness will occur. And in the small, nonthreatening things, that should be true, but if the learning is generating reactions such as it's not true; if true, it doesn't apply to me; and even though it applies, I can do it better, you'll need to repeat yourself or find multiple ways to say the same thing far beyond the number of times you think is reasonable. If people are resisting, they'll hear only the parts that fuel their belief that this is an idea whose time hasn't come. If you want them to change their minds, you have to keep repeating your explanations so people can work through all the stages.

Stage 2: Invitation

After people are aware that the new knowledge must be incorporated, you invite them to change in the following ways:

- **Train Them in the New Skill**
  This is an obvious one. Ask George to help people apply the balanced scorecard to their work.

- **Coach the Expert on How to Help**
  While George may be the world's gift to balanced scorecards, he may not be a good coach. For example, if he takes a my-way-or-the-highway stance, it will be more difficult for his colleagues to see beyond his attitude to the real value of his knowledge.

  If this might be an issue, work with George before you assign him. Point out that new knowledge can be difficult for people and how he handles the interaction will make a big difference. Suggest he look for areas of common ground rather than emphasizing how much different and better the balanced scorecard is. Continue this coaching until you're comfortable that George is an instrument of the change, not an impediment to it.

- **Agree on Rules of Engagement**
  People resist adopting new knowledge if they feel they'll lose something in the process. Before George starts to work with the other accountants, overtly and publicly discuss the rules of engagement such as:
  - *Who gets the credit?* Will Rose get the credit for bringing George in or will he get it for doing the job? Next time you're looking to assign a really exciting project, will you think of Rose or George? You need to work out what getting the credit looks like in this new environment.
  - *Who decides how the new knowledge will be incorporated?* Does Rose have to do whatever George says or can she decide where it fits? Again, if the control is with Rose, you're going to up the chances she'll try it out.
  - *Can I say no?* That is, can Rose refuse to use this new knowledge? In the invitation stage, I'd say yes. Allow people the option, right now, of letting someone else go first. If there's success, they may be more willing to take a stab at it.

- **Change Seniority Assumptions**

  In virtually all work teams, some people are considered more senior by virtue of their expertise. They take the lead in projects and have more influence on the group's direction, but unless the senior people are also the ones with the new knowledge, you'll need to change these assumptions. Since George has the new knowledge, he should take the lead in a new project rather than one of the regulars.

  This will put noses out of joint, which is another reason it's so hard to introduce new knowledge. But in an environment open to new knowledge, it makes sense (sense, didn't say it was easy) that project leadership devolves to the most knowledgeable.[8]

- **Use the Rank Xerox Approach**[9]

  To minimize reinventing the wheel, Rank Xerox asks people not to do the usual and claim they can do it better even before trying out a new idea. Instead, they urge them to follow the new process or knowledge by the letter for the first go around. After people have had some experience with it, they can add their own touches and improvements in later iterations.

  If you can get your group to agree, it is a good method to try. It's predicated on people trusting others (in this case, George) enough to suspend their normal tendency to want to improve before trying and just take direction. It might work and it might not. The openness of your group to take on new learning will be key. If they are generally resistant, this is not a good approach to use. If they are pretty open, it might be very effective.

- **Normalize Incompetence**

  To learn new knowledge, you have to work through four stages:

Figure: 10.1

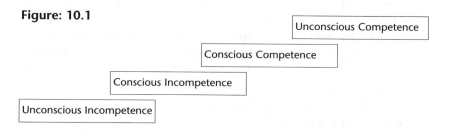

---

[8] Assuming all other skills—like project management—are equal between candidates.
[9] Thomas A. Stewart, "Beat the Budget and Astound Your CFO," *Fortune* (October 28, 1996):187.

In the first stage (Unconscious Incompetence) you don't know what you don't know. We all went through this with respect to driving a car. When you're very little, you don't even know cars exist. In the next stage, Conscious Incompetence, you struggle to acquire the knowledge. When you first get behind a wheel, you can't keep the car between the white lines and traffic frightens you. At the stage of Conscious Competence, you are able to use the new knowledge but only if you work at it. For example, you can merge into highway traffic but only if you really pay attention. Then, in the final stage, Unconscious Competence, you drive while talking to friends, listening to music, and talking on your cell phone. It's just so much a part of you that you can do it without thinking.

We'd all prefer to be at the final stage of learning, but we can only get there if we go through an uncomfortable period of being very bad at what we're learning. As youngsters, that's just a way of life as we learn how to cope with the world. But once we know our way around the world a little better, we seem to lose that willingness to be incompetent temporarily in order to learn.

As a manager, you can help to reintroduce the acceptability of being temporarily incompetent. One way to do it is simply to acknowledge it by saying things like, "Well, if this were easy, we'd have done it a long time ago," or "Nobody can be good at this right away." Whatever indicates that you think being temporarily incompetent in a good cause is not just okay but noteworthy.

Praising partial success is also important. Keeping between the white lines is an accomplishment when you start, even if you can only do it at 10 mph. Similarly, in a management situation, you can say things like, "I think we're really making progress" or "Gosh, this is harder than I thought."

Finally, you can be a model. It may not make sense for you to acquire the new knowledge everyone else is struggling with, for example, the balanced scorecard, but you can mention your struggles with trying out other things which are more managerial (for example, how to normalize incompetence!).

- **Change the Rewards**
  Clearly, people will only attempt, and more importantly, sustain, their learning behavior if it is rewarded in some way. That reward doesn't have to be money—your praise is a powerful motivator,

as is assigning those who integrate knowledge quickly to the new and exciting projects. You may want to change *what* you reward. If sharing credit is important, then rewards might need to be for team rather than individual output. This is such an important aspect of encouraging sharing and learning that there is an entire chapter (Chapter 12) devoted to how you can do this.

In this stage, you're setting up conditions so people see why they should learn the new knowledge and take steps to incorporate it into their thinking.

Stage 3: Requirement

Most people will come on board during the awareness or invitation stages but there is always that small minority who can't or won't. Sometimes, their resistance has to do with who they are—they may have a stronger than average aversion to appearing incompetent as they learn. Other times, it is because the person honestly doesn't believe that the direction chosen is the right one, despite all the discussions you have had with her. And sometimes, this resistance is a symptom of other problems in relating to work and work colleagues. Whatever the reason, people who have not switched to the new way of doing business after others have successfully done so, need to be called on their behavior.

If they are not, several undesirable things will happen. First of all, these resisters will of course not be doing business the new way and so you will not have a unified approach to business. Secondly and even more importantly, the signal you send to all the other people who have already changed is when was push comes to shove, acquiring the new knowledge didn't really matter. Thus, when they run into difficulties or roadblocks as they continue to move from Conscious Competence to Unconscious Competence, they're more likely to abandon the attempt because it's really not all that important.

If you want to avoid backsliding to the old way, you must make it clear to that small minority of resisters that they must also change. To do this, you must confront, insist, and then finally sanction.

- **Confront**

  Confrontation has a bad connotation but, it doesn't have to be ugly or extended. However, it is essential to confront someone who isn't performing. Let's say Janet had agreed to use the balanced scorecard in her audits but you notice that her reports are the usual. The conversation could go something like:

You:	*Janet, I got the Bathhurst report. Can we talk about it?*
Janet:	*Sure, Ted. What's up?*
You:	*I notice you're using the old format for the report.*
Janet:	*Yes, Ted, I know we're supposed to be using the balanced scorecard, but it just didn't seem right for this client.*
You:	*In what way?*
Janet:	*Well, they're largely manufacturing, you know.*
You:	*And?*
Janet:	*I know the scorecard applies there too, but... it just didn't seem right.*
You:	*We had agreed to use it in our last group meeting. Didn't you agree at that time?*
Janet:	*Oh sure, but I thought I'd try it on the next account.*
You:	*Juniper Products? So you'll use it next time?*
Janet:	*Absolutely.*

People often think that confronting means you have to drill the person into the ground. Not at all. In fact, as you can see from this conversation, you can let Janet off the hook by allowing her another chance. That's perfectly okay. You've accomplished what you wanted—to make it clear to her that you've noticed she isn't using the new knowledge and that you don't think it's acceptable. That's all you need to do right now.

- **Insist**

  Sometimes confronting doesn't work. Despite your agreement, the next report comes in, and it's business as usual or with at best a minor bow in the direction of the new knowledge. You need to speak with her again and the conversation could go like this:

You:	*Janet, how did the Juniper Products project go?*
Janet:	*Oh, just fine. No problems.*
You:	*I see you used some of the scorecard elements.*
Janet:	*Yes, well, like we agreed to.*
You:	*I was wondering why you didn't use them all.*
Janet:	*I didn't think we needed to.*
You:	*Well, the ones you used aren't that much different from what we've always used. The new ones are the ones you left out.*
Janet:	*They didn't seem to apply.*
You:	*Janet, we're having a problem. On the one hand, you've agreed to use the scorecard but on the other hand, I see you using it in a way that isn't all that different from business as usual. What gives?*
Janet:	*Nothing, Ted. Nothing. But I thought it was best to go this route with Juniper.*
You:	*That's not what you said when we spoke last time.*
Janet:	*Well, things change.*
You:	*Like?*
Janet:	*Like I was really rushed and I just didn't have time to make it pretty. Juniper got what it needed—they're happy. Isn't it what it's all about?*
You:	*That's one part of our job, certainly, but it's also providing a service that is of maximum benefit to the company and the full use of the balanced scorecard is a way we decided to go.*
Janet:	*I still don't see why we can't do it the old way. It still works.*
You:	*Janet, we've been over this before. You know the reasons why we've decided to change. I need your commitment that you will use all the elements of the scorecard the next time.*

Janet:	*Sure.*
You:	*What assurance will I have that you'll do that?*
Janet:	*Don't you trust me?*
You:	*You have said you'd do it the last two times and nothing much has changed, so I need some assurance that things will be different.*
Janet:	*I'll do it. Don't worry.*
You:	*'I don't think that's good enough. Can you think of a way that I can be sure it will happen?*
Janet:	*Well, do you want me to report in to you every day? Or punch a time clock?*
You:	*No, but I can think of a couple of ways. You and I could sit down at set stages to review progress. Or you could bring George in to consult.*
Janet:	*I don't need George telling me how to do my business.*
You:	*Fine, then let's make it status reports every couple of weeks. Agreed?*
Janet::	*I think this is a waste of time. I'll do it. I said I would.*
You:	*Sorry, Janet. I'd feel more comfortable this way. So, in two weeks, I'd like to see the project plan you've worked out with your client. Agreed?*
Janet:	*Fine, if that's what you want.*

Once you've given people a chance to comply with the new direction and they haven't, it's reasonable to ask for some proof that, this time, they'll do it. Otherwise, you could enter a never-ending cycle of confrontation with no result. At this point, Janet's agreement is nice but not absolutely necessary. You need to do what is required to ensure that the balanced scorecard is used.

- **Sanction**
  It doesn't happen very often, but every once in a while you get an employee who can't or won't incorporate the new knowledge. It is worth trying to find out why and making adjustments if

needed, but at some point, you need to make it clear that you will sanction continuing with the old behavior. The conversation might go like this:

You:	*Janet, I'd like to talk about the Juniper report.*
Janet:	*I thought you might.*
You:	*You're still using the old approach, even after you'd discussed using the new one with the client. This really isn't acceptable.*
Janet:	*Look, Ted, the old way—as you call it—works perfectly well. We don't need to change just for the sake of changing.*
You:	*I know you don't agree with this approach, but it's the way we're going to do business now.*
Janet:	*I think it's a waste of time.*
You:	*I'm sorry you feel that way, but I've given you all the leeway I can to come on board of your own accord. I'm going to have to set things up so that the scorecard is used on all projects.*
Janet:	*What does that mean?*
You:	*It means that from now on, I won't assign you as lead for projects. You'll have to work with one of the other accountants.*
Janet:	*What! But I've been a project leader for the last three years. I'm good at it. You know that.*
You:	*Yes, you are at the old way, but not at the new. And I don't see any evidence that you're trying to go in the direction I need you to.*
Janet:	*That's not fair. But OK, if it's all that important, I'll do it next time.*
You:	*Sorry, Janet. You've said that before and it hasn't happened. So for the Stanley project, Rob will lead and you can work with him.*

Janet:	*Rob! He's only been here a year! I can run rings around him.*
You:	*He's done four or five scorecards in the last year. He knows what he's doing.*

It's unlikely you and Janet can come to an agreement you'll both feel good about. But if it's important, you need to take actions which make it clear that changing what she is doing is not an option. One of two things will happen. Janet will continue to resist and make life difficult for Rob. If she's getting in the way of unit productivity, you may have to go the next step and move her out of the unit completely. It is also possible that taking a step that has embarrassed her will make it clear she needs to get on board. She may start using the scorecard effectively and you might eventually be able to reward the behavior by reinstating her as a project lead. Whatever the fallout, you need to draw a line. If it's important that this knowledge be widely used, you must insist everyone use it.

Employers May Comply but Don't Expect Them to Like It

Managers know that much of work depends on getting along well. Thus, they are often reluctant to take these final steps since they so clearly bring the conflict to the surface. Even if they do raise it, they will spend a long time trying to get the person not just to do what they want but to like it also.

At this stage, after awareness and invitation, it's not likely it will happen. You can insist they comply, but you can't get them to like it or even see its justice. So while in the other stages it is important to strive for agreement, it's probably not realistic to think it'll happen if you've reached this stage with an employee. The best you can hope for is compliance. It is not optimal, I agree, and this employee may eventually be happier elsewhere, but it is important to demonstrate that all employees must change. So while it's natural to want them not only to do it but admit that you were right all along, don't hold your breath.

Problems in Advancing Through the Stages

You let people know why and what they need to learn, support them through it, and eventually make it a requirement. That sounds pretty standard, but when organizations try to help people change to new ways or acquire new knowledge, they rarely go through all three stages. How they act usually falls into two main types: the Jump Ahead to Stage Three and the Stall at Stages One and Two.

Jump To Stage Three

The first kind go directly to Stage Three: Requirement. Their natural tendency is to kick butt and take names. They demand, "You will invest your intellectual capital or else." There are more of them around organizations than we'd like to admit and although I'm making fun of them, they're quite sincere in their wish to make the changes required. However, they haven't factored in two things: people change slowly and they're scared while they're changing.[10] No matter how quickly the organization needs to change, these two tenets don't. To effect true change in both people and culture, there must be a settling in period which allows people to get their heads around the idea that, despite the threat and inconvenience, they should share and be open to learning. Then they need to have a period to try out the new behavior, integrate it into what they already know, and to assure themselves that they will benefit from the change. The majority of people will make the changes required during these two phases if the period is long enough and the information and support are effective.

The reaction of most organizations to this settling-in period is that they can't afford the time if they want to stay competitive but remember:

- Just as you cannot compel people to cough up their ideas and commitment, so you can't compel personal change or learning. Even though you need people to move faster, the traditional levers don't work.

- The corporate landscape is littered with the corpses of organizations that have tried to fast track Total Quality, empowerment, teamwork, and many other initiatives which depend on people

---

[10] More about these can be found in Chapter 13.

learning and changing. The success has been dismal (70 to 80 per cent failure rate) and the organization spends a considerable amount of time cleaning up the mess or burying it. It seems to take about the same amount of time to do things right as it does to do them wrong.

- Finally, although it's important to allow time for people to come on board, it's not black and white. In any large change, some people are enthusiastic from the start. You can begin working with them, which will start to move you in the right direction even before the majority has committed to this new way.

So, it's like being late for an appointment. You want to get there as quickly as you can but if you drive too quickly, you may end up in an accident and not get there at all. In addition, you'll have wounds that need time to heal and prevent you from achieving other things. So it's not that you can't afford to take the time. It's that you can't afford not to.

Stalling at Stages One and Two

Another type of manager or organization is more the "let a 1000 points of light bloom" (I think I got George Bush and Mao Tse-tung mixed up here). He is excellent at Stages One and Two, spending a lot of time making sure people understand what they need to learn and why. They get training, modeling, and coaching, and their award and reward systems are redesigned. And after all that, they sometimes still don't get the shift to a culture that supports intellectual capital.

Companies can stall because they equate the activity intended to implement intellectual capital with the change itself. That is, they believe being trained in tapping intellectual capital is the same as actually tapping it or that understanding the need to change is the same as changing. They throw themselves enthusiastically into the activity and don't assess whether it is making a difference. Some companies have successfully implemented Stages One and Two, but still failed because they don't realize they must eventually enter Stage Three.

While the majority of people will come on board during the first two stages of the process, there is always a minority who cannot or will not, even if aware of the need and after the support and training. So at some point, the organization and the manager must require the change. It is essential to require the same standard of all employees. After all, if one section or person is allowed to stall at Stage Two, why should I go through the agony of change? And if the others aren't obliged to change, you send an important signal to those people who already have: *It didn't really matter.*

But if it does matter, these new behaviors must be made a part of the culture. That is, as in any other culture, they must be associated with sanctions and rewards. Undertaking personal change is too difficult to do if it has no consequences. Unless the change is required of all, people will revert to the familiar old ways and the hopes of making permanent change to the culture are lost.

An important part of imbedding new behaviors involves imposing sanctions on those who don't exhibit them. The sanctions can run from mild to severe, depending both on the behavior required and the person involved. They can include confronting the person with the difference between his words and his actions, denial of promotions or plum assignments or, in some cases, removal from her position or even from the company. These are difficult to contemplate and it's understandable if managers are reluctant to undertake them, but if you don't, all your good efforts in the first two stages will be for naught.

Sharing Knowledge

Most of this chapter has made the assumption you've got some expert in your group chomping at the bit to impart his knowledge and your challenge is in getting the group to accept it. Sometimes however, the scenario is different. Instead of reluctant learners, you have reluctant sharers.

Earlier, we examined how to encourage knowledge to come forward. But this is a slightly different. In this case, you know the employee has the knowledge the team needs but is reluctant to share it. Often people or groups of this mind-set claim their knowledge is so special that it can't (or mustn't) be shared. They are the corporate equivalent of the mystic healer with knowledge too arcane and abstract for our poor brains to comprehend. But that's almost never true. It's more likely that locking up their knowledge is a way to retain power or influence.

To convince your expert to share his knowledge, you need to work through the model of change discussed above. Make him aware of why it's important to share the knowledge. Pay special attention to why he thinks it's so important for him to hold onto his knowledge. If it's his way of feeling important, help him to paint a picture as coach and resident guru that might also fill those needs. If it's his way of ensuring he'll always be valued added, help him adjust his view of value from hoarding to sharing. Reward him for the small sharing he does.

It's unlikely you'll be able to require him to cough up the knowledge because that's the nature of knowledge workers—unless they contribute willingly, it doesn't work. If you can't convince him that sharing his knowledge will meet his needs as well as hoarding does, you won't have a lot of success.

If you're unsuccessful (and it's rarer than most people think), you may have to try other avenues. You might bring in another expert on a short-term assignment. Your own expert will protest naturally and perhaps even maintain that you haven't given him a chance. But if you've honestly tried to take him through awareness and invitation, bringing in someone may be the equivalent of moving onto the requirement stage. You won't be popular but if the knowledge is important, you may have to stand the daggers. And who knows, your reluctant expert may realize that hoarding the knowledge isn't securing his value.

There's no guarantee this will work, but on the other hand, there are relatively few employees who feel so strongly about keeping their knowledge to themselves that they can't be convinced to share in the first two stages. If you do run into one and you must have the knowledge, you need to find a way to introduce it to the group.

What about Speed of Integration?

If you're just starting out in encouraging people to take on new and threatening learning, the first pass through will take longer than you'd like or can afford. As with any other complex skill, employees need time and practice to understand how to use it effectively. The competitive advantage only occurs when you have a group that grabs onto the new knowledge and runs with it as a matter of course. It is a competitive advantage not simply because of the speed of integration but because other organizations have to follow the long and rocky path you've just traversed to get to this level of learning and sharing. That path alone can be a barrier to entry into competition with you. So, it is a competitive advantage to have an organization that learns and shares quickly and deeply, but developing it is not a quick fix. And it is a case of more haste, less speed.

Summary

It's a lot of work. You almost understand why many managers find it easier just to exhort their troops: "Shoulder to the wheel," "We're all in this together," and leave it at that. If exhortation worked, I'd be the first in line to do it, but it doesn't. Creating a climate where people are open both to learning and sharing can't be captured in a slogan. It takes consistent and persistent work to keep signaling how important integrating new knowledge is for your business. It is part of your role as both teacher and keeper of the flame. It's a slog at the beginning, but once it starts to work, you'll be flying. Another way to help your team fly is in the next chapter, which is specifically about teams working together.

Main Points

- The speed with which learning is integrated into an organization is key.
- Learning needs to be both fast and deep.
- Learning doesn't happen if people deny the truth of the learning, believe it doesn't apply to them, or want to reinvent the wheel.
- To help learning, managers must lead staff through three stages: awareness, invitation, and requirement.
- Failure to work through all three stages will result in failure to learn.

CHAPTER 11

ᏛᎧ

Teamness

In the previous chapter, we discussed the importance of employees sharing their knowledge and learning from others. We focused on one-to-one learning and sharing and while that is a critical component of fostering intellectual capital, much of today's work is done in groups. The greater specialization of people's work means that they need the help of one or more of their colleagues to turn out a complete product. In addition, the content and culture of a knowledge economy usually means a new idea is developed through a series of open-ended discussions, collaborating on many aspects, reviewing and refining many iterations.

Teams need to respond quickly, flexibly, and in a coordinated fashion to the market demands, and they can only do that if they work well together. If there is conflict or dissent, sharing and learning are the first casualties. Therefore, a manager needs to encourage his employees to function well together. This chapter is about encouraging this teamness. These thoughts can apply to both intact work teams and task groups. We'll concentrate on intact work teams since they are arguably both the most difficult area to create teamness and the most important.

Teams, Teams, Teams

Studies have shown that, on average, executives spend up to 20 per cent of their time trying to resolve feuds between subordinates. That is one full day out of every week spent resolving issues relating to employees who can't or won't work together! Unfortunately, with the demand for knowledge workers so great, many managers have to deal with people who have trouble working well together. You can't and shouldn't bend your group out of shape to deal with prima donnas, no matter how necessary their skills. Instead, you need to use your greater experience to teach these people, both for the sake of their careers and for your own sanity, how to work together.

Some of you may be thinking: "I can skip this chapter. I have a great team. They hang out together; we have great Christmas parties. And when Mathilda's father died, everybody pulled together so she could get away. I'm doing fine in the team area."

There's a difference between a group that gets along well and one that works well. A group that socializes doesn't necessarily work well together, for example, at resolving work conflicts. In fact, the opposite may be true. A work group that has established close personal bonds may worry more about keeping friends than confronting work problems. On the other hand, a group that never socializes may be very effective if they deal honestly and openly with teamness issues.

Of course, one has an effect on the other. If you like a colleague, you'll go that extra mile, and if a group doesn't like or understand each other, they won't deal with teamness issues well. However, getting along well doesn't guarantee productive teamwork.

Teamwork requires behavior such as:

- sharing information
- sharing work
- looking out for the other's interests
- allowing someone else's best interests to supersede your own occasionally
- dealing with interpersonal issues directly and quickly
- really listening to and encouraging everyone's contribution.

This isn't an exhaustive list, but it gives you an idea of what is required. If your group doesn't engage in these things as a matter of course, keep reading.

A Typical Ineffective Team

Let us look at an example of a work unit not at the level of teamness required to truly leverage its intellectual capital.

Claudia has years of experience and Joe is the new kid on the block with lots of ideas but little background. Whenever Joe suggests a new way to do things, Claudia comes up with a million reasons why it won't work. Worse, her poor opinion of Joe drips from every word. Similarly, Joe's view of Claudia as a barnacle on the ship of progress is evident. The conflict shows up in a number of ways like:

- The Employees Blame Each Other
- Employees Tattle on Each Other
- The Manager Orders Employees to Sort Things Out
- The Employees Go for Coffee
- The Manager Does a Team-Building Exercise

I'll discuss each problem briefly and then cover how the manager can resolve them using the teamness concept.

The Employees Blame Each Other

A project is late, poorly done, or misses the mark. The warring factions point fingers. One insists the other didn't produce his share, goofed off, or sabotaged the project. Unable to decipher who really did what to whom, the manager assigns the two parties to work only on projects that don't intersect. He ends up managing *around* people rather than through them.

Separating the combatants stops the sniping and can be an effective cooling off period, but it's not a long-term solution if a well-functioning team is the objective. In fact, by adjusting the work to skirt the problem, the manager is tacitly condoning the behavior.

Employees Tattle on Each Other

Joe sidles in and says, "Boss, I've noticed Claudia giving customers a hard time if they don't make up their minds right away. I think you should do something." The manager is alarmed. Naturally, he doesn't want customers badly treated and he knows Claudia has a short fuse.

He also knows that Joe has an ax to grind, so he checks out the allegation with other employees. Joe's report is confirmed. He speaks to Claudia who demands to know her accuser. The manager, reluctant to inflame an already difficult situation, won't disclose Joe's name. She refuses to discuss the issue until he does.

The manager had a laudable objective in trying to correct unacceptable behavior to customers, but in doing so, he has exacerbated the tension in the group. He has encouraged tattling by acting on Joe's report and gossip by discussing it with other staff members. Claudia is now focused on the backstabbing, not changing her ways.

It's an untenable position. The manager can't ignore the customer service issue but, by handling it this way, he has done further damage.

The Manager Orders Employees to Sort Things Out

The manager, in exasperation, may order Claudia and Joe to sit up and fly right: "I don't expect you to like each other, but I do expect you to get along. I don't want to hear any more backstabbing and tattling." And he gets his wish. He doesn't hear any more about it. The problem isn't solved; he just doesn't hear any more about it.

Claudia and Joe still stab and gossip—they just get more sophisticated at concealing it. The war is alive and well and the only person who doesn't know it is the manager. The work is still late, incomplete, and poor quality but it can't be the lack of teamwork since his little speech seems to have worked.

The Employees Go for Coffee

Sometimes, Claudia and Joe themselves recognize the poisonous atmosphere. After a particularly acrimonious meeting, they go for coffee. Pleased at the initiative, the manager beams approvingly. Over coffee, the two scrupulously avoid work issues and instead talk about Claudia's passion for golf and Joe's new family. They return from coffee, feeling better about each other.

I'm all for going for coffee together, and it's certainly better than no communication at all, but it doesn't solve the problem. Knowing Claudia's handicap or little Billie's cute way with toilet paper doesn't solve a work conflict. It is true that the more people understand others as people with hopes, desires, and needs, the better the work environment. However it's still not a substitute for working through conflicts.

The only way to resolve them is to address them directly. Talking babies and golf, papers over the crack so we can pretend it isn't there, but the next time the wall needs to bear the weight of a tense situation or tight deadline, the crack will break through again.

Managers often succumb to this thought process themselves when they encourage sporting days or other group activities. I had one boss who insisted that every time his "team" met (we lived all over the country), we cooked dinner together. I developed a healthy respect for my colleague Don's way with pasta, but it did not in the least affect my opinion of him as a backstabbing, underhanded viper.

The Manager Does a Team-Building Exercise

Team-building exercises are usually formal off-site events including all members of a work group with their supervisor. Their intent is to increase productivity by having the group members get to know each other better. It's usually run by an experienced consultant (and if you're going to do it, you should use one).

Managers with troubled groups hope running one will make everything warm and fuzzy and everyone will be fixed, but team-building exercises (TBEs) conducted under these circumstances almost never produce the kind of kick start hoped for. Not surprisingly, because knowing each other better is not the driver of good teamwork.

TBEs help us understand others' preferences and styles—who needs a precise plan before moving forward and who prefers to jump in feet first. These can be valuable pieces of data. However, they will not, in and of themselves, help the group to function better unless they're used to engage in teamlike behaviors. I'll compromise and go with a loosey-goosey plan because I know you're chomping at the bit to get started. You'll take the time to tell me what's going on because it's important to me even if you don't think I really need to know. Unless this happens, TBEs are entertaining but ultimately not useful ways to spend a day.

TBEs can add richness to a team's collective understanding of itself. That alone is a compelling reason for doing them, but they're an adjunct to resolving work conflicts, not a substitute for tackling the real issue—requiring team behavior on the job.

Tackle the Real Issue—Requiring Teamness

Even with the best intentions, your actions can make things worse. You may damage teamness on the road to another objective such as customer service. There is one simple, but *not* easy solution that can resolve all the problems outlined above: focus on the real issue— requiring team behavior from group members. Let's take each of the problems outlined above and discuss how the manager can require teamness.

The Employees Blame Each Other

The project is not delivered on time. Claudia and Joe are in your office, trying to absolve themselves and pass the blame. Here's how the conversation might go if you were requiring teamness:

Claudia:	*Harry, this is another example when Joe didn't produce.*
Joe:	*I didn't produce! I didn't produce! How could I when you didn't give me the data?*
You:	*All right, all right. I'm very disappointed this didn't get out today; it's going to hurt us all the way down the line.*
Claudia:	*Well, I did the best I could. I can't perform miracles!*
You:	*You're saying Joe didn't give you the analysis on time.*
Joe:	*How could I if I didn't get the data from her until yesterday?*
You:	*OK, Joe, just hold. Let's hear Claudia and then you. Claudia, Joe didn't give you the analysis on time?*
Claudia:	*Exactly. He delivered it yesterday at four.*
You:	*Did you remind him you needed it?*
Claudia:	*Why should I? It's not my job to keep track of his work.*
Joe:	*She didn't because she knew she'd only given me the data that same day.*
You:	*OK, Joe. Let's finish with Claudia's side. So, Claudia, even though the analysis didn't arrive when it should, you didn't ask about it?*

Claudia:	*Well, no, why should I? It's not my job.*
You:	(Make your expectations for teamness clear.) *Claudia, it's everybody's job to make the work a success. It's not acceptable to do nothing.*
Joe:	*Exactly. She didn't ask because she knew she'd been late with the data.*
You:	*Well, Joe, let's talk about your part. How much time did you need to do a good job on the data analysis?*
Joe:	*Three days, two in a pinch, but certainly not one.*
You:	*And did you make that clear to Claudia?*
Joe:	*Well, no, why should I? If she'd think about others, it wouldn't be a problem.*
You:	*And when you didn't get the data in time, did you ask Claudia about it?*
Joe:	*Well, no.*
You:	*Sounds to me like both of you have some work to do on acting like a team. I expect people to help make things work. It doesn't sound like either of you put much effort into that.*

Typically, there's a lot more finger-pointing going on. You don't need to sort out who did what to whom in the finest detail. Just gather enough information to decide whether the employees have engaged in team behavior. If not, focus on that and make it clear you require it. Don't get into a battle of who's right or wrong. First, you probably won't be able to figure it out, second, it's irrelevant, and third, it side-tracks everyone from the real issue: teamness.

The Employees Tattle on Each Other

One employee tries to get the other in trouble, using you. How do you handle this situation while still encouraging teamness?

Joe:	*Harry, Claudia gives customers a hard time if they don't make up their minds right away. I think you should do something.*
You:	*Have you spoken to Claudia about this?*
Joe:	*Well, no, I mean I couldn't do that.*
You:	*Why not?*
Joe:	*Well, it's not my place.*
You:	*I think it's everyone's responsibility to point out when things aren't going well.*
Joe:	*I couldn't do that. I mean, she doesn't report to me.*
You:	*No, but she's part of the team. If there's a problem, I expect you to take some responsibility for addressing it.*
Joe:	*Tell her what she's doing wrong? Harry, she'd take it better from you. After all, you're the boss.*
You:	*How can I talk about something I didn't see?*
Joe:	*Come on, Harry. Claudia would snap my head off if I said anything.*
You:	*Well, Joe, if you don't feel comfortable dealing with this one-on-one, I'd be prepared to put customer service on the agenda of the next team meeting. But I'd expect you to raise the issue of how to treat customers. Agreed?*
Joe:	*The agenda thing's a good idea, but I think you should talk about it. It'll carry more weight from you.*
You:	*No, Joe. I know this'll be difficult, but if you want to have this resolved, you need to take some part in getting it fixed. I didn't see what actually happened. You have to raise it.*
Joe:	*Ah, Harry, I'm not good at this.*
You:	*Well, it's a tough one, for sure. Let's talk about how you could tackle it in the meeting. Any ideas?*

We'll leave this conversation here and go into how to coach Joe later. A couple of comments on this one. The manager didn't require that Joe address the issue of Claudia's behavior head-on. Instead, he provided a vehicle for broadening it into a general discussion. While direct feedback is necessary in the longer-term, attacking it head-on at this early stage may be counterproductive and an acceptable interim step is a discussion of the issue at a high level. In this, as in any other personal change, small steps are usually best. Once Joe has some confidence handling what comes up in this controlled environment, you can push him to raise other issues more directly.

Joe may think you're wimping out. Obviously, he wants to dump the problem in your lap. In fact, he still thinks it's his job is to identify sticky, unpleasant situations and yours to resolve them. Anything which deviates (especially something requiring him to take responsibility for sorting it out) is likely to prompt a feeling that you're inadequate, not him. It is your job as teacher to help him understand that he and the others must take responsibility for the well-being of the team.

It is difficult living with this covert disappointment. You want to be seen as a dynamic, in-charge manager. Sitting back and letting others work out the problem isn't your style. But the extent to which you give in to the old, comfortable way, robs Joe of the time and space to learn the new one. You build teamness by building capacity and skills in individuals. Everyone must learn new ways of relating to be successful and your job is to foster that. You may have to live with the perception that you're not a "real" leader until employees begin to understand both that your role as team leader is exactly what you're doing and that their own behavior must change for them to become truly a team.

The Manager Orders Employees to Sort Things Out

It's tempting to just tell employees to sort things out for themselves. Although I've said as much myself, I now believe it's an inadequate discharge of a manager's duties. Just as you're learning how to lead a team, so employees are learning how to be team members. While they might eventually figure it out on their own, a manager has a responsibility to foster how quickly and how well people change. He can do this by helping to resolve the situation. Let's continue with the conversation started above:

You:	*No, Joe, I know this'll be difficult, but if you want to have it resolved, you need to take some part in getting it fixed. I didn't see what actually happened. You have to raise it.*
Joe:	*Ah, Harry, I'm not good at this.*
You:	*Well, it's a tough one, for sure. Let's talk about how you could tackle it in the meeting. Any ideas?*
Joe:	*Yes—get you to do it.*
You:	*Sorry, no can do. What about raising it as a general topic? For example, how about something like: "Some of us are real experts in the product line. Sometimes, it's hard to remember that the options can confuse customers. I think we need to remember to slow down and take our time."*
Joe:	*No way, Harry. Claudia will see through that in a minute. She'll jump on me right away.*
You:	*What do you think she would say?*
Joe:	*Are you saying I'm short with customers, Joe Black?*
You:	*And what could you say?*
Joe:	*Well, I don't know. . . back off, I guess.*
You:	*Why don't you say what you think? How about, "Well, Claudia, I've noticed it a couple of times. It must be kind of frustrating dealing with know-nothing clients when you're so knowledgeable."*
Joe:	*And she'd say, "I never do that. Don't accuse me of being rude to customers, Joe Black."*
You:	*What could you say then?*
Joe:	*Well, I guess I could say, "I'm not trying to accuse you of anything."*
You:	*Right, and maybe add something like, "But it's easy for all of us to get pressured by the amount of work we have and customer demands."*
Joe:	*Well, that's true enough, and Claudia helps out the new employees too.*

You:	*Great, say that too.*
Joe:	*Sure, I can say that, but Claudia's still going to be mad.*
You:	*Well, you may be right. But things are never going to get fixed if we don't speak up. I'm really glad you're going to do this, Joe.*
Joe:	*Well, we'll see.*

It's possible Joe's predictions are right and Claudia will get angry at the meeting. She may be upset either because Joe doesn't phrase things tactfully, or she resists the feedback, or he's wrong. It's possible the conversation will be somewhat acrimonious.

Don't despair. It's a natural outcome when you violate expectations of how people are supposed to relate to each other. If people are used to conflict being buried, they'll often react angrily to attempts to name it and discuss it. Getting angry forces the conflict back underground and returns things to the status quo. That's not a good state, not viable in the longer term, but at least it is not painful right at the moment. So, raising team issues may look like it didn't work. However, you've started the process simply by challenging the assumption that certain issues are not discussable. The next time will be easier and the time after that, and again, until there's no heat at all but a lot of light.

Getting to a state where issues can be laid on the table without offense requires practice. It's your job as teacher not to let this opportunity to strengthen teamness be forced underground. You need to keep insisting that the issues be raised to the light. If you don't, no one else will. You're the only one with the position power to require demonstrations of teamness.

However, don't look for perfection either from yourself in how you handle the situations nor in the players involved. If this were easy, you would have aced it long ago. Expect to make mistakes, to raise issues at the wrong time, to push too hard, not to push hard enough, to zig when you should have zagged. That is all par for the course.

Nor should you expect steady improvement. Things will improve but not in a straight line. In fact, things are likely to get worse before they get better. Claudia may believe you're taking Joe's side. You may need to discuss your motivation with her and even then, she may prefer her own interpretation of favoritism. Do it anyway. If you consistently raise important issues without respect to who's to blame, over time she and all the others will come to believe that you are sincere.

The Employees Go for Coffee

Even after the conversation and coaching, Joe may not bring up his concern at the meeting. If you prompt him during it, he may deny he has anything to raise. If that happens, just let it drop, but talk to him later. Here's how that conversation might go:

You:	*Joe, got a minute? I wanted to talk about today's meeting.*
Joe:	*Well, not really Harry. I mean, I've got to get this stuff up front.*
You:	*It will just take a minute.*
Joe:	*Well, OK.*
You:	*I was surprised you didn't raise handling customers.*
Joe:	*Well, I thought about it and decided it wasn't worth it. It's OK. Claudia and I went on our break together today and everything's fine.*
You:	*So, you talked about it?*
Joe:	*About the customer stuff? Well, no, but things are fine, honestly.*
You:	*You mean, you don't think Claudia will be rude anymore?*
Joe:	*Well, I don't know about that. No, I meant the situation between Claudia and me is all cleared up.*
You:	*Well, I'm glad that's settled, but it doesn't solve the rudeness issue. I think it's an important one.*
Joe:	*Harry, I just don't feel comfortable bringing it up.*
You:	*Joe, I understand that. It's difficult to raise these questions, especially when someone might take offense, but do you think it's an important one?*

Joe:	*Well, yes. We're going to scare away all our customers.*
You:	*I agree. So, if it's important, it needs to be raised. We can't be an effective team if we can't talk about what prevents us from being the best we can be.*
Joe:	*I suppose so, but why can't you raise it?*
You:	*If I had seen it, I would, but I didn't. Every team member should raise issues affecting the team.*
Joe:	*I guess you're right.*
You:	*So, you'll bring it up next week?*
Joe:	*I guess so.*

At this point, poor Joe's probably pretty sorry he brought up the matter in the first place and may not raise others for fear you'll make him take some responsibility for them. Since that's exactly what you would do, he's not wrong. There is no easy answer to this, but over time, Joe should come to feel more comfortable raising teamness issues after he has had some success in resolving them. To help him, ensure the whole team has conflict resolution training, but remember that training is *not* a substitute for requiring teamness—it's just a support. In addition, don't send just Joe on the course. He's not the "problem" to be fixed; everyone needs the help.

The Manager Does a Team-Building Exercise

If Joe raises the issue at the meeting, that in and of itself, will be an advance in teamness although it probably won't solve the underlying conflict between Claudia and Joe. They will probably continue to have problems working together. Reports may still be late or incomplete. Again, you have a role in helping to resolve this. A day or so after the latest piece of unacceptable work (but not much later), get both of them in a room. Make certain you have adequate time to talk; otherwise, when things get tough, someone will make the excuse of another commitment to avoid continuing. Here's now that encounter might play out:

You:	*Claudia, Joe, I've called you in today because of the continuing trouble you seem to be having. Last week's report was an example. I want to talk about what's not working and how to make it better.*
Claudia:	*Well, Harry, you already know what I think.*
You:	*I'm not sure I do. What do you think the problem is?*
Claudia:	*Well, obviously, Joe doesn't have enough experience to do the job.*
Joe:	*What do you mean by that?*
You:	*Joe, please let Claudia finish. I'll make sure you have airtime too.*
Claudia:	*He's bellyaching about having to do the analysis in a day. I could have, no problem.*
Joe:	*So why didn't you, then?*
You:	*Joe, please. So, Claudia, you could have done the analysis in a day. How does that relate to the situation?*
Claudia:	*What I said. Joe doesn't have enough experience to do a quick turnaround.*
You:	*Everyone knows you've got the most experience, but it makes sense to me that less experienced people will take a little more time. Doesn't it to you?*
Claudia:	*I suppose so.*
You:	*So, help me again. How does that relate?*
Claudia:	*Well, if Joe would just do things the way he's supposed to, he could be as fast as anyone.*
Joe:	*I suppose you mean the new analysis. Boy, are you rigid. Your way is the only way.*
You:	*You did a new analysis, Joe?*
Joe:	*Yes, and Ms Know-it-all didn't want me to.*
Claudia:	*Because it was a waste of time. It didn't tell us anything we didn't already know.*

Joe:	*But we didn't know that until it was done.*
You:	*Hold it, hold it! Slow down a bit. First of all, Joe, calling people names isn't going to get us anywhere. Let's just cool it on that, OK? Let's see if I've got this straight. Joe did a new analysis and Claudia thought it was a waste of time.*
Claudia and Joe (together):	*Right!*
You:	*So why did this cause a problem?*
Joe:	*Exactly. I didn't see why I couldn't try something new.*
Claudia:	*Not when it made us late with the report.*
You:	*Joe, if you hadn't tried out the new analysis, could you have completed the analysis in a day?*
Joe:	*I guess so.*
You:	*If a quick turnaround was needed to help Claudia, I don't see fooling around with something new.*
Joe:	*Well, maybe. But I want to do things my way.*
You:	*Sure, but not when other team members suffer for it.*
Joe:	*Well, maybe.*
You:	*And Claudia, I'm concerned that you're discouraging Joe from trying out something new.*
Claudia:	*I know what works.*
You:	*And how did you get so experienced? Didn't you experiment yourself when you started out? Maybe Joe needs the same latitude.*
Claudia:	*Well, maybe.*
You:	*I'm glad we talked this one through but I'm concerned how you two can work out other differences. What can you do to improve the relationship? Claudia?*
Claudia:	*I suppose I could let Joe fool around with the analysis when it isn't urgent.*

You:	*OK, but what else could be done to tackle other problems you might have?*
Claudia:	*I don't know. Talk about them, I guess.*
You:	*Good idea. And you, Joe?*
Joe:	*I guess I could have mentioned I needed the data earlier. And I guess I could bring up what's bugging me when it happens.*
You:	*I know this is tough to do, but I think you've hit on what's important. You can't solve things you can't talk about. I'm really pleased you're both willing to do that.*

This one conversation will not solve the problems between Claudia and Joe. It's likely you'll have to haul them back in for another talk or even a series of talks. This is to be expected. Changing ingrained ways of relating is difficult and can only be done in stages, especially when mutual distrust must be overcome. Each time you work with them, you help build their skills. The first time, they committed to talking about the problem. Likely, this discussion will occur only when things have gotten to the boiling point again. If you can talk to them about that incident, you can get them to agree to raise a problem before it escalates and not after the fact. Although it's time-consuming, messy, and possibly frustrating, pulling them back in signals your seriousness about working this out.

Once people have an inkling of what's required of a team member, holding formal team-building sessions can be very useful. Claudia and Joe can talk about where their work styles clash. Possibly Claudia is offended Joe won't tap her fount of experience. Joe, on the other hand, may truly have some interesting new ways of doing things. If these understandings surface, they help team members adjust their own behavior and be more tolerant of others.

A formal team-building session is quite concentrated and focused as opposed to the slow build-up of skills illustrated here. Don't try to tackle this yourself—use a consultant. It can be a powder keg when very difficult personal issues arise. For example, Claudia may realize she's been trying to control work because her personal life is so out of control. This may be a devastating insight. Someone experienced in helping people through this is needed. Team-building exercises are powerful adjuncts to teamness but their power can cut both ways. Only people skilled in this type of intervention should attempt it, otherwise, you're courting disaster and more importantly, damage to one or more team members.

Steps To Developing Teamness

In these sets of conversations, you've seen how you could use the concept of teamness to shape your group's interactions. In all cases, the conversations have followed the same flow of making it clear what you expect, talking about how to be a team member, discussing how to improve, getting at the root cause of the problem, and requiring that everyone take responsibility for the well-being of the team. Let's talk a little about each one of these.

Make It Clear What You Expect

Employees often don't know what being a team member means. Although it may seem self-evident, it isn't, and that's the reason professional sports teams don't just throw a group of top athletes in a room and hope for the best. They work at working together. You need to do the same with your team. Set the expectation that they will (at minimum):

- share information
- share work when necessary to get the job done
- look out for the other's interests
- allow someone else's best interests to occasionally supersede their own
- deal with conflict directly and quickly
- listen to and encourage everyone's contribution

You don't have to publish a list, but you should take any opportunity to make these clear.

Talk About How to Be a Team Member

In addition, people often have trouble imagining what they could do differently to resolve a difficult situation. They're so used to acting one way, they can't break the mold. Encouraging them to think through the situation and coaching them on what they might do or say, are ways to help promote an understanding of teamness.

Discuss How to Improve

Help team members apply the solution to one team problem more generally. You can start by asking them to identify how they would handle a similar problem in the future and then gradually expand it to a principle of operation. The broader the view of teamness, the more it will govern all situations.

Get at the Root Cause

As noted above, identifying actions to improve the situation is an important step along the road to teamness but unless they come from a real understanding of and respect for the differences of others, these actions are merely mechanistic or pro forma. This is where team-building exercises can be very powerful. It can move Claudia, for example, from simply *allowing* Joe to experiment to realizing it helps the group innovate. Claudia moves from tolerating an idiosyncrasy to respecting a difference.

Require Everyone to Take Responsibility for the Well-Being of the Team

Only the leader can require and enforce teamness, but every team member must eventually take responsibility for acting as a team member and for calling others who stray. In the beginning, it's to be expected that work unit members will be hesitant. Most would prefer to avoid conflict. That is understandable, but you have to keep requiring teamness by pushing the responsibility back onto them. Help them set up the right situations, coach them on what to say and how to act, but don't do it for them. Otherwise, you'll end up being the only one who cares about and is working towards teamness. And a one-person team isn't a team at all.

Keep Plugging at It

This is hard on you and hard on your employees. You'll find that right when you think you've got it licked, something happens to show you in no uncertain terms that you do not. Don't be discouraged if things don't work out wonderfully or change immediately. This kind of change never goes quickly or smoothly, but if you keep focused on raising the issues and coaching team members, you will eventually make a difference.

Outside Help

You will need help to do a formal team-building exercise, and there are other times when outside help can be useful: training for staff, coaching for you, and if you are part of the problem.

Provide Training for Staff

There are many excellent trainers and training to address interpersonal conflict questions but some are little more than feel-good training—the equivalent of pouring money down the drain. The best recommendation is from someone who's taken the course. Failing that, look for training objectives that fit yours, then send one person from the group. If she likes it, everyone can take it. Even mediocre training can help, but given the investment in time and money, it's worth having someone research the product.

Provide Coaching for You

Most managers progressed because they were good with finances and other resources. If they were also good leaders—people *wanted* to follow them as opposed to *had* to—it was a bonus for the employees but otherwise not very important. This is changing. Organizations are beginning to see good leaders as an essential component to effective management of knowledge workers. The problem is that most managers weren't recruited for their leadership skills, they haven't been reinforced or rewarded, and they are not easy to develop overnight. You can't discuss team problems with your employees, you may not have work colleagues sophisticated or trusted enough to confide in, and it may be a career-limiting move to do so with your boss. You may need some help. A good consultant, executive coach, or human resources professional can help.

Are You Part of the Problem?

If you've managed the group for more than a year or so, you should consider whether you have reinforced or even created any difficulties that exist. For example, if you've typically kept warring parties separated, you've tacitly supported the idea that this unteam-like behavior was acceptable.

Even more difficult to contemplate is that your management style may be causing part of the problem. For example, you may tend to reassign projects when progress isn't fast enough, or you may favor one person over another. It may be that, however inadvertently, you've created the problem that now needs solving.

To address this problem you may have to recognize the truth of what Einstein said: "The significant problems we face cannot be solved at the same level of thinking we were at when we created them." If you try to resolve the problem with the same resources, mind-set, and experience that created the problem in the first place, it's unlikely you'll have much success. You need an infusion of new thinking, a challenge to your own ways of looking at things, and perhaps even new skills. If you conclude you played a part in creating the problem, the right thing, the courageous thing, is to seek outside help.

How do you know if you're part of the problem? Frankly, you don't. Large silences when you talk of teamwork may give you a clue, but that might as easily be resistance. You can handle this in one of two ways. The first is to proceed, in the absence of compelling data to the contrary, to work on teamness collaboratively, and bring in someone only if that doesn't work. The second option is to ask for help from someone immediately to offset the possibility you have a blind spot.

I'd lean toward the former. It'll be harder and may be a false start, but the more you deal with the issues of teamness directly, the better model you are for the staff, the more learning you'll acquire, and the more effective you'll be in the long run. But it's not going to be easy.

All this takes time and it's uncomfortable to boot. You have other fish to fry—like running the business. I wish I could help. If I could speed up how quickly people change, I'd bottle it, sell it, make billions, and retire to write esoteric novels that explore the darker side of life. Wanting it doesn't make it so. Losing weight, quitting smoking, are all *easy* compared to changing how you relate. It's going to take time and it's going to be messy. You'll have to keep pushing even when everyone else has thrown in the towel and is urging you to do the same.

On the other hand when you have been able to deal successfully with these teamness issues, real teams have a power and excitement that can be matched by little else in the work world. They give meaning and value to even the most mundane work. It is one of the great work experiences that you can give to yourself and to those who work for you. It is worth the effort, and it is essential if you really want to tap the intellectual capital of your people.

Summary

Today, more and more work is being done in teams, but if the team can't or doesn't exhibit teamness behaviors like sharing information and work, it will not be effective. The manager has a role in setting expectations and coaching members to meet them. Along the way, she may need coaching herself, especially if she suspects she has inadvertently caused part of the problem.

Both individuals and teams need to be encouraged to engage in the kind of behavior which will leverage the organization's intellectual capital. They can be encouraged to do so by the type of reward system put in place. This is covered in the next chapter.

Main Points

- Because the demand for knowledge workers is so great, every worker is needed, even if their ability to work well in a team is not well-developed.

- Since so much of today's work is done in teams, it is important to foster this skill in all team members.

- Teamness consists of sharing information, sharing work, looking out for the others' interests, dealing with interpersonal issues directly and quickly, and encouraging everyones' contribution.

- Managers often have to deal with difficult interpersonal relationships in order to develop an effective team.

CHAPTER 12

೦೦

Rewarding Knowledge

In their 1997 report, *Fortune* found that the single most reliable predictor of being "most admired" as a company was the ability to attract and retain employees.[1] And of course, *Fortune* being *Fortune* and not Frances Horibe, their definition of "most admired" is not "gosh, you're a really fun person and let's do lunch soon," but whether you can light up the eyes of those on Wall Street, Bay Street, and all the other financial streets around the world.

It makes eminent sense that the ability to hold onto good employees translates into profits. People have always *been* the means of production; what's new is that they also now *own* the means of production—their brainpower. Given this consolidation of power in employee hands (and minds), it's not surprising an organization's ability to attract and retain them is key.

In previous chapters, we've talked about how managers can attract and retain employees by consulting, involving, and encouraging learning, but in addition to these, how a company rewards its employees contributes heavily to their satisfaction and retention. There are three main types of reward:

- **Money.** This includes bonuses, incentive programs, profit sharing, stock options, as well as just plain salary. It is often assumed

---

[1] "Key to Success: People, People, People," *Fortune* (October 27, 1997): 232.

that money is not just the main, but the only way, to keep people. We've already broached this, but we'll explore its role farther in this chapter.

- **Personal.** A well-timed pat on the back, a "well done" written across a report, a moment of public praise for some background work, is by far and away the most powerful way to recognize people. When the money is taken for granted and the plaques gather dust, these are remembered. It is a powerful motivator in and of itself and gives meaning to the money and the awards.

- **Award Programs.** Many companies have formal award programs. "Employee of the Month" certificates, "Most Valuable Contribution" plaques, instant awards, all have a process in place to hand them out, but doing it well can be the difference between the program creating the pride it's intended to or producing just another hunk of wood. The latter part of the chapter will be all about that.

Money Rewards

Paying more for any commodity in demand is an understandable and automatic assumption. Knowledge workers command a higher price in the marketplace than their low-knowledge counterparts and money has a role in attracting and retaining these employees. But while this view is understandable, it is also puzzling that managers seem to focus primarily on money when trying to attract and retain knowledge workers. Let's talk about why it is a puzzling phenomena.

Competing on Price

The first puzzlement comes from the difference between how we operate in the external and the internal marketplaces. One of the hard fought understandings (which some industries have yet to get, surprisingly) is that competing on price in the marketplace is the road to disaster. Your competitor will always match your price and force you into further concessions until your margins are so narrow, or nonexistent, that it may not make sense to stay in business. Price is important but the true competitive edge comes from the service you provide around the products and how quickly and frequently innovations to them reach the market.

So, knowing that competing on price doesn't work externally, why does it make sense to do it internally? The same logic applies. In fact, professional sports is a cautionary tale for us all. Yes, individual players are certainly much wealthier than they would have been in the pre-outrageous salary days, but has any game improved because of the inflated salaries? I don't think so. Over the longer term, paying higher and higher salaries for your "players" doesn't improve your game either and can be a recipe for disaster if your attractiveness to customers stays stable as your salary costs rise.

The Law of Diminishing Returns

Except for some rare cases, money starts to lose its value as a motivator past a certain point. Once people feel their lifestyle is comfortable, increasingly larger amounts of money are needed to act as an inducement. If you are in a McJob, a raise of $5000 would be a powerful inducement, but if you're presently doing OK, would the same amount cause you to change jobs and cities? Probably not for the money alone. Would $50,000? Getting interesting. At the other end of the scale, money can stop having any effect at all. Seinfeld was offered $5 million *a show* to do one more season, and he turned it down.

Since most knowledge workers are paid a decent, even comfortable, wage, unless you're able to offer over-the-top money, you're probably out of luck.

Do You Really Want that Type of Worker?

Even if you were able to successfully bait your lure with money and snag scarce knowledge workers, how long will you keep them? A knowledge worker who came to you primarily because of the money, will be off like a shot when a better offer comes along. Are they any way to build your intellectual capital? Mercenaries have a bad name no matter their field of endeavor.

You Know Money Alone Doesn't Work

You probably know from your own experience that money is not a prime motivator. Think about it. Have you ever been in a job where the money was okay or even excellent, but you were so miserable, so unvalued, so trampled on, that you just couldn't take it? Did the money keep you at that job or did you move heaven and earth to get out? Most of us do the latter. At some point, the money simply isn't enough to keep you.

Similarly, even when you've gotten a big raise, how long did it take before it stopped having a glow? How long before you stopped noticing the difference it made in your paycheck and began to think of it as your due? One paycheck? Two? Your employees aren't any different. More money doesn't necessarily buy loyalty or the urge to contribute.

Naturally, like all other sweeping generalizations, there are some exceptions. Sometimes people hang in with a job because they don't want to lose the pension or the stock options, but if their prime motive for staying is to avoid losing their due, how motivated and innovative will these knowledge workers be, how eager and excited about contributing to the company? You've retained their hands and presence when what you need to retain are their minds, spirits, and hearts. Money might keep them there but it won't matter unless you can also engage their intellectual capital.

Of course, money is still important but in today's knowledge economy, its importance in motivating and retaining knowledge workers can be overblown. As Arie de Geus notes in his *Harvard Business Review* study of long-lived companies: "Money is not considered a positive motivator in a [long-lived] company. If money is insufficient, people will become dissatisfied, but adding money above the threshold of sufficient pay will not motivate people to give more to the company...the essence of the underlying contract is mutual trust. Individuals understand that in exchange for their effort and commitment, the company will help them develop their potential."[2]

So money is certainly important, but it isn't the driver many people think it is. Assuming it's the be-all and end-all precludes looking at other rewards that can be your competitive edge in attracting and retaining employees.

Personal Rewards

It's interesting to look at the awards I've collected over the years. There's that handsome plaque I keep shifting to make room for more

---

[2] Arie de Geus, "The Living Company," *Harvard Business Review* (March-April, 1997): 58.

recent stuff, and the letter from the board, extolling my contribution on some long-forgotten project. My name's misspelled. Then, there's the crumpled note, with the scrawly writing that I can barely make out but know without looking: "Fantastic job, Frances! Way to go!" That's the one I reread, smooth out, and keep in a place of honor, if not in the cupboard, then certainly in my heart.

So, why is the crumpled piece of paper so important? I think we all know. It's the one vested with meaning and purpose, the one I remember my boss's face lighting up with excitement and enthusiasm. The others, while more handsome and I am sure equally well intended, lack the same power. We need to harness *that* power in rewarding employees.

Despite how important it is to recognize people's contributions, by and large, managers are incredibly bad at it. Generally, they just don't to it, or if they do, it's as if every word of praise deducts a dollar from their personal bank accounts. Some managers praise only when the race has been won. They studiously avoid kudos during the race or in the trials, perhaps believing applause will weaken the will to get to the finish line. When I try to think of any of my employees who were like that, I can only come up with an ex-cleaning lady. If I mentioned how clean the fridge was, it never got cleaned again. If I praised how meticulously she dusted, she stopped being as careful. It took me a long time to figure out that she saw praise as permission to relax rather than a spur to more effort.

Over the course of your career as a manager, how many of your employees have had a similar problem—one, two, three if you've been really unlucky? That's still a tiny minority, and even if there are a couple around, does it makes sense to shape your use of such a powerful tool so a handful won't get the drop on you? If you do, you lose an important way to mold the behavior you need in your team.

Finally, there are some managers who simply don't understand how important approval is to employees and are careless in their attention. When you are running as fast as you can and trying to cope with everything that's coming down the pipe, it's hard to remember that people need to be reminded they have made, and are making, a difference, and yet, you are usually the only person who can give them that. Yes, there are other sources—peers, family, friends—but it isn't the same. About work, your praise is the most important because you represent the company. So try to carve out some time to do it.

What to Praise and How to Do It

There's so much worthy of praise as we move through and into this information age. Personal change certainly, since it's the stuff of heroes, but there are plenty of others—progress toward the strategic goal, making the jump from today to tomorrow, delivering on the present mandate while adjusting to the new. But be careful how you choose. Here are some things to keep in mind:

- Praise Something the Employee Cares About
- Praise Patterns as Well as Extraordinary Effort
- Praise the Characteristic/Trait Not Just the Activity
- Praise Only What You Believe In
- Separate Praise and Opportunities for Improvement
- Tell the Person How You Really Feel

Praise Something the Employee Cares About

I had a boss who was truly trying to praise more, but never got it right. "Gosh, I really like how you get right to work in the morning; gee, you staple well; I really admire how neat your desk is." Okay, the last one may appeal to neat freaks, but generally, these "kudos" damn with faint praise. Praise what the employee cares about.

Things you might say:
"Your design was really elegant. I don't think I've ever seen a more efficient one. You did a great job."
"I see how much effort you put into including everyone. I know it can be frustrating, but I can see the progress."

Things you probably shouldn't:
"This will really help our third quarter profits." This might make *you* happy but the employee?
"This exceeds the standards, although just barely." Most people prefer praise that doesn't have a sour aftertaste. Don't deduct the pride from the praise.

Praise Patterns as Well as Extraordinary Effort

It's easier to know when an employee has put in a great deal of over-time or come up with a home run. It's less obvious when people doggedly work toward their goal. Yet, given how important is it is to make haste slowly, the latter is very worthy of praise. Home runs are flashy and sexy but consistent one-base hits are what really move the game forward.

Things you might say:

"I've noticed you're holding your own in the discussions. I know this is hard for you, but it looks like it's working."

"The reaction to your presentation was really positive. I think you honed in on what they needed."

Things you probably shouldn't:

"It's great that you've conquered that." Again, this is doubtful. It gives me the impression that no more improvement is necessary. There aren't very many times when I can imagine you'd want to send *that* message.

Praise the Characteristic/Trait Not Just the Activity

A particular behavior usually triggers the praise—a report well done, a project delivered early. However, to encourage more of the same, praise the characteristic rather than the behavior.

Things you might say:

"That report was great. Really concise but covering all the objections. You're really good at zeroing in on the main point."

"You were absolutely right about the sales projections. Nobody can beat you in nosing out what the customer wants."

Things you probably shouldn't:

"I'm glad you got the project in early." Sounds a bit naked, doesn't it? More like stating the facts than praise. You need to add something personal like: *"You're so efficient. These things appear almost before we know we need them."*

Praise Only What You Believe In

When leaders are convinced of the power of praise, they often overuse it. It's neither necessary nor useful to go on a recognition rampage. You dilute the power if you spread it around indiscriminately.

That doesn't mean avoiding lavish or frequent praise. Quite the contrary—I think you should praise just as lavishly and as frequently as your internal praise meter will allow, but always about what is praiseworthy. If you don't believe it yourself, people will sense it, and your praise will rightfully be dismissed as insincere.

Things you might say/ Things you probably shouldn't:
I'm not going to fill anything in here since this depends on what you think. One person's genuine praise may feel phony to another.

Separate Praise and Opportunities for Improvement.

Few things are ever perfect; almost everything can stand some improvement. It's natural to say, "That was great but next time, you could..." It's also natural not to hear the "That was great" part and hear only the "but." So, stifle the suggestions when you're praising.

You can still make the suggestions, but it's a matter of timing. Praise first. Full stop. Go away. Do something else. Come back later to say: "Jeff, I had some ideas to make things even better." It may be more efficient to knock off the praise and the criticism in one go, but it's not effective.

Things you might say:
"I liked the presentation. Clear and to the point. You could tell by the discussion that the others did too."
"Your ability to gain consensus is phenomenal. I don't think we could have gotten to this point without you."

Things you probably shouldn't:
"The presentation went really well, but you have an annoying habit of clearing your throat frequently. It's very distracting."
"I'm pleased you reached consensus, but we had to give a lot away to get it. I wouldn't have compromised on the scheduling."

There are times when it's appropriate to mix praise and suggestion but that's usually when the main intent is correction and not recognition. That's perfectly okay, just don't expect the praise to be remembered.

Tell the Person How You Really Feel

I admit this is for the advanced among you. If you can, tell the employee how you feel about what's happened.

Things you might say:
"The way you handled that argument—I was really proud of you."
"It was a tough call, but I think the right one. I admire your ability to take a stand."

Things you probably shouldn't:
"You've done an excellent job, don't get me wrong, but I don't think it's fair to other employees that you get all the attention." Well, yes, it is how you feel and might even be quite legitimate, but it's not praise. Praise is about the person without caveats, conditions, or consequences.
"I just feel overwhelmed by your achievement. You're a real Einstein. I feel honored to be in your presence." Overblown gushing is just as bad as silence. Say what you mean but mean it from the heart.

Notice how frequently the word *you* figures in these conversations. This is about praise so it's "You did a good job" not "The project is going well." See the difference? The second is about the work, the first is praise. Also, praise goes into specifics. People, particularly knowledge workers, need to know exactly how and what they're doing well. Just as you may have trouble knowing when an output of a knowledge worker is what you want, they are also sometimes not sure that their production is what the organization needs. Your praise will both feed the need for recognition and encourage them along the right path.

Keep these points in mind when you praise. It may seem like a lot but it's worth it to see someone's shoulders straighten a little more, to see the aw-shucks smile, to find out that the do-I-care employee has a wife who can repeat what you said word for word. You have a tremendous power to influence through recognition. Using it will provide meaning and value to the work and thus increase the likelihood that your knowledge workers both feel committed to the company and want to stay.

Award Programs

Personal recognition is a powerful way to reward employees one-on-one. Formal recognition programs can have the same power but, they can run the gamut. They can be excruciatingly embarrassing and even phony events or they can be moments, rare in our lives and cherished because of that, when our hearts are touched in such a special way that it never leaves us. They can be moments when the best of who we are and can be is honored.

Needless to say, we all hope that our company's recognition programs are more inspiring than embarrassing, but in my experience that generally isn't the case. Organizations often spend a lot of time and effort setting up these programs, only to have them languish after the first flurry of interest. Nominations typically drop off to almost nothing and award winners often spend all of thirty seconds reading the plaque before tossing it into a drawer.

Formal recognition programs often lose sight of their true intent. If they are just a matter of form, they're worse than useless, so why bother? Unless formal recognition programs help people stand a little taller and a little prouder, they have no value. So, the critical factor in recognition programs is their ability to create a sense of pride and honor in their recipients.

Decide What You Want From an Award Program

It seems kind of obvious to say "decide what you want from an award program," but it's often not done. In some companies, it seems anyone can win an award for anything— showing up consistently, using the dental plan least, moving mountains, and doing their regular job—all seem to be equally important, at least if the awards attached to them are any indication.

If you're revamping your awards program (or starting one), think about what's important to the company. Loyalty or labor? Money or moxie? Fearlessness or fortitude? If just showing up isn't enough, a perfect attendance award should be questioned. Awards are messages to the staff about what matters.

Also, as with any incentive, you get what you actually reward rather than what you say you're rewarding, so make sure the reward is aligned to your strategic intent. If you're promoting teamwork but still providing big incentives for individual sales achievement, there's a disconnect. The implicit message is, "Forget the rhetoric, just sell like always." Individual incentives in a team environment may be appropriate if you explain how they fit together. If you don't, it's like two people paddling in opposite directions. At very least, you won't go anywhere. At worst, you'll overturn the canoe.

The Dos of an Award Program

One of the peculiar characteristics of knowledge workers is that a great deal of their job satisfaction comes from the knowledge itself—simply knowing a lot, being able to manipulate it, being able to create new knowledge. They derive satisfaction and self-worth from these internal events, which makes it that much harder for external events, like awards, to have meaning and power to shape their behavior in the direction the company desires. Thus, it's critically important that award programs for knowledge workers reward what is clearly valued. There are some things which will help this happen:

- Have Clear Criteria for the Award
- Make the Awards Winnable by All
- Set Up a Ceremony
- Make Each Award Count
- Focus on Personal Recognition
- Consider Letting Peer Groups Choose Award Recipients

Have Clear Criteria for the Award

Getting really clear criteria is a challenge. The interpretation of: "*outstanding achievement*" may vary greatly. Outstanding to me means I've stayed late four days this week but to you it means scaling Mount McKinley in shorts. Try to set out the intent as precisely as you can without getting wrapped in reams of rules.

Clear doesn't necessarily mean tough. You don't have to leap tall buildings in a single bound, but you destroy the credibility of the award if employees' reaction to an announcement is "*He* got the award? Are you kidding?" Clear also doesn't mean exclusive. It doesn't matter how many people get the award. In fact, if the whole company's eligible, that's great. A nonexclusive award might be for exceptional customer service. A significant percentage of the employee population might win this award without its power and pride being diminished.

It is possible to have a few awards whose criteria are less strict. There might be one that can be given on the spur of the moment by a manager catching an employee doing the right things. The awards are often things like dinner for two at a local restaurant, a piece of software for home computers, or even just flowers. These instant awards have the virtue of immediacy, but be prepared for a wide variability in their awarding, with some using it (to your mind) to win popularity and others (to your mind) being too stingy. It's perfectly okay to have a few awards like this, as long as the others have clear criteria.

Make the Awards Winnable by All

Sometimes awards can really only be won by certain categories of employees. "Highest sales" will never go to the shipping clerk even if his work has been instrumental in customers reordering. "Exceptional innovation" may be more generic, especially if it is understood that creativity can be applied to filing systems as well as to product development. If you want to keep the possibility for highest sales, you may want something like "Outstanding achievement in your area of expertise" which would allow both the top salesperson and the top janitor to be eligible.

Set Up a Ceremony

A ceremony or some sort of public recognition opportunity is usually a good idea. The ceremony itself can be lavish spectacle or impromptu staff meeting, a sit-down dinner or coffee all around, the worldwide VP of operations presiding or the unit supervisor. The only important thing is that the words of thanks mean something. The VP or supervisor needs to say what was accomplished, why it's important, what personal qualities of the recipient made it possible, and how proud the company is that this employee has chosen to use his creativity and energy in their service. If the manager can convey that message, the trappings can be as simple or elaborate as you like.

When you're setting up the ceremony, check with the recipient first. Some people are extremely private and having to accept an award publicly (however much they might want the recognition) would be a punishment rather than a reward. The award presenter still conveys the same message, but it might take place in an office cubicle rather than on a stage.

Make Each Award Count

Take a leaf from the marketing department or from politics. Don't announce bunches and bunches of goodies all at once but one at a time so each gets its moment in the limelight. Make it special so the people receiving can feel it.

Focus on Personal Recognition

As already mentioned, the award should be the tangible expression of the personal recognition, not a substitute for it. By all means, hand over the plaque, trophy, painting, carving, or whatever, but accompany it with words that will stay in the recipient's heart and infuse the award itself with the meaning you intend. It is how award programs can have the power to inspire and motivate in the way we all want them to.

Consider Letting Peer Groups Choose Award Recipients

Most managers feel pretty negative about this, seeing it as another loss of control. Actually, there are some good reasons why you shouldn't let peer groups take on this task or delay doing it. If the behavior you're awarding is unclear, retain the process until people understand what's expected. For example, what constitutes team-work or innovation in your context may need some sorting through. Those you honor will illustrate what you're aiming for.

However, handing the process over to employees can have great benefit. Employees almost always know who's doing a great job and who's great at snowing the boss. In addition, there is wonderful power in an award given to you by your peers. And of course, it's a tremendous show of confidence in employees for management to hand them this activity.

The fear that awards will turn into popularity contests is I think overblown. Provided employees buy into the strategic goal, they'll be fine. In fact, as they get rolling, you may have to encourage the awards committee to be less stringent rather than more. If employees take the award seriously, they'll want to make sure it means some-thing.

The Don'ts of an Award Program

Because understanding, working with, and creating new knowledge is a motivator in and of itself for knowledge workers, their need for external awards is lower than it is for other types of workers. However, since companies want to use awards to encourage these workers to continue to contribute, they need to be especially mindful of designing programs that feel phony, routine, or ill-conceived. Some things to avoid in designing an award program:

- Don't Use the "Catalogue" Approach
- Don't Do It for Things Already Rewarded in Another Way
- Don't Start an Award Program When There Are Morale Problems
- Don't Do It as a Substitute for Adequate Pay

Don't Use the Catalogue Approach

Some companies publish a glossy, full-color book of awards available to employees, with the value of the item (clock, CD player, software, stereo system) rising with the importance of the award. For a particular award, an employee usually has the choice of several gifts of comparable value. The intent, laudable in itself, is to allow the employee to chose an award that best suits his tastes. However, this feels like company frequent flyer points. I'm happy to get them, sure, but does it make me proud to be part of this company, able to stand a little straighter, gratified my contribution has been recognized? I don't think so. The value of the award is not how in much it costs but in the sentiment behind it. Awards are not about acquiring consumer electronics. They are about pride.

Don't Do It for Things Already Rewarded in Another Way

Again, this sounds obvious, but the awards lose their power if they're seen as a way to get extra kudos for an adequate job. If they are, you might as well issue them with the paychecks. To avoid this, focus on particularly problematic aspects of your business. For example, an award for Outstanding Improvement might steer people in the right direction.

Don't Start an Awards Program When There Are Morale Problems

For some reason, managers seem to think that awards will address morale problems. If the pay is too low, the supervisors tyrannical, the company policies unfair, the equipment outdated, the safety record abysmal, and the training nonexistent, an award program will not fool anyone into thinking that the company is a great place to work. In fact, in this kind of climate, the awards are seen both as a joke and a crude attempt to manipulate people into feeling good about a bad situation. Instead of pride and loyalty, you get "They gave me this outstanding achievement award. Ha! The real achievement is putting up with this place."

Don't Do It as a Substitute for Adequate Pay

Sometimes, companies have quite large cash awards for a selected few while the base pay for most is inadequate. In a kind of lottery mentality, the thought is that making a big fuss in awarding that one person a cash bonus will fire up others to achieve the same. Wrong. Awards razzmatazz may divert attention from the pay problem, but it's temporary. If you are underpaying, don't expect it to smooth over the problem. It may distract but it won't alleviate. Sooner or later, your knowledge workers will leave for companies that pay the going rate.

Summary

Rewarding people for their work is an important aspect of attracting, retaining, and tapping your human capital. However, an overemphasis on money can blind companies to other ways in which service can be acknowledged. This is particularly important since many of these techniques tap different needs in employees. If those needs (like recognition from peers and a sense of pride) are not met, then money alone will not be powerful enough to keep people engaged.

Money is often used as the only lever in attempting to leverage intellectual capital in part because the other approaches (like communication, consultation, and involvement) require some personal change either on the part of the managers, the employees, or both. In the previous chapters, we've discussed what kind of personal

SECRET REWARDS

A large firm has a secret reward. They offer stock options to people they really want to keep, but you only get to know the *existence* of the reward if you're a VP. Whether the secret is that they value the person or that he's getting stock options is unclear to me. Whichever it is, it's got to be one of the stupidest employer tricks I know about.

Firstly, this is a company that believes that man [sic] lives by money alone, and that they can make the barriers to leaving so high you won't jump. And, as a way to make sure people show up for work, it's fine as long as you aren't all that concerned about whether they bring their minds along with them.

By keeping the award secret, they've also broken a fundamental rule of recognition; other people have to know that you've been recognized or you haven't been. It's the old question about whether a tree falling in a forest makes any sound if no one's there to hear it.

Anyhow, these kinds of secret awards don't stay secret—I know and I'm not even in the company. Eventually, it gets out. And what does it say? That whatever the company pontificates to the contrary, there really are two classes of people. Ones they *really* care about and the others.

Finally, the company doesn't even have the guts to tell people that they value some more than others, and it expects me to give my intellectual capital to it?

If you really value someone's contribution and want them to stay, by all means reward them with stock options or whatever, but do it publicly and honestly. Yes, you may take some flack for picking out certain individuals, and you need to address this. Is it appropriate in your team environment to reward individuals? How does that jive with your mission and values? These are difficult questions with no easy answers, but avoiding them sends a message that, whatever you say, you aren't really serious about creating an environment where everyone feels truly valued.

change is required. In the next chapter, we'll discuss how to encourage personal change.

Main Points

- Money doesn't have the power to attract and retain knowledge workers that most people think it has.
- Money is important but so is personal recognition.
- Most managers need to increase the amount and quality of the personal recognition they give.
- Companies should put greater effort into making their award ceremonies promote a sense of pride and accomplishment.

CHAPTER 13

ᕲᕣ

Being Willing to Change

Much of what we've talked about in the management challenges of structural capital have had to do with the ability of both managers and staff to change their ingrained ways of thinking and doing. Whether it's living with less control as a manager or accepting new learning as an employee, personal change is the hallmark of moving to this new world both of information and of intellectual capital. Personal change is difficult for everyone and needs special attention if the fruits of sharing, learning, and teamness are to be realized in the workplace.

Why can't you fake the new attitudes and mind-sets we've been discussing? After all, there's lots of it going on in organizations: people pretend to support changes they'd lie in front a speeding truck to prevent; they mouth teamwork, caring, and respect and use humiliation, belittling, and manipulation as their modus operandi. Such hollow adherence won't sustain long-term or fundamental organizational change. For the ideas of intellectual capital to become the way of operating, organizational beliefs that support it have to achieve the same automatic adherence as personal ones. For example, you believe truth is important but know there are times when it's inconvenient, embarrassing, and perhaps even threatening to tell it. You might tell the truth even if it meant losing your job, but you'd probably lie to save a life. You have an intuitive sense of those boundaries and don't have to work them through every time you might benefit from lying—you've already settled what's right for you. And people trust your word because you act consistently and within that internal frame.

Once beliefs like fostering intellectual capital reach that level, the same benefits accrue. Employees know you want their ideas because you listen even when it's inconvenient or opposite to what you want to hear. They see you accepting both the bad and the good, but these beliefs don't become automatic without rethinking what's important and what you believe. In short, you have to struggle with some personal change. Without this inner journey, it's all window dressing. You can get people to the window to ooh and aah about the pretty picture, but you won't get them to buy.

Why Is Personal Change So Hard?

Personal change is difficult to accomplish in life as well as at work. Why is that? If I knew the complete answer, I'd be a whole lot slimmer, healthier, and richer. No, I take that back. I probably do know *why* it's hard. It's *making* the change that is the conundrum. (More of that later.) Personal change is hard because:

- It's a Surprise
- It's More Profound than Anticipated
- Meaning Is Vested Even in Details
- It's a Life Issue
- It Has Unanticipated and Unwanted Consequences

It's a Surprise

Everyone seems to start out believing that if they'd only fix the other guy, life would be perfect. We want the benefits of change but we all seem to assume that it should leave us alone. It's something of a surprise when we realize that we have to change also. For example, we want employees to be more innovative but to have that happen, we have to change by allowing and perhaps even encouraging ideas we don't agree with. It's human nature to want the gain without the pain, but things don't work like that. Things get better because the people in the system do different things. You're part of a system that is changing, and you have to change too.

It's More Profound than Anticipated

Once everyone has gotten over the shock that *they* might have to change, almost no one is prepared for the level required or how much it attacks fundamental beliefs.

A social welfare organization was undergoing massive change due to deficit reduction. The social workers' jobs were to help welfare recipients move out of poverty by funding career training. To respect the clients' right to shape their own lives, the social workers felt that the choice of training should be the clients, but the new government required that any assistance directly further self-sufficiency. Thus social workers couldn't approve training if they didn't believe clients had the aptitude.

While the social workers accepted self-sufficiency as a worthwhile goal, the new rule was contrary to their training as well as their personal philosophies. They were helpers, facilitators, and supporters not enforcers, administrators, or economists. It was not simply that they cared about helping people; it was how they defined themselves. Beyond that, the new ruling made them question the value of all their past work to the clients, the organization, and society. By respecting clients' freedom of choice, they wondered whether they'd created dependency on the very system they thought they were liberating clients from.

So even though the social workers might accept the new goal, they must revamp their beliefs in a fundamental way to commit fully to it. They not only had to do things differently but had to change their definition of how they could contribute. When change forces you to consider the value of your work, it's understandable that it might find this difficult to accept.

Meaning Is Vested Even in Details

It's pretty easy to see the big adjustments—change of jobs, a change of bosses, a new process—but in fact, change reaches more deeply into our daily lives. To illustrate, let us look at the debate in a convent in Australia during Vatican II—the reform of the Catholic Church in the sixties. The nuns debated whether to wear new, shorter habits. The younger sisters pointed out how much easier it would be to work in them. They also felt more contemporary dress would be less intimidating to parishioners.

The older nuns were deeply offended by this emphasis on efficiency. To them the wearing of the habit was a link to hundreds of years and thousands of women who had gone before them on whose work they built theirs. It was a daily reminder of an honored and honorable tradition of service and sacrifice. Faced with this, convenience was irrelevant.

From the outside and from another time, this may seem like a fairly simple, even trivial, change—just a redesigned uniform. Except that, as human beings, we vest meaning in everything we do. It wasn't just about a piece of clothing; it was about tradition, honor, and loyalty. It isn't just a piece of work; it's pride, self-esteem, and dignity. The debate was not about hemlines but about values.

While in theory we're just talking about new or old clothing or knowledge, in practice, we're talking about issues vested with a meaning and power which provide sustenance to the user and are a compelling reason why change is unwelcome. It is both our strength and our roadblock.

So, why should I give up the knowledge I possess which has meaning and power simply because somebody else thinks another way is more efficient or more effective? How can you be sure this new way will give the same sense of personal value? In fact, you can't, which explains why personal change is so reluctantly undertaken.

It's a Life Issue

We spend much of our lives adapting to what life throws at us. Some of us do it well and others don't. Some embrace change as opportunity and others see it as threat. If someone had grown up in a family whose parents divorced when he was young, or if they moved a great deal, he may find change upsetting and try to keep most of his adult life, including work, stable. Another person who experienced the same life events may react very differently, welcoming change because it is all she's ever known. Individual reactions are difficult to predict, but generally, it's safe to say that these types of life inclinations spill over into work and help to determine how we react to the need for personal change at work. People's experiences affect how far and how fast they can adapt to work change.

It Has Unanticipated and Unwanted Consequences

Change always seems to have unexpected and unanticipated consequences. Even people who welcome the change are often surprised by its outcomes. Let me use a personal example. I have always wanted to take time off to write. I thought through the financial side, the risk, the possible downsides, and then went ahead.

While I believe I did what was right for me, there were unexpected consequences. I was unprepared for how much difference the lack of a paid, defined role would make. I began to notice that the first thing anyone seemed to ask was "What do you do?" In the past, I had a title, an organization, and through them, an easily communicated capsule of my life. I was unprepared for the assumptions that writing was a cover-up for an inability to keep a job. Not everyone reacted this way. In fact, the vast majority reacted with interest and even admiration but I was unprepared for even that small minority of doubters.

What I have learned—in my gut and not just in my head—is that nothing is purely good or purely bad. However satisfying the result, it didn't come without a price. The price was worth paying; I just didn't realize I'd have to ante up. So it is with all of us. If we look forward to the change, we see the positives and don't realize all the negatives. This is true even if we think we know what we're getting into. If we resist the change, all we can see are the negatives and none of the positives. And you know what? Both are right.

Even if the change is desired (and a lot of time, it isn't), there will be a period when the unexpected consequences will be slapping you in the face every other day. Yes, I want to learn, but I wasn't prepared for the feelings of incompetence. I want people to share their ideas, but I didn't know they'd challenge what I did as their boss. I want things to change, but I didn't think that meant I'd have to change, too.

Change comes as a package deal with both up and down sides. To successfully adapt, you have to see and appreciate both, no matter which view you took at the outset. Thus, it's not surprising that change is a difficult process. It forces us into pathways we didn't expect, in more profound and more varied ways than anticipated, with consequences we didn't realize were possible.

How People Change

There are many theories about how people change and all make intuitive as well as logical sense, but they all boil down to two major tenets: people change slowly, and they're scared while they're changing. If you keep these in mind, you'll understand a lot of the sometimes bizarre behavior you see.

People Change Slowly

People change slowly—more slowly than executives want them to, more slowly than might be needed, and perhaps even more slowly than they themselves might want. You can put just-in-time techniques in place, but you can't ensure just-in-time change because it forces you to give up control, change values, and change your self-image.

Give Up Control

We all like to do things our way, know what to expect, and control our work lives, but the essence of personal change is a willingness to enter that no-man's-land where you don't know what to expect and can't do things your way because there is no "your way" in the new situation.

Change Values

All the examples we've seen speak to this issue. Personal change, whether at work or in one's personal life, often has to do with a reexamination of what we care about. For example, a colleague I know started to suffer severe health problems in his fifties. He knew he needed to lower his stress levels, exercise more, and pay more attention to healthy eating habits. However, his career had always come first. He had made many sacrifices and many more would be necessary to get where he wanted to go. However, to be healthy, he needed to change the value he placed on career. In order to make lasting and sustained personal change, he will have to learn to value success less and to value health more.

Changing what we value is a difficult task. We often don't do it in our personal lives unless some crisis or other important event forces us to and even then it can take a long time to make the change. Thus, it's not surprising that personal change at work is also a lengthy process.

Change Your Self-Image

We all have an image of who we are at work—dynamic, competent, can-do, nurturing, or tough. As the implications of radical change hit, we begin to question what we thought we knew. Can I deliver the way I used to? Do the same rules about taking care of people apply? What does *"tough"* mean now? Is my intuitive sense of priorities still reliable, or do I need to use a different yardstick? If the answers come out any distance from what we're used to, we need to change something. For example, in the past, the managers you most admired were those who made tough decisions, but did it with an eye to alleviating the distress it caused employees, and you've always seen yourself as tough, given that definition. Nowadays, based on who you see being promoted or getting the plum assignments, it looks like the company believes "tough" is making the decisions no matter who it hurts. Given that definition, you need to decide either that you aren't tough or you don't want to be. Anyway you slice it, it means rethinking some part of who you are.

Of course, this doesn't mean change in everything. Most of who you are and what you do will stand you in as good stead in the new world as it did in the old. The problem is you don't know which bits are keepers and which need changing. Thus, everything seems to be up for grabs and may well be.

They're Scared While They're Changing

The second important thing to remember about personal change is that everybody engaged in it is scared. Even if they want to change, even with lots of support, they're still frightened and for good reason.

It's a Step into the Unknown

People fear—and rightly so—that however much they desire the promised land, the journey to it will be through desert and hardship. They must leave the stability and comfort of a present they understand for an uncertain future. Moreover, they have to go through all the pain *before* they know whether it'll actually get them what they want. It's paying the piper before you know whether you'll get the tune you want, or any tune at all.

It's an Emotional as well as a Logical Adjustment

Almost all change is undertaken with at best an intellectual understanding of what will happen. The profound emotional changes that accompany it are never understood. It's nobody's fault, and you can't fix it. It's just the way change happens—first you get it with your head, and then you get it with your heart. They have to come in that order and you can't do both at once. Knowing that you have to change and actually changing are two completely different things. While words are necessary to signal a change is needed or coming, only experience itself will change the heart.

An example is lifetime employment. People understand that they can no longer expect it. There are many things you can do to adjust logically—like keeping your résumé up-to-date and contacting headhunters, but there are deeper matters to accept. You won't have the comfort of familiar faces and tasks; being not yet out of one job but not yet into another will be a way of life; this isn't about your worth but about the way the world is going.

If understanding doesn't eventually advance from the head to the heart, the change will never really take. Even if you go through the motions of developing your network, and so on, you'll always be trying to shoehorn yourself into the old way. For example, you might take a mediocre but stable job rather than gambling on an exciting one with a definite end-date. Thus both emotional and logical adjustment to the change are necessary.

It Takes Courage

The personal courage that undertaking change requires cannot be underestimated. It is frightening and unsettling to look at who you are, how you relate, and what you believe in. This is the stuff of heroes and heroines, but we need to have sympathy for those who cannot summon up the courage. For whatever reason, whether it is the timing in their lives, the cynicism that has crusted over their souls, or a fear so overwhelming it paralyzes rather than energizes, some people will not be able to screw their courage to the sticking place. That realization alone will be devastating.

Personal change is an inner journey for all of us. The hills we have to climb, the rivers we have to ford are individual and private. To adapt, we must change but how hard that change will be or whether we can make it, will be determined in part by that corner of ourselves which is neither public nor about work.

So, personal change requires an openness and willingness to abandon our old safe and successful ways that can be breathtaking in its scope and depth. Not everyone is ready to make the journey and even those who are, need to pursue it at their own pace. Organizations can encourage, support, and even require it but whether it will happen is not entirely within their control.

The Three Stages of Fostering Personal Change

Because fostering personal change is arguably the most difficult part of a manager's role in tapping intellectual capital, we need to spend some time examining how to do it. You will remember the model we're using:

1. Awareness of the Need for Change	2. Invitation to Change	3. Requirement to Change
• Explain why it's important • Explain what needs to change	• Train on new behaviors • Coach • Change systems to reward desired behaviors	• Promote/reward those who demonstrate the new behaviors • Sanction those who do not

Let's walk through a typical situation at each stage.

1: Awareness of the Need for Change

To promote awareness of the need for change, you need to bring the contradiction between what is being done and what is being espoused. In addition, you need to make your expectations for the appropriate behaviour clear. For example, you've noticed Tom and Marjorie aren't sharing information each needs to do their work and instead, blame each other for the lack. Your talk with Tom might go something like this:

COMMENT		CONVERSATION
• Check Tom has had the training	**You:**	*Tom, you've done the conflict resolution course, haven't you?*
	Employee:	*Yes, a couple of weeks ago. It wasn't half bad.*
	You:	*I liked it too. I got a lot out of the unit on raising difficult issues.*
	Employee:	*Yeah, that was good.*
• Check he's ready to use the skill	**You:**	*Did you feel you got enough out of it to try using it?*
	Employee:	*Well, I don't know.*
	You:	*Really? I thought it was pretty comprehensive. What do you think was missing?*
	Employee:	*Ah, well, I guess I'd have to think about it.*
• Offer coaching or further training but keep going	**You:**	*Well, if you think of anything, let me know. Until then, can we talk about the staff meeting this morning?*

	Employee:	*Sure, what about it?*
	You:	*I felt the discussion got out of hand.*
	Employee:	*Well, you stepped in and got it back on track.*
	You:	*Thanks, but I guess I would have preferred you and Marjorie to use some of the techniques from the course to help the discussion.*
	Employee:	*Well, you know Marjorie. Always ready for a scrap.*
• Don't be detoured— stick to the point	**You:**	*I can talk to Marjorie, but I'd like to talk about what you could have done to make things better.*
	Employee:	*Ah come on, Barry, you got things back on track. What's the big deal?*
• Bring the issue to the surface	**You:**	*Good question. Is resolving conflict just my job?*
	Employee:	*Well, no, but you're the boss. You can do it with more authority.*
• State the expectation	**You:**	*That may be true, but if we're a team, we all need to take responsibility for it.*
	Employee:	*Well, I see your point, but Marjorie won't.*
	You:	*I can talk to Marjorie. Let's focus on how you can make a difference.*

At this point, you can move on to discussing how Tom can implement his new skills.

It is important to check whether the training has provided enough to apply to a real setting. If an employee has fewer of these skills than most other people, he may need more time or instruction.

However, don't let Tom use this as an excuse not to apply the skills. You sometimes have to make a judgment call about whether further training is really required.

Also, you note Tom tried to deflect the conversation to Marjorie. This is understandable. From Tom's point of view, Marjorie is the problem, not him. You may want to obliquely acknowledge you know it takes two to tango ("I can talk to Marjorie."), but keep drilling down on Tom's responsibility to use his skills to resolve the issue.

Stage 2: Invitation to Change

It's not unusual for an employee to need some help in making the transition from the classroom setting to real life. You can provide that through coaching.

	You:	*So, Tom, what could you do to help the situation next time?*
	Employee:	*Well, I don't know.*
	You:	*Can I make a suggestion?*
	Employee:	*Sure.*
• Describe an incident	You:	*I saw you immediately engage Marjorie when she said that she wanted to see the data before the customer did.*
	Employee:	*Well, yes. She doesn't need to.*
• Keep describing	You:	*Uh-huh. And then we got into an argument about who needed to see what when.*
	Employee:	*Right and she wouldn't back down.*
• Ask for suggestions	You:	*So what could you have done to make the exchange more productive?*
	Employee:	*Well, I suppose . . . I guess I could have kept my cool better.*

• Make suggestions	**You**	*Sure, that would have helped. And also, the course talked about focusing on areas of agreement. Are there areas where you and Marjorie agree?*
	Employee:	*No—she just wants to protect her little empire.*
• Ignore the character assassination and move on	**You:**	*I'd say you both agree the customer needs good information. Wouldn't you say so?*
	Employee:	*Sure, but she doesn't have to see it first.*
	You:	*Marjorie disagrees with you.*
	Employee:	*I know what the customer needs.*
	You:	*But Marjorie doesn't agree with you.*
	Employee:	*Then she's wrong.*
	You:	*How do you know that?*
	Employee:	*Come on, Barry. I've been at this for seven years. I know my business.*
	You:	*And Marjorie knows hers. Isn't it possible you both might learn something about customer's needs if you talked about that rather than who's to blame?*
	Employee:	*I suppose.*
	You:	*So you could try to find areas of agreement next time rather than areas of disagreement.*
	Employee:	*Well, I guess I could give it a try.*

In this example, you would also talk to Marjorie along the same lines you did with Tom. Here you've helped an employee link the classroom and a situation charged with emotion. Tom may have been so entrenched in the battle he didn't realize he had an option.

At some point, you may want to address the character assassination issue. If Tom and Marjorie start working together well, it will die of its own accord, but if it doesn't, this may call for another coaching session.

Stage 3: Requirement to Change

In the previous stages—awareness and invitation—you supported change. Usually, that's enough for an employee to make the change. When it isn't, you also have a role in *requiring* the change. Changing is difficult. For Tom to do what you talked about, he'll have to operate quite differently. He'll have to ignore the slights and take the high road. While it's easy to see that this is the more productive route, it's not necessarily the obvious one in the midst of finger-pointing, nor is it, let's face it, the most emotionally satisfying. Scoring off an enemy may be more attractive than struggling with a personal change, but this is not an acceptable way to take responsibility for the well-being of the group. You need to point this out by both supporting and requiring the change.

	You:	*Tom, got a minute?*
	Employee:	*Sure.*
	You:	*How'd you think the meeting went today?*
	Employee:	*Well, it could have gone better. Marjorie was up to her old tricks.*
	You:	*I thought you were going to try something new.*
	Employee:	*I thought about what you said, but honestly, I don't think it'll work. I mean, Marjorie won't change and without that, what's the use?*
• Remind him of your agreement	**You:**	*Let's stick to your part. How come you didn't try to find what the two of you had in common?*

	Employee:	*Because it's not going to work. Like I said, until Marjorie...*
• Don't let him off the hook	**You:**	*How do you know if you don't give it a try?*
	Employee:	*What's the use? Marjorie's going to act the way she always does...*
	You:	*How do you know that for sure?*
	Employee:	*Oh come on, why shouldn't she?*
	You:	*Well, you're trying. How do you know she won't too?*
	Employee:	*She sure didn't today.*
• Keep focusing on his behavior	**You:**	*Of course, neither did you.*
	Employee:	*Well, true. OK, maybe I can give it a shot. But only if you get her to do it too.*
• Make the requirement clear	**You:**	*Sorry, Tom, that's not good enough. I expect you to make the effort even if Marjorie doesn't. I will speak with Marjorie, but I'm talking about your responsibility. I expect you to continue trying.*
	Employee:	*Barry, come on. How can I if Marjorie won't change?*
	You:	*We don't know that yet, and we'll deal with that if it happens. In any case, I still expect you to step up to your side of the equation.*
	Employee:	*Geez. I don't think this will work.*
	You:	*I know it'll be tough, but if we aren't all trying to solve the problems, I don't think we're going to get through.*

In this conversation, you make it clear to Tom that making somebody else's change (i.e., Marjorie's) a prerequisite of his is not acceptable. It is the pattern that makes conflicts unresolvable. You must play a role in breaking the cycle.

You may be reluctant to undertake this conversation. None of us wants to be the heavy. But avoiding this step means, in some quiet way, you're sabotaging personal change. Training people to resolve conflicts and then not requiring they do so sends the unmistakable message that the form and not the content is OK. You've wasted the money training for skills that weren't required and most importantly, signaled that employees don't need to change.

These are hard conversations to have, but it is often these potentially threatening or embarrassing ones that can result in the greatest learning.

A corollary of requiring new behavior is that you must follow up—you must ensure that people actually do what you required of them. It is something managers hate to do and typically aren't too good at. It's uncomfortable to keep coming back to an issue, but once you have required the behavior, you need to make sure it happens. Otherwise, you signal your lack of commitment.

The follow-through doesn't have to be negative. It is also important to praise the effort Tom is making. That's the easy part—it's the other that causes heartburn—when Tom hasn't done what he said he would.

You:	*Tom, you were going to talk to Marjorie off-line. Has that happened?*
Employee:	*Just haven't had a minute, Barry. I'll do it soon.*
You:	*We talked about this two weeks ago.*
Employee:	*Yeah, but you know how crazy things have been around here.*
You:	*Yes, but some of the craziness is because you and Marjorie are having trouble.*
Employee:	*Well, I'll do it as soon as I get a minute.*
You:	*OK, by the end of the day today, could you e-mail when you two are set to meet? Then we can talk after that.*
Employee:	*OK.*

Follow-up isn't usually fun. It can be an unpleasant conversation, but isn't it better to know there's a problem than merrily gathering daisies, assuming all is well? You'll be forgiven if you're tempted to answer, "Let me think about it."

If you follow-up again and find that Tom hasn't taken the action you require, you need to decide how far you want to take this issue. By repeatedly ignoring your explicit requests, Tom has laid himself open to disciplinary measures. On the other hand, that's a serious step to take and not many work relationships are productive after such formal processes are invoked. Other equally serious steps might be to make it clear to Tom that there isn't a good fit between him and the team and that he needs to be looking for other employment.

What you do will depend on how important it is that Tom engage in the behavior you want. If it is important, then you can't let it drop. And if it wasn't, then you shouldn't have traveled down this path at all.

DRIVE-BY COACHING

The following is a recreation of a series of e-mails between a boss (Carl) and his subordinate (Kerry).

Carl: *Kerry, I felt that your behavior at the meeting last week was inappropriate. Even though Dan was rude, a modicum of respect is required for senior managers.*

Kerry: *Carl. Thank you for your note. I can't agree with you. Firstly, I didn't feel I was rude, although I was assertive. I didn't think it was appropriate for Dan to speak the way he did.*

Carl: *Got your note yesterday. Sorry I haven't had a chance to reply until now. I don't disagree that Dan was out of line, but that doesn't gives us permission to respond in kind. I feel it's very important to rise above these personal idiosyncrasies.*

Kerry: *Carl, I disagree with your assessment of my behavior. I saw it as assertive, not as rude.*

This series of e-mails could go on forever. Will it resolve the problem in a way that will help both parties understand each other better and change? It's doubtful.

Requiring change forces us into difficult conversations and it's natural to want to avoid them or at least minimize the contact. Transmitting these types of expectations by e-mail, memo, phone message, or any other way that isn't person-to-person is less painful for Carl. However, it's more painful for Kerry. Carl is making it easy for himself at her expense.

Equally important, this drive-by coaching is flatly ineffective. No matter how carefully you word the message, it's impossible to get the benefits of real coaching. Coaching is not about proving who was right but about opening a dialogue in which both parties are open to changing their views and their behavior. A paper war of memos isn't coaching but just a series of one-way messages. Without dialogue, it is an order to change, and, as you know, personal change is not orderable.

Because you sometimes have to *require* personal change even if you can't make it happen, you need to up the chances the recipient will see it in his own best interests to change. You do this by coaching in person or at least in real time.

You may have to put your expectations in writing if you don't trust the recipient (e.g., he'll deny you asked him to change). This may be necessary if the recipient is having great difficulty making the transition, but it's still only a follow-up to, not a substitute for, coaching.

Will All This Make Employees Change?

You can't *make* employees change but just because you can't mandate how much change people make, doesn't alter how much change the organization needs. You need people to share their knowledge. After appropriate coaching and support, an employee may still need to operate as a loner. This failure doesn't remove the need for knowledge sharers.

If after numerous coaching sessions, you conclude the employee can't or won't change, you have a couple of options. If he's stymied in an area pivotal to success, such as teamwork, you may have to help him find another position. Or, you and/or your work unit may agree to live with the idiosyncrasy. And there may be some value in that. Having everyone fly in formation can sometimes prevent new ideas from coming into a group. If you decide to live with it, you then have to deal with the fact that you have required the change of others but not of your "wild duck." Sometimes, groups are willing to live with two sets of rules—one for them and one for a special case—because they recognize that it is warranted. Other times, however, it's a signal to the rest of the group that you really don't require the change. So, it's a judgment call.

You don't have your hands on all the levers that drive personal change but that doesn't absolve you from the need to require it. However, it is possible the employee can't or won't change despite your best efforts.

Summary

To tap a company's intellectual capital, some substantial changes must occur which are not just organizational or structural but personal. Unless change occurs at the level of attitude and behavior, an organization can't fully mine the gold of its people. However, it is difficult both to change oneself and to foster change in others. This chapter covers how to encourage personal change as a way to move the organization to become one that can use its intellectual capital effectively. In the next section, we begin to address the kind of organizational change that is necessary if the company wants to leverage another part of its intellectual capital—customer capital.

Main Points

- Personal change is required in order to implement most if not all of the techniques and suggestions for leveraging your intellectual capital.

- However, personal change is difficult because it's a surprise; it's more profound than anticipated; because it reaches down into even the details of work; and it is a life issue.

- People change slowly and they're scared while they're changing. If these two precepts can be kept in mind, much of the bizarre behavior taking place in organizations is more understandable.

- Managers can foster personal change by helping employees to be aware of the need to change, by inviting them to change, by requiring the change, and by following through.

Section Three

The Human Side of Customer Capital

We've already discussed the fact that customer loyalty is a survival issue. Unless they're fanatically loyal, you may be forced to compete on price which is almost never a winning game. If an organization can leverage its customer capital, it will increase the likelihood of sustained viability and growth. However, more and more research is showing that loyal customers are a function of loyal employees. If employees are satisfied with, and motivated by their work, their daily interactions with customers will be more positive and this, in turn, will increase the likelihood that customers will not only buy, but return to buy again. Employees loyal to the company create customers loyal to it too. So a major management challenge with customer capital is the creation of this loyal workforce who will in turn leverage your customer capital for you. Chapter 14 will talk about that. Because this is such a central issue to your competitiveness, you also need to know how you're doing on it and Chapter 15 will deal with ways to assess employee loyalty. The final section will bring together all the various themes from the whole book in a concluding overview.

Customer Loyalty Is Employee Loyalty

Whether your customers continue to buy your goods and services determines your company's success. However, as we've seen, it's not enough that your customers be satisfied with your products. Customer loyalty has to be almost fanatical in order to be assured of their continued patronage. There is growing evidence that customer loyalty at that level is driven by how loyal employees feel to the company. Let us review some of the research we covered early in the book.

Gallup found that there was a strong correlation between company profits and employees' belief that they had opportunity to do what they do best every day, that their opinions counted, that all workers were committed to quality, and that there was a direct connection between their work and the company's mission.[1] In other research, it has been found that employee attitudes about the job and company are two factors that predict their behavior in front of the customer, which in turn predicts the likelihood of customer retention and customers' recommending the product to others, the two factors that predict financial performance.[2]

So the research is strong and growing that you get customer loyalty if you have loyal employees. A friend gave me a perfect example

---

[1] Linda Grant, "Happy Workers, Happy Returns," *Fortune* (January 12, 1998): 81.
[2] Sherman Stratford, "Bringing Sears into the New World," *Fortune* (October 13, 1997): 183.

of how employees control customer loyalty. She was buying a piece of hardware for her home computer when the salesperson pointed out that her credit card had expired. When she got home, she phoned the credit card company to renew her card. The operator took her information and told her when to expect the new card. As the operator was wrapping up, my friend asked why she hadn't received the card automatically as usual. The operator, sounding somewhat harassed, sighed and went into the database. He reported that a card had been sent out to her several days before. "Where is it?" asked my friend, and the operator snapped back, "Well, how should I know? Lost in the mail, I guess." My friend promptly cancelled her card. She was incensed not merely because the card was lost but because the operator hadn't checked whether one had been issued and when prompted to do so, clearly didn't care that a credit card with her name on it was floating around unaccounted for. The credit card company lost that account because the company operator's attitude was *I don't know and I don't care.*

Presumably, his boss or his boss's boss does care whether they lose customers, but they have not been able to communicate that to this employee. This is how you can lose your customers and their loyalty one by one. As *Fortune* columnist, Thomas A. Stewart, points out, "A customer's decision to be loyal or to defect is the sum of many small encounters with your company."[3] Your employees control these small encounters.

So, how do you build employee loyalty as the royal road to customer loyalty? Certainly, all of the things we've been talking about in the rest of the book, like encouraging new knowledge to come forward and involving employees in decisions, will make a difference. However, there is an old standby that has much power. Mission and values statements, although often dissipated or ill-used, can be a compelling reason for employees to be loyal to the company.

The Old Standbys: Mission and Values

Mission and values statements are old hat in some ways, and like ATMs, which were once a competitive advantage, are now just the

---

[3] Thomas A. Stewart, "A Satisfied Customer Isn't Enough," *Fortune* (July 21, 1997): 113.

cost of doing business. The logic for creating mission and values statements that people believe in still holds true. If people believe in what the company's doing, they're more likely to contribute their intellectual capital to it. If they don't, they're less inclined to engage their brains or even stick around. Knowing this, company executives spend a couple of days in some secluded spot thrashing a mission statement out. Then they hang the result on a wall back at the office with a sense of a job well done.

Unfortunately, when talking about "creating a mission that people believe in," companies have focused on the "create" part and forgotten the part about "people believing in it." That's what this chapter will be about—how to do the "people believe in it" part.

Having a mission can be an important way to focus energy in the corporation, but creating it is only the first and least step to make it useful. Talking it up and posting it on walls are also necessary but not sufficient conditions. To be effective, it has to go from the wall into the heart. The statement has power only to the extent that it influences behavior and action. Otherwise, the only profit from it goes to picture framing companies. The same goes for corporate values. Values such as respect, service, quality, professionalism, and responsibility are just words unless they propel action.

When your mission and values are on the wall but not in the heart, one of three things can occur. The first is that the organization acts on many values and missions but not shared ones. For example, you may believe nothing should go out the door unless it's perfect, while I think that as long as nobody notices, we're in business. Both are values, but they're going to have trouble living in the same organization, and we're going to disagree on the wisdom of shipping a marginal product.

The second possibility is that the company has a shared mission and values but with quite different definitions. Let's use the example of a mission:[4] *We design innovative software driven by our customers' needs and support their effectiveness with it with values of customer service, professionalism, and mutual respect.* Your definition of professionalism is that a design has to ensure nobody could be hurt using the product, no matter how they abuse it. I may believe that our professional duty is to design a sound product, but that the

---

[4] Just to clarify, I think of mission as the statement of the business you are in, not as the vision or any number of variants in between.

customer has a responsibility to read the instructions and act in the interests of his own safety. Again, we're going to have very different views of how much work has to go into a design. I see you as unrealistic; you see me as callous.

Finally, the organization may have a truly shared value or mission that isn't reflected in major decisions. In the example above, the value of *customer service* implies playing straight with the customer, but if it's company practice to leave products on the shelves past the expiry date or to "prove" that the customer misused the product rather than fix the design, these violations prompt grave doubts about the leadership.

Any of these three conditions are not merely useless in engaging employee loyalty, but harmful to it. At the very least, it sends mixed messages about what the company stands for; at worst, it confirms that it doesn't walk its talk.

If values and mission really are shared and drive decisions, they can create a sense of belonging to a collective endeavor which infuses meaning into even the most repetitive and boring job, because it is linked to that piece of us which wants to be of service, to contribute to a higher good, or to make a difference. Faith in the core of what the company is and a belief that everyone acts in accordance with it can be a compelling reason to contribute one's intellectual capital to the greater good.

Dr. Loretta DiFrancesco, a nutritionist and senior manager at Kellogg Canada, believes that Kellogg really does live its mission of "Grain-based food for a healthier world." For example, the recent Special K cereal advertisements focused on encouraging women to put less emphasis on their body weight and more on their overall health and well-being. The nutrition group is actively involved in all the marketing plans at Kellogg, starting with the brainstorming and culminating in having approval rights on all the marketing copy and media produced. In fact, when I asked for an example of the nutrition group successfully insisting that the marketing group reposition a product to avoid inadvertently misleading consumers, Loretta answered, "That's not how we work. The nutrition group isn't the watchdog and the marketing people aren't trying to get around us. We work as a team and *both* use the mission to make our decisions."

Shared values and mission in a company are far more powerful than rules. They guide people toward the right path even when there's nobody looking over their shoulder or when no one will ever know whether they've made the right decision. As in our example at Kellogg, it does away with defenders and attackers of a company's core. A strongly shared sense of mission and values will act as a self-regulating mechanism for everyone.

The Stages of Mission and Values

Your company probably has values and a mission, but as mentioned above, it is possible to have both and still make little impact on the loyalty of your employees. If what the company does and what the mission says are at odds, knowledge workers will feel the lack of connection and be reluctant to invest their intellectual capital in a company which is at best unable to deliver on its mission or at worst, is hypocritical. Executives often don't realize that they must move the mission off the wall and into the heart in order for it to have the desired effect of aligning knowledge workers to the company's strategic direction.

One can't expect to go directly from creating a mission and values to having everyone act on them, although there are a distressing number of organizations who seem to believe they can. In fact, moving the mission and values off the paper and into the heart progresses in stages. These are outlined below.

Table: 14.1
The Stages of Mission and Values

STAGE	WHAT IT LOOKS LIKE	ACTIONS INDICATIVE OF THIS STAGE
1. On the wall	*"Oh, new decoration. Hey, see the game last night?"*	*Your strategic direction and mission/values are consistent.*
2. Read it	*"Accounting's customers are the salespeople as well as the buyers."*	*The mission/values statement has been distributed widely.*
3. Understand it	*"So we're supposed to be customer driven. What's that mean in accounts receivable?"*	*Managers and employees can relate mission/values to daily work.*

Table: 14.1 cont'd

4. Can quote it	*"Well, that's what we're here for, right? To serve the customer."*	*Used as a matter of course in publications, newsletters, and speeches.*
5. Understand why tough choices were made	*"OK, I can see why we have to stay open late. People can't get to us during the day. I'll have to shift my schedule, but I suppose it's doable."*	*Reasoning behind decisions includes reference to mission/values and is widely communicated and understood.*
6. Make tough choices based on it	*"This can't go out. In a month, the customer would be back for a replacement and be mad to boot. It'll have to be redone."*	*Difficult corporate and individual work decisions are guided by mission/values.*
7. Use it for all choices	*"Where does Joe get off being so high-handed? But he's a customer—even though a miserable one—so I guess I'd better make it right for him. Not that I'll get any thanks for it."*	*You use mission/values to guide your decisions daily, and you can say that about everyone in the company.*

Unless your company is at the fifth or sixth stage of the chart, you're probably not getting the mileage you need. Up to this point, the activities are easy to put into place, hardly inconvenience managers at all, and also don't require much from employees. But around Stage 5, things get a bit more difficult, and people begin to understand that a living mission/values cannot do so outside the heart. It must live within to be alive. Unless choices are guided by what you believe in, no matter how inconvenient or uncomfortable, mission and values statements will be of little value. Stage 5 is the make or break point in this process and where progress frequently stalls.

You may think that it is impossible to work through all these levels, but I've seen it happen. I was working with health professionals charged with recommending a revamp to the health system. Every faction was represented, from diverse fields such as acupuncture, geriatrics, and social work, not just doctors and nurses. As they deliberated, all began to recognize the complexity not simply of providing adequate health care to a large and diverse population but also of responding to issues like alternative/native therapies and to the special needs of populations such as the disabled. The more they struggled, the greater became their understanding that not everyone's interests could be addressed. And it was not just because funds were limited. Just as frequently, one group's values (e.g., to use only scientifically validated treatments) conflicted with another's reality (e.g., acupuncture has been practiced for hundreds of years without scientific validation).

The participants began to realize that, because the choices were so tough, the decisions must inevitably be best possible—not perfect—solutions. They came to understand, not just in their heads, but in their guts, that all must compromise if a solution that was even adequate was to be crafted. It is the kind of major breakthrough organizations as well as governments, need. It is possible to achieve this level of buy-in to your organization's mission, but it takes effort. Let's talk specifically about what needs to be done.

Getting It Off the Page and Into the Heart

Earlier in the chapter, we talked about three ways a lack of connection between people and the company's mission/values manifests itself. They were:

- There are many values and missions in the company, but they're not shared.

- There is one shared mission and set of values, but they mean different things.

- There is one truly shared mission/values, but they aren't reflected in major decisions.

In the next section, we'll talk about how to deal with each of these situations so that your mission and values can contribute to retaining and engaging your intellectual capital.

Many Values and Missions

In this situation, everyone uses their own values and sense of mission (or lack thereof) as the way to guide their work behavior and there has been little or no effort to align them to the "official" version. In these organizations, the mission/values statements literally are just pieces of paper on the wall. In that case, people who trample on customers and employees are as likely to get the next plum assignment as the manager who is really trying to live by the mission. There is no necessary logic to decisions. Sometimes they make sense because people guided by the mission made them. Other times, they seem to be taking the company in exactly the opposite direction because a decision maker has powered through what was good for him even if it wasn't good for the customer or the company.

As a starting point, you do need a statement of your mission and values. Most companies have these and the development can be a worthwhile exercise for executives. It forces them to seriously consider where they're going and where they want to go. If things work well, they discover honest differences in both perception and operation which may have made working together difficult. The process can lead to an executive team that is much better able to move forward.

However, the very usefulness of that exercise for executives is the reason why employees at all levels should engage in the same kind of debate. Just as executives needed the chance to reflect on what the mission and values meant to them, so do employees. An immediate reaction is often to dismiss this option for two reasons. One is the time it will take, and the second is that it's not the job of employees to set the direction of the organization. Both objections are valid but let's take into account a couple of points.

There is no doubt that it will take time to set up a process to consult, although not as much as you might think, and Chapter 4 suggested a consultation process that works. The question is not so much whether it takes time, as whether you think you're going to get something worthwhile from it. Anything that is simply announced without some kind of involvement is not usually an object of compelling interest (bonus and layoff announcements aside). And yet, to make the mission and values work for you as a way to invite your knowledge workers to feel part of a greater whole, engagement is exactly what you need. So, as the first step to moving the organization forward together, the consultation may well be worth it.

With regard to the second objection, executives should set the direction of the organization but I don't know why that precludes asking employees whether they agree. As you will recall, there is an important difference between consultation and being compelled to act on its results. It's analogous to being consulted by a friend on whether she should take a job offer. You can be flattered that your opinion is being sought without assuming it will materially affect your relationship if she decides contrary to your advice. You want to set up the same conditions for consultation within your organization.

So, you may want to consider using a more broadly based approach to crafting the mission and values as a way to engage the commitment of your knowledge workers. You may find that the consultation process is as valuable as the results in its ability to challenge employees to think about what the company is really about and what they need to do to make it so.

Mission/Values Definitions

An organization can have a common set of mission and values but with different definitions of what they mean. In the example of the mission used above, *We design innovative software driven by our customers' needs and support their effectiveness with it*, your view might emphasize the "innovation" aspect with a bow to customer needs, while I think that giving the customer what he wants is the pivot of the mission. We'll differ on how innovative we're supposed to be. I see you as stifling it and you see me as not being grounded in the realities of the marketplace. With these conflicting interpretations, we're going to have trouble going in the same direction.

The answer is not to lock a group of seers and lexicographers in a room to come up with the perfect definition. Instead, the answer is to use the mission in actual decision making and by doing so, develop a better and more precise understanding of what each part of the mission and values means to the company. At each critical decision point, you need to refer back to your mission to understand how you should act. If you do this in the face of a real live decision, people will naturally fall into discussions about what the mission and the values mean to them. From that, they can both make the decision at hand and further their and the organization's understanding of what the mission and values mean pragmatically.

It will be critical for decision makers to record how their thinking evolves on what the mission and values mean in practical terms, and equally important, to distribute these understandings widely throughout the organization. If the executive committee decides that "professionalism" means you design products assuming a modicum of common sense on the part of the user, you need to communicate this all the way down the line so that the engineers fighting it out earlier in the chapter (a product shouldn't injure no matter what, versus the customer has a responsibility to read the instructions) understand what is required. The engineer who has an opposing view may not like the conclusion, but he now knows what the standard is and can start aligning his thinking to it.

Aligning Mission/Values and Decisions

The third possibility is that everyone believes that the mission and values are worthwhile but there are major decisions that don't align with them or, at very least, are not perceived to. A famous example of alignment was the Tylenol scare of some years ago. If you remember, someone had introduced poison into one of the Tylenol bottles. Before it was clarified whether this had been done at the factory or in the store or whether any other bottles were affected, the Tylenol executives ordered the removal of all Tylenol from all stores. Their swift action was based, not on considerations of potential liability or profit, but on their values. This values-based action confirmed people's faith in Tylenol's reliability and their sales suffered hardly at all.

Imagine what might have happened if there had been no agreement that major decisions must be aligned to the company's values. In that case, I can imagine, in the chaos and lack of information of the moment, Tylenol executives would be arguing that it couldn't possibly be their fault (as turned out to be true) and therefore, they should just sit tight and leave the product on the shelves. If they had done that, everyone would have believed that Tylenol cared more about its profits than its customers' well being. Even though the disaster was not due to their production processes, there would have been the perception of hypocrisy. It is both important to live by your values and be seen to be living by them.

There is no doubt that making decisions consistently according to your values is difficult and it is far simpler to make decisions based on the pressures of the moment. You will be frequently faced with the decision whether to stay loyal to your values or just this once, ignore them. If you do the latter, employees will know. This is exactly what the rumor mill is set up for. Each "exception" to the rule further undermines your credibility until you have firmly established your reputation for speaking out of both sides of your mouth. So aligning every tough decision to your mission is not easy, but it is essential if you want your knowledge workers to believe in both you and the mission.

Summary

Mission and values statements were popular for good reason—organizations that were truly aligned behind them were powerhouses in their industries. They have become important again as it becomes increasingly clear that knowledge workers who are committed to the mission and values are more likely to be loyal employees who will in turn create loyal customers. Because employee loyalty (and therefore customer loyalty) are such critical elements to an organization's success, companies need to be able to constantly assess how they're doing on employee satisfaction and loyalty. The next chapter shows you how to do that.

Main Points

- Loyal customers are the lifeblood of an organization.
- Research is showing that customer loyalty is determined by employee loyalty.
- Employees will be loyal if they believe that the company adheres to its mission and values.
- Companies often have trouble retaining employee loyalty because they have not put enough time and energy in ensuring that the mission and values are truly shared.

CHAPTER 15

⁓

Assessing Employee Loyalty

Needless to say, almost everything you're doing needs to have a positive impact on the bottom line. You might vary when it does (i.e., a long-term investment versus an effect on this quarter), or how (lowering expenses rather than increasing revenues), but unless all this theory about intellectual capital allows your organization to be more competitive or more effective, why would you bother?

Thus, the issue of employee satisfaction has always been a gray area. Yes, we care about it because we're good human beings and prefer people to be happy rather than unhappy. We might even concede that satisfied employees are more loyal, but when push comes to shove, does it make any difference? In the long ago past (i.e., five or six years ago), and using the industrial model (Worth of a Company = Book Value + Goodwill), where goodwill was an unimportant percentage of the equation, the answer was typically, no.

But now that goodwill or intellectual capital can account for up to 90 per cent of a company's wealth creation potential, employee satisfaction has taken on a new importance. Studies consistently show a correlation between employee satisfaction and superior financial performance. For example, Sears found that financial performance was a lagging indicator—it only tells you that you're already in trouble, not that you are going to be—but employee attitudes are a predictor of financial performance.[1] Several other studies

---

[1] Sherman Stratford, "Bringing Sears into the New World," *Fortune* (October 13, 1997): 183.

also suggest that you need to track how your employees feel about working in your company, and that if you can improve that, it will positively influence your financial performance.

So, how satisfied your employees are does make a difference and their satisfaction and loyalty makes for loyal customers, which in turn affects profitability. Therefore, as a company, you need to know how employees feel about what you're doing, how you're managing the company, and how you're managing them. Two ways you can do this are company-wide employee surveys that regularly test for employee satisfaction and a 360-degree feedback program that allows employees to comment on the management skills of their bosses. Typically, these should be done in sequence—get the employee survey going regularly before you introduce 360-degree feedback. We'll go into the reasons why later.

At this point, some managers will feel they don't need to read any farther. "I know my employees," they say. "I don't need surveys or anything else to tell me what they're thinking and feeling." Well, maybe, but a 1997 survey[2] showed an alarming difference between what managers thought and what employees actually believed. For example, 85 per cent of senior managers believed that they supported customer service goals, but only 55 per cent of the workers agreed that they saw that in managers. Fifty-five percent of managers said they involved employees in decisions but only 26 per cent were aware that happened. And 61 per cent of managers felt that they treated employees as valued business partners, while only 27 per cent of workers thought so. A 30 or 40 per cent spread between what you believe and what your employees believe doesn't suggest that you can move forward together easily. You can't do anything about promoting employee loyalty and therefore customer loyalty if you are operating under these kinds of misperceptions. Doing an employee survey or 360-degree feedback is a way that you can ensure that you really do know how employees feel and what they believe.

---

[2] "Trust Levels Poor in Canadian Companies," *The Training Report* (July 1998).

Regular Employee Surveys

There are excellent reasons for doing an employee survey: it will provide data on how employees are feeling; it shows employees that management cares about their opinions; it taps ways to improve the company. There are many reasons why you should go ahead, but how you roll it out will determine its success.

Discussions Before Launching the Survey

This is the most critical, least used step in doing a survey.

If a survey hasn't been done in living memory, it is almost guaranteed the results will be less than what we might wish for. No matter what you tell them, employees will feel that this is their only kick at the can, their only chance to tell you what they really think, so they do. They let you know not just about what you're doing but about all the sins of your predecessors. Yes, you are going to be blamed even for things you didn't do. People will express *all* their feelings, including past perceived wrongs that still rankle. I have seen people complain about how a downsizing was handled even though it occurred ten years before and under another set of managers. The pain may be suppressed but it doesn't go away. Thus, the survey feedback is almost always significantly harsher than you expect.

Executives are often taken aback by this criticism, and hurt that their efforts—like running the survey—aren't recognized. They are understandably incensed that employees blame them for mistakes they had no hand in. The automatic inclination is to dispose of these unfair and hurtful items as soon as possible. Usually that means acknowledging the report, perhaps even sending a nice letter of thanks to participants, and then quietly shelving the whole thing.

That is exactly the wrong thing to do. Employees know you did the survey. If they never hear of it again, they'll conclude that you didn't want to hear what they had to say, that you only want good news, and finally that it was all window dressing anyway. By doing the survey and burying it, you create more distrust than if you hadn't done it at all. So don't proceed unless the executive group agrees that employee surveys are likely to have unfavorable results if this is the first one or in times of great change, but the survey is still worth doing. It should be agreed that the survey results will be widely available, although the "level of aggregation"—that is to say, whether the results are reported at the company level or for each manager—may be discussed. An action plan to remedy the problems will be generated and the executive group is willing to be held publicly accountable for its achievement.

This may sound like all the reasons for *not* doing a survey, but remember, ignoring a boil doesn't make it go away. Just because you didn't cause it, doesn't mean you don't have to attend to it. Sometimes you have to lance it, let the poison drain, and begin the healing process. And you can't heal unless you are willing to undergo the pain first.

Building the Survey
Keep it simple

People who have never done a survey are often enamored with the idea of getting reams and reams of data. That can soon get out of hand. So, some rules of thumb:

- keep it short—one page, no more than five to eight questions
- questions should all be multiple choice with check-off boxes or numerical ratings
- provide a comments section at the end
- individual anonymity must be assured

Know What You Want to Measure Before You Start

Knowing that 63 per cent of the company feels satisfied or very satisfied with management is helpful but it isn't enough. For example, that number might actually be composed of the rating from regional operations (98 per cent satisfaction) averaged with those from marketing (28 per cent). The regional operations manager probably just needs to continue doing whatever he's doing, but the marketing manager has a big challenge on her hands. However, you can't do this kind of breakdown of the overall company figures if you haven't asked employees *where* they work. Thus, you need to know what kind of breakdowns of the data you will want before you conduct the survey. Otherwise, you may not be able to figure out what the data mean when you get them.

Make It Statistically Valid, if Possible

This isn't as esoteric as it sounds. If the survey results aren't what were hoped for, managers tend to get defensive. One of the classic routes is to attack the survey itself— the questions were biased, they weren't the right ones, the analysis was incompetent, not enough people were asked, too many were asked, and so on. And sometimes they're right. For example, you may inadvertently bias the results by the way you ask the questions—Do you really like the management style? versus How do you feel about the management style? Unless you set up your data collection in an unbiased way, managers can quite legitimately accuse you of running an unfair or unusable survey. You can avoid this avenue of discussion by demonstrating that commonly accepted survey practices were used.

If you have someone with a statistics background on staff, you're in business. If not, you can hire this help or use a commercially available survey instrument. The latter are likely to be relatively expensive but have the advantage of rigorous testing to ensure validity. If time or money prevent this, make the survey very, very simple, with the results reflecting the company as a whole without a breakdown of results by unit, geographic location, hourly or salaried workers, and so on.

What to Do with the Results

No matter how much preparation is done up front, the first shock of seeing the results is likely to be substantial. Executives are running as fast as they can, and they'll interpret the results as indicating their efforts are not appreciated. The CEO or most senior manager can do several things to up the chances the managers will move ahead on these results: let each manager see his results before they are generally released, send a positive message, do a group action plan, communicate, and take action with reluctant managers.

Let Each Manager See His Results Individually First

Each manager who can be identified in the survey, e.g, the head of marketing, sales, R&D, should have a chance to digest the news in relative privacy. This allows them time to get over the shock of their results without an audience. By avoiding embarrassing them in public, they are likely to feel less defensive and more willing to accept changes they might have to make to their behavior in order to respond to the feedback from the survey.

Send a Positive Message to All Managers

After these private sessions, discuss the overall corporation results. The CEO can diffuse a lot of anxiety by saying something like: "It doesn't matter how bad or good this first survey is. What matters is what we do with it. I'll be looking for suggestions on how to make the next set of results even more positive than this one." I think you'll see shoulders around the room relax and several prepared defense texts quietly dropped.

During this meeting, beware of diminishing the value of the session by moving quickly past the embarrassing results that pinpoint one manager. It is better to say something like: "Well, this is disappointing, but again, it's just where we are. What do you think we can do about it? Burt, this is mostly your area. Any thoughts?" This openly acknowledges it wasn't what you'd hoped for but that you're following through on your promise. No blame is attached, just a focus on how to do better. When managers realize they're not going to get slammed, they'll be more willing to spend the time talking about what to do than trying to explain the results away.

Even so, you will run into one problem. Sometime during the discussion, someone will say, "That's ridiculous. We're not trying to hide anything/damage the market/get rid of R&D. They're completely wrong about that." Everyone will nod sagely and skip to the next set of responses. They miss the point. The truth is irrelevant to this exercise. Perception is reality. As we all do, employees treat what they believe as fact. Even if the employees are incorrect, the very smallest problem you have is to correct the perception.

Try to prevent these quite fruitless discussions by saying: "We might see responses which are a little hard to swallow because we have a different take on things. I'd ask you to remember that what people believe to be true is what they'll act on. When you look at your results, please consider all feedback, not just the ones you believe are true."

Do a Group Action Plan

In deciding how to address the issues raised, try for concrete, measurable actions. Don't respond to feedback that managers don't communicate with a blanket statement such as: "Managers will communicate more." That's too vague. Specify how—regular meetings, briefing staff on recent decisions within a certain amount of time, or sharing quarterly results. And whatever it is, be specific.

One of the actions that should *not* be undertaken is another full-scale data collection. Sometimes, you don't know exactly what the results mean. For example, a recent survey showed that employees didn't feel they were in the loop. There are two possible interpretations. Either the managers really weren't communicating, or something was preventing employees from understanding the information. As you can see, the solution you target will depend on the problem you're addressing. In this example, a random sample of employees was asked what they thought this feedback meant and the managers concluded that the problem was a mix of both issues. Some managers weren't transmitting the company messages, but, in addition, some of the communication was confusing and open to misinterpretation.

There is a temptation to reanalyze the existing data (which usually won't tell you anything much) or to do another, more focused survey. Don't do it. Hold a few focus groups or get managers to ask staff what this means, but don't let collecting more data *be* the action. The action is fixing the problem.

Communicate and Track the Success of the Action Plan

Once you've agreed on actions, assigned responsibilities, and set deadlines, send the plan to all employees. If the results are disappointing, say so.[3] They're going to figure that out for themselves anyway—you might as well admit it up front. Talk about how you'll address the problems identified. If there are some that can't be tackled, right now or ever, explain why, otherwise, people will assume you're hiding something.

Report regularly to employees on the progress being made in implementing the plan, remembering that it's the success of the actions, not just the completion of the plan that's important. The

---

[3] However, one of my reviewers, Cliff Cullen, points out, a survey is successful no matter how many problems are pointed out. That's the point of doing it, after all.

plan is successful only if employees believe their concerns have been addressed. A further survey, perhaps a year or six months after the first, might be in order, although smaller scale efforts—like a cross-sectional focus group of employees—can also be a way to assess how you're doing.

Take Action on Managers Who Are Not Taking the Plan Seriously

There will be managers who, despite your best efforts, feel that this is just so much fluff and will do nothing (or as close as she can get away with). The reluctant manager can probably come up with plausible excuses why nothing's happened. If you agree, let it pass, recognizing you may take a hit in the rumor mill. If it needs addressing, take the underperforming manager aside and have the same kind of talk you'd have about financial results. How can I help? Do you need some training? This is what I require within this time period. I need your commitment on this.

Doing a survey is an important way to signal your concern about employee morale and loyalty, but just because it's the right thing, doesn't mean it's easy. Through all the difficult times, never forget that it can be a positive force in showing people that you really do value what they think and that you're willing to change how you run the organization to reflect the new realities of the information age.

360-Degree Feedback

As companies recognize the importance of people management and cooperative skills, they look for ways to assess an individual manager's effectiveness. Whereas employee surveys are excellent vehicles to take the pulse of the organization, they're typically blunt instruments when it comes to individual feedback. If the VP can say, "It's not me but my subordinate managers causing the problem identified in the employee survey," and equally, the managers can say, "We'd get much better scores if only the VP would smarten up," we have the perfect recipe for inaction. As long as you're pointing the finger at someone else, you don't have to think about what you need to do to increase employee loyalty and morale.

So, a more precise instrument than employee surveys is needed. Because management skills are largely intangible and not easily amenable to third party observation, the usual route is to ask the recipients of these skills—employees—how well the manager is doing. This approach reverses the usual managerial assessment of employee performance—it is the employees assessing their bosses. This turnabout (and hence the name, 360-degree feedback) can be a very powerful instrument for change at an individual level.

Deciding Whether or Not to Do 360-Degree Feedback

Everyone fears feedback unless you know beforehand that everyone's going to tell you how wonderful you are, and even then, it has to be unanimous. If even a couple of employees grumble, even about minor things, we obsess over those few. What's the matter with them—or you? So, nobody likes feedback. On the other hand, deep in our little hearts we know it's probably good for us, like spinach and exercise, but it doesn't make it any easier to put yourself in the way of potential criticism.

A 360-degree feedback exercise can be precisely right for your company, but there are some times when it might be less effective or even damaging. Work through these points and decide whether they apply to your organization:

- You Have Never Used Any Kind of Employee Feedback Before
- You Have a Lot Of Turnaround Situations
- Many Units Have New Managers
- There is a High Level of Fear of Revenge from Senior Managers

You Have Never Used Any Kind of Employee Feedback Before

If you've never sought employee feedback before, you're likely to get a lot of negative comments, including old baggage. It feels unfair enough to managers even if the level of aggregation is pretty high—that is, if the comments are about all the managers in sales, not just you. The comments feel even worse when they're about your unit. It's also a threatening situation for employees even if they believe the survey is anonymous. It's one thing to be one of hundreds or thousands filling out a company-wide employee survey—your responses will be buried among all the others. It's another to be one of five or 10 subordinates who are passing judgment on the manager to whom you say good morning every day.

You can make excellent progress with an employee survey. Once you've made progress on corporate-wide issues, you may want a greater precision about how each division or unit is functioning. Before embarking on a 360, it is usually better to do a series of general employee surveys.

You Have a Lot of Turnaround Situations

I've been in situations where my mandate was to improve a poorly functioning group. You're often faced with having to right years of managerial neglect in a fairly short time. Even if the people welcome the change of managers in general, they won't welcome the changes. If the previous manager allowed conflicts to depress productivity and you insist they be resolved, you're not going to be popular. Even though both employees and the company will be happier in the longer term, it's quite typical to go through some bad times while these issues are being addressed.

So if a 360-feedback process is introduced while a manager is trying to address difficult interpersonal and group issues, the feedback may reflect employees' resistance to change rather than the manager's people skills. If there are only a few of these turnaround situations in the company, they could be identified beforehand and an understanding reached that these managers' scores may not be a good reflection of their abilities. However if there are many groups with these types of issues, delaying implementation is advisable.

Many Units Have New Managers

Similarly, you may want to delay implementation of a 360 when there are a large number of units whose managers are relatively new. Until managers and staff have had some time working together—say, about a year—it's usually not possible to get an adequate reflection of that particular manager's strengths and weaknesses. Remember, as with the employee survey, employees are likely to comment on all the problems management is creating for them and not just on the ones by this particular manager. If that happens, it will be almost impossible for the current manager to know what to address in his own behavior.

There is a High Level of Fear of Revenge from Senior Managers

If managers fear punishment when their results are known and subordinates don't believe their responses are anonymous, it's a recipe for disaster. You may think that this doesn't exist in your organization, but your belief isn't enough. If employee surveys indicate an acceptable level of confidence or you have information from highly credible employees, you may be okay.

Don't use any of these caveats as an excuse to avoid a 360 exercise. Sometimes, conducting it may help rectify the conditions discussed above. For example, if you think retribution is a problem, instituting a 360 is a powerful message you want things to change. On the other hand, don't barge ahead, blithely and blindly. If you proceed in the face of any of these conditions, take special pains to ensure the implementation is well done and the feedback well handled.

Questions to Ask

Are You Willing to Do This Too?

Don't ask other managers to commit to this process unless the most senior person does too. If you're not going to put your managerial skills up for comment, why should they? In fact, if you're not willing to do so, drop the plan right now. It smacks too much of do what I say, not what I do.

Is This Voluntary for Managers?

Can a manager choose not to participate? If yes, how will you encourage participation and how will you address problem managers who avoid the whole process? If not, how will you deal with the perception of coercion? One option is allowing a somewhat lengthy implementation period. For example, you might give managers two years to start using the system, although even that may not address the issue—it may just be seen as *slower* coercion. Another option might be mandatory participation, but the first round's results would stay private with no *public* action plans.

How Will the Feedback Be Used?

Will the feedback results be available only to the manager to whom it is addressed? What about the employees who filled it out? What about the manager's supervisor? How will the information be distributed? Do the managers in question get to see it first? What gets distributed? The raw scores? The answers to all the questions? A summary of the results? To whom do people go to get help interpreting the results? What will be done with the results?

How Formal Will the Follow-Up on the Results Be?

If no follow-up is done, the 360 was a waste of time, money, and paper and in addition, will add significantly to the cynicism quotient in the company. So, something must happen as a result of the exercise. Follow-up can be a very formal reporting process, with each manager's data available both to his staff and supervisor. The manager meets with his staff to identify needed improvements in his managerial style and makes a commitment in writing to his supervisor to accomplish them within the next year or other agreed upon time period. You may have to set up a monitoring system to ensure these steps are followed. While some companies have used this level of formality very successfully, it is the most threatening way to introduce the process to managers since it is the most public. It not only publicizes the manager's weaknesses but also the actions he must take to rectify the faults. It gives him little opportunity to make personal change quietly and on his own timeline—both of which we'd all prefer when embarking on a difficult journey. While these factors should not drive your decision on whether or not to use this more formal approach, pay special attention to setting up an accompanying process to work with managers who are struggling.

The opposite end of the scale is a very informal follow-up process where each manager decides himself what to do with the results. The problem here is that if the manager can squirrel the results away in the bottom drawer, how do you know the process has made a difference, and just as importantly, how do the employees know? If you don't know the results, how do you address persistent problems?

There are no easy answers to these questions. One way to find your way through these minefields is to return to the objective of the exercise—to your values. If the objective is personal growth for the managers, a process that encourages rather than whips them toward the goal is preferable. If the development of cooperative and interpersonal skills is of predominant importance, a more public stance that can be more easily monitored might be more useful. The latter may also be appropriate if it is important not only to conduct the feedback process but also to show that it is making a difference. However, if respect is the driver (and managers are people too), a more informal one might be right.

No matter what you decide, someone will be unhappy. If it's formal, managers will object to this public display of their dirty laundry; if it's informal, employees will doubt whether it is serious exercise. Even so, keep focused on what most closely aligns you to your values and will move the yardstick forward.

What Will You Say Before the Results Are Released?

Say in some public way what you said privately during the employee survey. "It doesn't matter what the results are. What matters is what we do with them. It's our ability to grow, not how tall we are to start, which matters." As with the employee survey, this type of statement signals to everyone that the focus will be on improvement and not on blame.

Will This Process Be Repeated?

This is a logical extension of this whole process. What's the point of a one-time deal? In employees' minds, it simply confirms how bad things are. Why do you need to do that? It is only in the action plan that follows the first results, and then the second and third cycles that everyone can begin to see progress. Don't shortchange the process by assuming a one-time shot is an inoculation for life.

Implementation

The skill of helping managers and staff understand and work with the results of a 360-degree feedback exercise is a special one because of the exceptionally threatening nature of the exercise. An expert in the process (usually an external consultant) should do this.

Most of the larger consulting firms have a 360-degree feedback process. The consulting firm will usually use a questionnaire that has been tested for validity. The manager distributes the questionnaire to a number of her subordinates and peers. Sometimes the manager's boss also fills one out. The questionnaires are completed anonymously and returned to the consulting firm. The consultant does an analysis and presents the results to the manager. At the same time, the consultant works with the manager to plan how she will introduce, explain, and discuss the results with her staff. This would include what questions of clarification the manager needs to better understand the feedback and what behavior changes the manager is willing to commit to as a result of it.

Although the feedback process itself is usually best handled by external professionals, the implementation—that is, how the process is rolled out in the organization—should be done internally. Particular attention should be paid to briefing both staff and managers on the process and handling the aftermath.

Voluntary or mandatory, spend a good amount of time explaining what will happen, to whom, and when, well before the process is implemented. Both employees and managers need to get their expectations right. It's going to be hard enough to work with the feedback without a lot of, *"But I didn't know that was going to happen!"*

How to Handle the Aftermath

Getting everyone to do the 360 exercise is just the first step. Difficult as it is, the real payoff comes in changing individual management styles to align them more closely to your values. However, these alterations are also exceptionally difficult because they involve personal change. There are three things specifically related to handing the aftermath of this process:

- Build in the Capacity to Deal with Difficult Reactions
- Protect the Mangers to Give Them Time to Change
- Require Improvement but Support It Too

Build in the Capacity to Deal with Difficult Reactions

Most managers will be fine. They'll be able to look at the results, discuss them with their staff, and start to tweak their behavior to be more in line with what is effective. Others will be shocked and hurt. The results will be unexpected and devastating. The person may see the results as a comment on him not only as a manager but as a person. It may come at a time when he has problems in his personal life. For these reasons and others we might not be aware of, the results may hit him exceptionally hard.

For these managers, a session with the consultant to discuss the results is necessary, but it won't be enough. Even if he gets through the meeting with his employees to discuss what he could do differently, the manager won't be able to move forward without help. You can contract with the consultant for extra time for those managers who react very negatively or encourage managers to use an internal counseling program, if you have one.

Protect the Mangers to Give Them Time to Change

It's not uncommon for employees, the managers themselves, and their supervisors to expect instant change, but personal change is a difficult and slow process. While we all know that, we don't often act as if we do. Every sign of improvement is greeted by a "Finally!" and every slip with: "See, I told you he wasn't serious. He hasn't bought into it at all. He's just doing this because the CEO is so hot to trot."

Even the most sincere manager won't be perfect every time. You need to protect managers during the period they're trying to change. One way is to announce the timing of the next cycle of feedback to give an indication of the window within which change is expected. You might also publicly recognize how difficult this process is and appeal to employees to cut the managers some slack. Couple this with your commitment to require improvement, or employees might interpret this as letting managers "off the hook."

Require Improvement but Support It Too

None of the above negates that fact that you must require improvement. The speed of improvement may be negotiable; progress is not.

You must make this clear to both managers and employees by including it in your performance evaluation process or some other less formal procedure. However it is done, it can't be a matter for barter.

But, you must also be prepared to support the changes. Managers may need extra training or coaching by outside experts, so release funds to management training needs identified as a result of this process. And most importantly, show your support for managers struggling to change ingrained patterns of thinking and acting by allowing them to make mistakes, to forget or to resist changing as fast as you need them to. This is not to say that you have to do this forever since some part of your job is to eventually require that people change, but you need to allow a period—probably longer than you feel comfortable with—during which your managers can undertake the change that is desired.

Is All this Planning Really Necessary?

All this preplanning may seem a bit excessive, but no matter how you slice it, the first time through this process is a risky proposition even for managers relatively confident of their skills. It is even more difficult for those who suspect (often correctly) that they're not as skilled as they need to be. Managers may tough it out, saying things like: *"Ah, this is a tempest in a teapot. All this pussyfooting around. Just give me the stuff and let's get on with it."* This tough guy stance is often a front for a manager who either doesn't know how to change or feels betrayed by the criticism. Neither suggests the information will be used to improve skills or help release the intellectual capital in his corner of the company. Without a move to change, however grudging it might be at the beginning, this process will not work. To some extent, you must rely on individual willingness to make these difficult moves. You can have a formal system to require change, but only a positive spirit will encourage managers to use the system to help them change rather than trying to outmaneuver it. This investment up front will help managers use rather than work the system.

Summary

There is increasing evidence that employee morale drives financial success. However, unless you have a measure of its state, you can't improve it or even understand it. When judiciously used, employee surveys and 360 feedback can translate the rhetoric of cooperative behavior and wise management into action. On the other hand, if poorly conceived or implemented, it can descend into defensiveness and entrenched positions.

The final chapter will help you to pull all of these ideas together and to plan how you will begin to leverage the intellectual capital in your organization.

Main Points

- Employee satisfaction is a predictor of financial success.
- It is critical that organizations know the state of their employee satisfaction.
- Two ways to gauge employee satisfaction are regular employee surveys and 360-degree feedback process.
- Both the surveys and the feedback exercises are valuable but important to implement well.
- A 360-degree feedback is more threatening to both managers and staff, so it should only be undertaken after a series of employee surveys have conditioned everyone to give and accept comments on their behavior.

The End of
the Beginning

Knowledge is now the coin of the realm, and the knowledge worker is the most important source of wealth in an organization. Companies are coming to terms with this and starting to assess how to leverage their intellectual capital. Understanding the differences between the information and industrial societies is difficult enough, but trying to introduce changes to use your intellectual capital to its best advantage is a daunting task. It will require not simply changing what we do but what we think and how we relate to each other.

In this book, we've focused on the management challenges which accompany leveraging your organization's intellectual capital. With respect to human capital, a manager's job is to encourage people to bring forward the knowledge that is in their heads, to encourage them to move their knowledge from tacit and implicit to public and explicit. In addition, the sheer volume of knowledge forces more and more employees to specialize to become truly expert in a particular field and the manager is left with the challenge of managing people whose work he doesn't really understand. To address this, the manager must share decision-making power more than ever before. Similarly, the organization must share its power by consulting and involving employees in strategic decisions. Employees can only use their knowledge to provide sound and useful advice on corporate issues if the organization helps them understand the complexities of the business environment. Finally, it's not enough to tap the knowledge which your human capital presently possesses. You must also ensure that knowledge workers continue to learn, in informal as well as formal ways.

The management challenges with respect to using structural capital are also daunting. These include setting up a plan and developing a mind-set within the organization which encourages a free flow of information to employees, even information which has previously been considered highly confidential. Similarly, unless managers can use expertise from other business divisions, having elaborate databases that identify the location of that expertise is of little use. Using structural capital fully requires a freer flow of people and knowledge than is typical of most organizations.

In addition, employees need to share their knowledge with others. Otherwise, the quality of the knowledge captured with your structural capital—databases, networks, and procedures—will not reflect the latest knowledge. To get employees to do this, they must believe there is some pay off for them in ceding their intellectual capital to the organization. On the other side of the coin, employees must become more willing to learn from others. This means that they must be willing to experiment, fail, and be temporarily incompetent as they struggle to incorporate new knowledge into their way of operating. The manager has an important role in showing employees why they need to share and learn, inviting them to do so, and eventually demanding it of them. All of this will mean some personal change, on the part of both employees and managers. Both parties must learn to operate in a more ambiguous, less controlled, and more fluid situation than may feel either comfortable or familiar.

Finally, organizations must look beyond money as a way of rewarding knowledge workers through personal and personalized recognition that not only warms the heart but also increases knowledge workers' commitment to the organization.

Because employee satisfaction is essential to achieve customer satisfaction and loyalty which in turn drives profitability, the management challenge of customer capital is to increase employees' commitment to, and satisfaction with, the company. One of the ways to do this is to ensure that the organization is true to its mission and its values. Organizations have to carefully monitor employee satisfaction regularly through regular employee surveys and 360-degree feedback processes.

As you can see, there are many management challenges to using your intellectual capital to true competitive advantage. It will require revisiting many concepts we thought we understood—like team-work, control, and management itself. Managers must adjust to their new roles as teachers, scouts, and keepers of the flame while, at the same time ceding more of their purely technical functions to employees. And as if all these changes were not enough, it is almost guaranteed that this new age will make even more new demands which we cannot even guess at.

Implementing the concepts behind intellectual capital is a challenge because no one knows enough about its implications to give you a foolproof road map. It is a work in progress. Some things in this book will work for you and others won't. You'll discover ways that aren't mentioned. You'll go down a lot of blind alleys before you make it through the maze. Intellectual capital is not a well-worn path with the bumps smoothed out.

Of course, managing your intellectual capital superbly isn't a substitute for good strategy and sound financial management. Running a successful organization still requires all of the management skills and talents of the past. The changes discussed in this book don't replace those skills, although they may change *how* they're used. For example, you will still need to do budgets and financial projections, but how much you involve employees and how much effort you spend helping them to understand what a budget means to their jobs will probably change. So, leveraging your intellectual capital must always be in the service of your organizational goals, but at the same time, the daily rigors of the mandate should not be the excuse for avoiding the changes required. They are the future beckoning you.

Not a Panacea or Cookbook but a Road Map

Managing intellectual capital can have a powerful influence on readying your company to face the new world. The book has been organized around the concepts of human, structural, and customer capital and although this helps us understand how important the management challenges are for each type of intellectual capital, it is not always easy to see how to implement the changes. For example, ensuring that the organization lives up to its mission and values will help to create employee loyalty and therefore customer capital. However, because they serve as an underpining to many other activities (e.g., whether you value sharing knowledge), it may make sense to start working on them immediately, if you have not been using them as effectively as you could. Similarly, some managerial activities flow naturally out of organizational ones. For example, managers will be most effective in pushing down complexity if the company has already freed up its flow of information and is regularly releasing financial and other strategic information. To help you implement the ideas of this book, I've included a road map of the order of the activities.

Some things to note about this road map:

1. It is not a straitjacket. You may find a different sequence makes more sense for your organization. For example, you might prefer to do an employee survey right away to get a baseline reading or change the reward systems off the top to signal you're serious about this new way of managing. Tailor the road map to your own circumstances.

2. When an activity is mentioned, it denotes the start but not the end. Communicating starts early but should continue indefinitely.

3. The first set of activities (free flow of information, learning program, and mission) are ones that you might want to do at about the same time. Similarly, the next group (consulting, involving, and free movement of people and knowledge) could occur in the next period. The same is true of the managerial/employee activities. The time frame for each of the columns of activities can vary greatly depending on how large the organization is, how open to the ideas, how supportive the executive group, and other factors that we can't predict.

4. The time you will need to get to the end of the road map will also vary, but however long you think it's going to take to do this—think in years rather than months—it will probably take just a little bit longer.

5. The number next to the name of the activity is the relevant chapter in the book.

One final point. It's critical to realize that the aim is to create an environment that supports the flowering of intellectual capital, not simply to get to the end of this road map. Don't confuse activity with accomplishment. Exercises such as communication and involvement are useful only if they result in people more willing to invest their intellectual capital. Keep your eye on the goal and not on the activities.

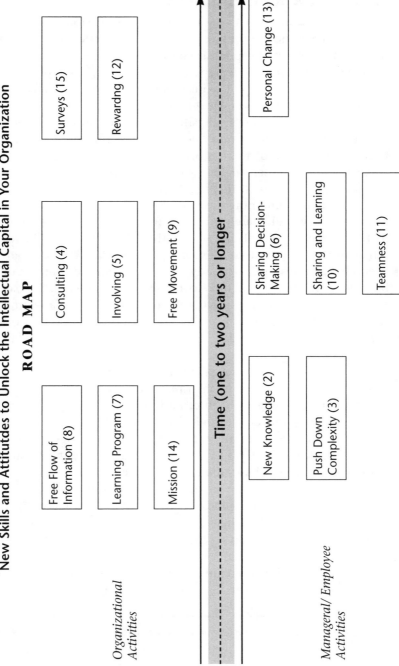

Managing Knowledge Workers:
New Skills and Attitutdes to Unlock the Intellectual Capital in Your Organization

ROAD MAP

Is This New Role Enough?

So now you know what to do and how to do it. However, whether this new role is enough for you is, in some ways, the pivotal point of managing intellectual capital. If you can't see a new role which has as much value and excitement as the old one, you won't move toward it, and if you don't, your organization won't be able to tap the full potential of its knowledge workers.

There is an important leadership role in the new environment of intellectual capital, but it won't be the same as the old one. Your role is changing to one of teacher and supporter rather than doer and decider, and while there are many positive things about being a doer and a decider, there is little as satisfying as helping others to grow and learn, to do something they were sure they couldn't, to see them run when they could barely crawl. There is little that is sweeter than to hear someone say, "I did what I thought you would have." It tells you not only that your expertise is appreciated but that you've been able to transmit it in a way which has allowed that person to become more capable and more confident by building on the base of your wisdom. Your workplace role is that of mentor—someone respected for your experience and your willingness to help others avoid the stumbles you made and climb the peak you may not make yourself.

So the new role isn't necessarily better, it's just different. The old and the new roles both have their pluses and minuses. If the world's rules about knowledge and information hadn't changed while we weren't looking, maybe we could stick with what we already know well. Well, they did and those who understand the times are thriving in them. Jack Welch, CEO of GE says, "Early in my career, and in many other careers, there was way too much focus on making the numbers, on delivering the goods. And a lot less on the softer values of building a team, sharing ideas, exciting others." [1] He understands, as you do, that this is the new role for leaders—to create an environment where people will invest their intellectual capital in their workplace.

Does it have the adrenaline rush of saving the world? Probably not, but as someone once said to me, "Maybe the satisfaction isn't a

---

[1] Marshall Loeb, " Jack Welch Lets Fly on Budgets, Bonuses and Buddy Boards", *Fortune* (May 29, 1995): 146.

peak but a roundness." So maybe it doesn't have the excitement of fighting fires; maybe it's more like the satisfaction of watching your son graduate from college.

The information age is a new work world and we are its pioneers. It is not that we always know where we're going or where we'll end up, but it doesn't stop us from moving forward. It is not that we are without trepidation, but we carry on in any case. There is hardship and difficulty, but we endure both because we have a vision of what we are building and it is worth the effort.

INDEX

ᏸᏱ